The Precipice

The
Precipice

Neoliberalism, the Pandemic,
and the Urgent Need
for Radical Change

Noam Chomsky
and C. J. Polychroniou

Haymarket Books
Chicago, Illinois

Published in 2021 by
Haymarket Books
P.O. Box 180165
Chicago, IL 60618
773-583-7884
www.haymarketbooks.org
info@haymarketbooks.org

ISBN: 978-1-64259-458-4

Distributed to the trade in the US through Consortium Book Sales and Distribution (www.cbsd.com) and internationally through Ingram Publisher Services International (www.ingramcontent.com).

This book was published with the generous support of Lannan Foundation and Wallace Action Fund.

Special discounts are available for bulk purchases by organizations and institutions. Please call 773-583-7884 or email info@haymarketbooks.org for more information.

Cover design by Jared Rodriguez.

Printed in Canada by union labor.

Library of Congress Cataloging-in-Publication data is available.

10 9 8 7 6 5 4 3 2 1

Contents

Foreword

C. J. Polychroniou

Over the course of the last couple of decades we, have become witness to the rise of a new political phenomenon, which may be loosely described as authoritarianism populism. It is a movement situated, ideologically, on the far right of the political spectrum, although there are some subtle differences with regard to policymaking on various issues between, say, Hungary's authoritarian-populist regime under Viktor Orbán, and those of Tayyip Erdoğan's in Turkey, Jair Bolsonaro's in Brazil and of Donald Trump's in the United States, respectively. However, what bonds authoritarian populist leaders in the early part of the 21st century is their affinity for forms of political behavior that result in repressive measures, undermine all forms of collective decision making—and indeed of the democratization process itself—and lead to the formation of autocratic regimes. Authoritarian leaders such as Orbán, Bolsonaro, and Trump employ a rhetoric that can be loosely defined as "neofascist" and xenophobic, if not outright racist, while seeking at the same time to gain popular support by using an ideology of extreme nationalism.

The reasons behind the rise of authoritarian populism appear to be intrinsically related to concerns about globalization, immigration, and a dilution of the national identity among growing segments of primarily lower and working-class citizens. These factors were surely at the heart of Donald Trump's surprising victory of the 2016 US presidential election over Hillary Clinton, even though he lost the popular vote by three million votes. Indeed, authoritarian populism received its biggest boost with the rise of Trump to power, and, by virtue of the fact that he held the highest position in the world's most powerful nation, made him the de facto leader of the authoritarian-populist current that has been spreading among liberal democracies over the last couple of decades.

Thankfully, Donald Trump ended up being a one-term president, losing the 2020 election to Joe Biden. Typical of his anti-democratic impulses, and just as he had hinted all along, Trump refused to concede defeat by claiming without a trace of evidence that the election was "rigged and stolen" and in-cited an insurrection. By doing so, Trump's apparent strategy to sue his way to election victory on the basis of baseless vote fraud claims was also carried out with the explicit intent of having his fanatical base become ever more convinced of the need to subvert the democratic process.

And here is the trouble. Trump may be out of office, but Trumpism is still very much alive and kicking in the "land of the free and the brave." The Republican Party is Trump's party, and the followers of the MAGA move-ment live in an entirely different galaxy than the rest of the population. To be sure, the United States remains most likely the most divided and polar-ized nation in the world. The differences among the citizenry are not merely political or ideological. They are epistemological. Indeed, what separates Trump's fanatical base, possibly 40 percent of the American population, from the rest of the body politic, are alternative conceptions of reality it-self! Trump's supporters reject science, have no faith in actual facts, and are drawn overwhelmingly into conspiracies. And the con artist that occupied the White House from January 20, 2017, to January 20, 2021, knew his polit-ical clientele all too well, and took full advantage of the situation by being a super-spreader of misinformation and constant lies, while proceeding at the same time to extend all sorts of big gifts to the very rich and the corporate world (huge tax cuts and massive deregulations) and backstabbing the poor and average Americans who voted for him.

But Trump wasn't just a liar and a con artist. He was America's worst nightmare, democracy's Trojan horse, the planet's greatest mortal threat. The forty-fifth president of the United States is responsible for the death of hundreds of thousands of Americans on account of his reckless stance on the Coronavirus pandemic, for bringing the nation on the verge of a civil war and the planet dangerously close to the tipping point with his denial of global warming, compelling one of the world's greatest minds and most revered public intellectual alive (i.e., Noam Chomsky) to label Trump "the worst criminal in history."

During the course of Trump's reign, I had the pleasure and honor to continue interviewing Noam Chomsky on the developments unfolding in the US and around the world. The interviews collected in this volume, which originally appeared in *Truthout*, cover the period from Trump's election in November 2016 to the 2020 elections. They offer brilliant analyses, immense insights, and breathtaking critiques by a staggering genius on Trump's presidency and the phenomenon of Trumpism. Hopefully, however, this little volume won't be read only by those who are aware of the existential threat that Donald Trump represented—and may still represent—for the future of democracy in the United States and of the sustainability of the planet, but also by those who were mesmerized by and idolized the greatest political con man in recent memory and the "worse criminal in history."

Trump in the White House

C. J. POLYCHRONIOU: Noam, the unthinkable has happened. Despite all forecasts to the contrary, Donald Trump scored a decisive victory over Hillary Clinton, and the man that Michael Moore described as a "wretched, ignorant, dangerous part-time clown and full-time sociopath" will be the next president of the United States. In your view, what were the deciding factors that led American voters to produce the biggest upset in the history of US politics?

NOAM CHOMSKY: Before turning to this question, I think it is important to spend a few moments pondering just what happened on November 8, a date that might turn out to be one of the most important in human history, depending on how we react.

No exaggeration.

The most important news of November 8 was barely noted, a fact of some significance in itself.

On November 8, the World Meteorological Organization (WMO) delivered a report at the international conference on climate change in Morocco (COP22), which was called in order to carry forward the Paris agreement of COP21. The WMO reported that the past five years had been the hottest on record. It also reported rising sea levels, soon to increase as a result of the unexpectedly rapid melting of polar ice, most ominously the huge Antarctic glaciers.

Already, Arctic sea ice over the past five years is 28 percent below the average of the previous 29 years—not only raising sea levels, but also reducing the cooling effect of polar ice reflection of solar rays, thereby accelerating the grim effects of global warming. The WMO reported further that temperatures were dangerously close to the goal established by COP21, along with other dire reports and forecasts.

Another event took place on November 8, which also may turn out to be of unusual historical significance for reasons that, once again, were barely noted.

On November 8, the most powerful country in world history, which will set its stamp on what comes next, had an election. The outcome placed total control of the government—the executive branch, Congress, the Supreme Court—in the hands of the Republican Party, which has become the most dangerous organization in world history.

Apart from the last phrase, all of this is uncontroversial. The last phrase may seem outlandish, even outrageous. But is it? The facts suggest otherwise. The party is dedicated to racing as rapidly as possible to destruction of organized human life. There is no historical precedent for such a stand.

Is this an exaggeration? Consider what we have just been witnessing.

During the Republican primaries, every candidate denied that what is happening is happening—with the exception of the sensible moderates, like Jeb Bush—who said it's all uncertain, but we don't have to do anything because we're producing more natural gas, thanks to fracking. Or John Kasich, who agreed that global warming is taking place, but added that "we are going to burn [coal] in Ohio and we are not going to apologize for it."

The winning candidate, now the president-elect, calls for rapid increase in the use of fossil fuels, including coal; dismantling of regulations; rejection of help to developing countries seeking to move to sustainable energy; and in general, racing to the cliff as fast as possible.

Trump has already taken steps to dismantle the Environmental Protection Agency (EPA) by placing in charge of the EPA transition a notorious (and proud) climate change denier, Myron Ebell. Trump's top adviser on energy, billionaire oil executive Harold Hamm, announced his expectations, which were predictable: dismantling regulations, tax cuts for the industry (and the wealthy and corporate sector generally), more fossil fuel production, lifting Obama's temporary block on the Dakota Access pipeline. The market reacted quickly. Shares in energy corporations boomed, including the world's largest coal miner, Peabody

Energy, which had filed for bankruptcy but registered a 50 percent gain after Trump's victory.

The effects of Republican denialism had already been felt. There had been hopes that the COP21 Paris agreement would lead to a verifiable treaty, but these thoughts were abandoned because the Republican Congress would not accept any binding commitments, so what emerged was a voluntary agreement, evidently much weaker.

Effects may soon become even more vividly apparent than they already are. In Bangladesh alone, tens of millions are expected to have to flee from low-lying plains in coming years because of sea level rise and more severe weather, creating a migrant crisis that will make today's pale in significance. With considerable justice, Bangladesh's leading climate scientist says that "these migrants should have the right to move to the countries from which all these greenhouse gases are coming. Millions should be able to go to the United States."

And to the other rich countries that have grown wealthy while bringing about a new geological era, the Anthropocene, marked by radical human transformation of the environment. These catastrophic consequences can only increase, not only in Bangladesh but in all of South Asia as temperatures, already intolerable for the poor, rise inexorably and the Himalayan glaciers melt, threatening the entire water supply. Already in India, some 300 million people are reported to lack adequate drinking water. And the effects will reach far beyond.

It is hard to find words to capture the fact that humans are facing the most important question in their history—whether organized human life will survive in anything like the form we know—and are answering by accelerating the race to disaster.

Similar observations hold for the other huge issue concerning human survival—the threat of nuclear destruction, which has been looming over our heads for seventy years and is now increasing.

It is no less difficult to find words to capture the utterly astonishing fact that in all of the massive coverage of the electoral extravaganza, none of this receives more than passing mention. At least I am at a loss to find appropriate words.

Turning finally to the question raised, to be precise, it appears that Clinton received a slight majority of the vote. The apparent decisive victory has to do with curious features of American politics, including the Electoral College—residue of the founding of the country as an alliance of separate states; the winner-take-all system in each state; the arrangement of congressional districts (sometimes by gerrymandering) to provide greater weight to rural votes (in past elections, and probably this one too, Democrats have had a comfortable margin of victory in the popular vote for the House, but hold a minority of seats); the very high rate of abstention (usually close to half in presidential elections, this one included). Of some significance for the future is the fact that in the eighteen-to-twenty-five age range, Clinton won handily; Sanders had an even higher level of support. How much this matters depends on what kind of future humanity will face.

According to current information, support for Trump from white voters—working class and lower middle class, particularly in the $50,000 to $90,000 income range, rural and suburban, primarily those without college education—broke all records. These groups share the anger throughout the West at the centrist establishment, revealed as well in the unanticipated Brexit vote and the collapse of centrist parties in continental Europe.

[Many of] the angry and disaffected are victims of the neoliberal policies of the past generation, the policies described in congressional testimony by Fed chair Alan Greenspan—"St. Alan," as he was called reverentially by the economics profession and other admirers until the miraculous economy he was supervising crashed in 2007–2008, threatening to bring the whole world economy down with it. As Greenspan explained during his glory days, his successes in economic management were based substantially on "growing worker insecurity." Intimidated working people would not ask for higher wages, benefits, and security, but would be satisfied with the stagnating wages and reduced benefits that signal a healthy economy by neoliberal standards.

Working people, who have been the subjects of these experiments in economic theory, are not particularly happy about the outcome. They are not, for example, overjoyed at the fact that in 2007, at the peak of the neoliberal miracle, real wages for nonsupervisory workers were lower than they had been years earlier, or that real wages for male workers are about at 1960s levels. Meanwhile, spectacular gains have gone into the pockets of a very few at the top, disproportionately a fraction of 1 percent. Not the result of market forces, achievement, or merit, but rather the consequence of definite policy decisions, matters reviewed carefully by economist Dean Baker in recently published work.

The fate of the minimum wage illustrates this pattern. Through the periods of high and egalitarian growth in the '50s and '60s, the minimum wage—which sets a floor for other wages—tracked productivity. That ended with the onset of neoliberal doctrine. Since then, the minimum wage has stagnated (in real value). Had it continued as before, it would probably be close to $20 per hour. Today, it is considered a political revolution to raise it to $15.

With all the talk of near-full employment today, labor force participation remains below the earlier norm. And for working people, there is a great difference between a steady job in manufacturing with union wages and benefits, as in earlier years, and a temporary job with little security in a service profession. Apart from wages, benefits, and security, there is a loss of dignity, of hope for the future, of a sense that this is a world in which I belong and play a worthwhile role.

The impact is captured well in Arlie Hochschild's sensitive and illuminating portrayal of a Trump stronghold in Louisiana, where she lived and worked for many years. She uses the image of a line in which residents are standing, expecting to move forward steadily as they work hard and keep to all the conventional values. But their position in the line has stalled. Ahead of them, they see people leaping forward, but that does not cause much distress, because it is "the American way" for (alleged) merit to be rewarded. What causes real distress is what is happening behind them. They believe that "undeserving people" who do not "follow the rules" are being moved in front of them by federal government programs they erroneously see as designed to benefit African Americans, immigrants, and others they often regard with contempt. All of this is exacerbated by [Ronald] Reagan's racist fabrications about "welfare queens" (by implication Black) stealing white people's hard-earned money and other fantasies.

Sometimes failure to explain, itself a form of contempt, plays a role in fostering hatred of government. I once met a house painter in Boston who had turned bitterly against the "evil" government after a Washington bureaucrat who knew nothing about painting organized a meeting of painting contractors to inform them that they could no longer use lead paint—"the only kind that works"—as they all knew, but the suit didn't understand. That destroyed his small business, compelling him to paint houses on his own with substandard stuff forced on him by government elites.

Sometimes there are also some real reasons for these attitudes toward government bureaucracies. Hochschild describes a man whose family and friends are suffering bitterly from the lethal effects of chemical pollution but who despises the government and the "liberal elites," because for him, the EPA means some ignorant guy who tells him he can't fish, but does nothing about the chemical plants.

These are just samples of the real lives of Trump supporters, who are led to believe that Trump will do something to remedy their plight, though the merest look at his fiscal and other proposals demonstrates the opposite— posing a task for activists who hope to fend off the worst and to advance desperately needed changes.

Exit polls reveal that the passionate support for Trump was inspired primarily by the belief that he represented change, while Clinton was perceived as the candidate who would perpetuate their distress. The "change" that Trump is likely to bring will be harmful or worse, but it is understandable that the consequences are not clear to isolated people in an atomized society lacking the kinds of associations (like unions) that can educate and organize. That is a crucial difference between today's despair and the generally hopeful attitudes of many working people under much greater economic duress during the Great Depression of the 1930s.

There are other factors in Trump's success. Comparative studies show that doctrines of white supremacy have had an even more powerful grip on American culture than in South Africa, and it's no secret that the white population is declining. In a decade or two, whites are projected to be a minority of the workforce, and not too much later, a minority of the population. The traditional conservative culture is also perceived as under attack by the successes of identity politics, regarded as the province of elites who have only contempt for the "hard-working, patriotic, church-going [white] Americans with real family values" who see their familiar country as disappearing before their eyes.

One of the difficulties in raising public concern over the very severe threats of global warming is that 40 percent of the US population does not see why it is a problem, since Christ is returning in a few decades. About the same percentage believe that the world was created a few thousand years ago. If science conflicts with the Bible, so much the worse for science. It would be hard to find an analogue in other societies.

The Democratic Party abandoned any real concern for working people by the 1970s, and they have therefore been drawn to the ranks of their bitter class enemies, who at least pretend to speak their language—Reagan's folksy style of making little jokes while eating jelly beans, George W. Bush's carefully cultivated image of a regular guy you could meet in a bar who loved to cut brush on the ranch in 100-degree heat and his probably faked mispronunciations (it's unlikely that he talked like that at Yale), and now Trump. The latter gives voice to people with legitimate grievances—people who have lost not just jobs, but also a sense of personal self-worth—and who rails against the government that they perceive as having undermined their lives (not without reason).

One of the great achievements of the doctrinal system has been to divert anger from the corporate sector to the government that implements the programs the corporate sector designs, such as the highly protectionist corporate/investor rights agreements that are uniformly mis-described as "free trade agreements" in the media and commentary. With all its flaws, the government is, to some extent, under popular influence and control, unlike the corporate sector. It is highly advantageous for the business world to foster hatred for pointy-headed government bureaucrats and to drive out of people's minds the subversive idea that the government might become an instrument of popular will, a government of, by, and for the people.

Is Trump representing a new movement in American politics, or was the outcome of this election primarily a rejection of Hillary Clinton by voters who hate the Clintons and are fed-up with "politics as usual?"

It's by no means new. Both political parties have moved to the right during the neoliberal period. Today's New Democrats are pretty much what used to be called "moderate Republicans." The "political revolution" that Bernie Sanders called for, rightly, would not have greatly surprised Dwight Eisenhower. The Republicans have moved so far toward a dedication to the wealthy and the corporate sector that they cannot hope to get votes on their actual programs, and have turned to mobilizing sectors of the population that have always been there, but not as an organized coalitional political force: evangelicals, nativists, racists and the victims of the forms of globalization designed to set working people around the world in competition with one another. Meanwhile, the privileged are protected and measures that provided working people with some protection are undermined, including the ability to influence decision-making in the closely linked public and private sectors, notably through effective labor unions.

The consequences have been evident in recent Republican primaries. Every candidate that has emerged from the base—such as [Michele] Bachmann, [Herman] Cain or [Rick] Santorum—has been so extreme that the Republican establishment had to use its ample resources to beat them down. The difference in 2016 is that the establishment failed, much to its chagrin, as we have seen.

Deservedly or not, Clinton represented the policies that were feared and hated, while Trump was seen as the symbol of "change"—change of what kind requires a careful look at his actual proposals, something largely missing in what reached the public. The campaign itself was remarkable in its avoidance of issues, and media commentary generally complied, keeping to the concept that true "objectivity" means reporting accurately what is "within the beltway," but not venturing beyond.

Trump said following the outcome of the election that he "will represent all Americans." How is he going to do that when the nation is so divided and he has already expressed deep hatred for many groups in the United States, including women and minorities? Do you see any resemblance between Brexit and Donald Trump's victory?

There are definite similarities to Brexit, and also to the rise of the ultra-nationalist far-right parties in Europe—whose leaders were quick to congratulate Trump on his victory, perceiving him as one of their own: [Nigel] Farage, [Marine] Le Pen, [Viktor] Orbán and others like them. And these developments are quite frightening. A look at the polls in Austria and Germany—*Austria and Germany*— cannot fail to evoke unpleasant memories for those familiar with the 1930s, even more so for those who watched directly, as I did as a child.

I can still recall listening to Hitler's speeches, not understanding the words, though the tone and audience reaction were chilling enough. The first article that I remember writing was in February 1939, after the fall of Barcelona, on the seemingly inexorable spread of the Fascist plague. And by strange coincidence, it was from Barcelona that my wife and I watched the results of the 2016 US presidential election unfold.

As to how Trump will handle what he has brought forth—not created, but brought forth—we cannot say. Perhaps his most striking characteristic is unpredictability. A lot will depend on the reactions of those appalled by his performance and the visions he has projected, such as they are.

Trump has no identifiable political ideology guiding his stance on economic, social, and political issues, yet there are clear authoritarian tendencies in his behavior. Therefore, do you find any validity behind the claims that Trump may represent the emergence of "Fascism with a friendly face?" in the United States?

For many years, I have been writing and speaking about the danger of the rise of an honest and charismatic ideologue in the United States, someone who could exploit the fear and anger that has long been boiling in much of the society, and who could direct it away from the actual agents of malaise to vulnerable targets. That could indeed lead to what sociologist Bertram Gross called "friendly Fascism" in a perceptive study thirty-five years ago. But that requires an honest ideologue, a Hitler type, not someone whose only detectable ideology is Me. The dangers, however, have been real for many years, perhaps even more so in the light of the forces that Trump has unleashed.

With the Republicans in the White House, but also controlling both houses and the future shape of the Supreme Court, what will the US look like for at least the next four years?

A good deal depends on his appointments and circle of advisers. Early indications are unattractive, to put it mildly.

The Supreme Court will be in the hands of reactionaries for many years, with predictable consequences. If Trump follows through on his Paul

Ryan–style fiscal programs, there will be huge benefits for the very rich. The Tax Policy Center estimates a tax cut of more than 14 percent for the top 0.1 percent and a substantial cut more generally at the upper end of the income scale, but with virtually no tax relief for others, who will also face major new burdens. The respected economics correspondent of the *Financial Times*, Martin Wolf, writes that, "The tax proposals would shower huge benefits on already rich Americans such as Mr Trump," while leaving others in the lurch, including, of course, his constituency. The immediate reaction of the business world reveals that Big Pharma, Wall Street, the military industry, energy industries, and other such wonderful institutions expect a very bright future.

One positive development might be the infrastructure program that Trump has promised while (along with much reporting and commentary) concealing the fact that it is essentially the Obama stimulus program that would have been of great benefit to the economy and to the society generally, but was killed by the Republican Congress on the pretext that it would explode the deficit. While that charge was spurious at the time, given the very low interest rates, it holds in spades for Trump's program, now accompanied by radical tax cuts for the rich and corporate sector and increased Pentagon spending.

There is, however, an escape, provided by Dick Cheney when he explained to Bush's treasury secretary Paul O'Neill that "Reagan proved that deficits don't matter"—meaning deficits that we Republicans create in order to gain popular support, leaving it to someone else, preferably Democrats, to somehow clean up the mess. The technique might work, for a while at least.

There are also many questions about foreign policy consequences, mostly unanswered.

There is mutual admiration between Trump and Putin. How likely is it therefore that we may see a new era in US-Russia relations?

One hopeful prospect is that there might be reduction of the very dangerous and mounting tensions at the Russian border: note "the Russian border," not the Mexican border. Thereby lies a tale that we cannot go into here. It is also possible that Europe might distance itself from Trump's America, as already suggested by [German] Chancellor [Angela] Merkel and other European leaders—and from the British voice of American power, after

Brexit. That might possibly lead to European efforts to defuse the tensions, and perhaps even efforts to move toward something like Mikhail Gorbachev's vision of an integrated Eurasian security system without military alliances, rejected by the US in favor of NATO expansion, a vision revived recently by Putin, whether seriously or not, we do not know, since the gesture was dismissed.

Is US foreign policy under a Trump administration likely to be more or less militaristic than what we have seen under the Obama administration, or even the George W. Bush administration?

I don't think one can answer with any confidence. Trump is too unpredictable. There are too many open questions. What we can say is that popular mobilization and activism, properly organized and conducted, can make a large difference.

Trump's First 100 Days Are Undermining Our Prospects for Survival

C. J. POLYCHRONIOU: The first 100 days of Donald Trump in the White House are characterized by complete disrespect for the truth and the freedom of the press and, overall, a style of political leadership that is not merely authoritarian but also smacks of Fascism. In your view, is all this part of a preconceived strategy or simply a reflection of the whims of a person with a very fragile ego?

NOAM CHOMSKY: I don't pretend to have any special insight into the mind of this strange person, though the people around him have been fairly coherent, in particular Steve Bannon, who seems to be the shadowed figure behind the throne.

What is happening before our eyes appears to be a two-pronged operation, I presume planned.

Bannon/Trump (and the pathetic Sean Spicer, who has to defend the latest shenanigans in public) have the task of dominating TV and headlines with one wild performance after another, the assumption apparently being that his fabrications will quickly be forgotten as the next episode displaces them, and the base will be satisfied for a time, believing that their champion is standing up for them. So, who remembers the millions of undocumented immigrants who "voted for Clinton," or the charge that that really bad guy Obama ("sad!") literally wiretapped poor Trump—a claim now downgraded to irrelevance, but not withdrawn—and so on? Look how well the birther tales played for many years, ending hilariously with Trump blaming Clinton for initiating the farce.

Meanwhile, the real work is going on more quietly, spearheaded by Paul Ryan, a different and more malicious kind of posturer, who represents the most brutal fringe of the Republican establishment and somehow manages to present himself as a man of ideas, maybe because—as Paul Krugman argues—he rolls up his sleeves and uses PowerPoint. The ideas are quite familiar. They are the standard fare of the component of the Republican establishment dedicated with unusual ferocity to enriching the rich and powerful—bankers, CEOs, and other types who matter—while kicking the vulnerable, the poor, and Trump's rural and working-class constituency in the face. All of this abetted by the ultraright billionaire cabinet and other appointees, selected very carefully to destroy whatever within their domains might be helpful to mere humans, but not to the chosen few of extreme wealth and power.

The consistency is impressive, if not breathtaking.

With the collapse of the shameful GOP health care proposals, we are likely to see this scenario enacted with real passion. The White House and its congressional allies have many ways to undermine the current health care system, which, with all its flaws, is a considerable improvement over what preceded it though still well behind comparable societies, let alone what the population wants and deserves, as polls continue to show—a rational single-payer universal health care system. That is a fairly resilient phenomenon over many years, with some variation, and quite remarkable in that there is virtually no articulate elite advocacy of this sane and popular position.

Of course, undermining the system will harm a great many people, but that cannot be a consideration. After all, Ryancare was going to add some 24 million to the ranks of uninsured, which might kill more than 40,000 people annually, according to an analysis by health care specialists Steffie Woolhandler and David Himmelstein. If the health system can be substantially damaged, and people really do suffer sufficiently, then the propaganda drumbeat can proceed to blame the disaster on the political opposition, and maybe even get away with it. A good deal is possible in the era of "alternative facts." We are already witnessing the early stages.

The lead character in the show does indeed present himself as a thin-skinned megalomaniac whose only ideology is Me. But his appointments, and the policies for which all of this is a cover, are too systematic to be merely random shots.

As I mentioned, the policies being formulated and enacted are drawn from the playbook of the most reactionary fringe of the Republican establishment. The abject service to private wealth and power is accompanied with an authoritarian and fundamentalist program to transform US society. The project is driven by the Bannon-Sessions vision of a society devoted to Judeo-Christian roots and white supremacy, eliminating such pernicious and threatening nonsense as arts and humanities, upholding the Betsy DeVos doctrine that public education has to be dismantled, while if science conflicts with religion, then too bad for science. Meanwhile, we are to wave a mailed fist at the world while cowering behind walls and rebuilding the "depleted military" that is the most powerful force in human history, dwarfing any collection of competitors. All of this resonates with at least parts of a society that has long been the safest and most terrified in the world.

The fundamentalist project goes well beyond getting rid of arts and humanities. Science is also in the crosshairs. Trump's budget cuts medical research. There's been considerable attention to his dismantling of the EPA [Environmental Protection Agency], now pretty much in the hands of associates of James Inhofe, the Senate's leading climate denier, who has explained that if God has decided to warm the Earth, so be it. But that's the least of it. For action and research on climate, EPA is a small actor. Far more important is the Department of Energy (DOE). Its Office of Science is scheduled to lose $900 million, nearly 20 percent of its budget. DOE's $300 million ARPA-Energy program is eliminated completely. That's in addition to deep cuts to the research programs at the EPA and the National Oceanic and Atmospheric Administration (NOAA), and a 5 percent cut to NASA's earth science budget.

In Congress, the science-deniers can scarcely contain their glee now that the wrecking ball has opened the path for demolition of the heresies of the modern world. Lamar Smith, who for years has used his position as chair of the House science committee to harass scientists, now feels free to openly acknowledge that "the committee is now a tool to advance his political agenda rather than a forum to examine important issues facing the US research community."

An appropriate comment on all of this was made by Stephen Colbert, when the Republican-run legislature in North Carolina responded to a scientific study predicting rapid sea level rise by barring state and local agencies from developing regulations or planning documents anticipating a rise in sea level. "This is a brilliant solution," Colbert said. "If your science gives you a result that you don't like, pass a law saying the result is illegal. Problem solved."

Most important of everything that is happening is the attack against future generations, in fact even against those coming of age today. Trump and allies, departing from the world, are cheerily leading the race to environmental destruction while the rest take at least halting steps toward averting a looming catastrophe—which doesn't weigh in the balance against fabulous profits tomorrow for the select few.

A few years ago Republican governor of Louisiana Bobby Jindal took a little time off from his campaign to drive the state even deeper into the abyss to warn that Republicans are becoming "the stupid party." The respected conservative analyst [Norman J.] Ornstein of the American Enterprise Institute described the current party as a "radical insurgency" that has abandoned parliamentary politics. . . . Has any other organization dedicated itself with such enthusiasm to undermining our prospects for decent survival? And not in the distant future.

What do you make of Trump's recent attacks over FBI Russia leaks? Clearly, this is not the sort of thing one would ever expect from a US president, so what do you think it's all about?

Very little that comes out of the White House would be expected from a US president. But another question comes to mind as well. What is this all about? When Obama was presenting himself to the public before the 2008 primaries, one of his proudest accomplishments—in fact, one of the very few of his senatorial career—was impassioned support for Israel's murderous invasion of Lebanon. He even went so far as to cosponsor legislation calling for strong action against any country that might impede the assault. Has anyone on the Trump team been accused of similar support for Russian crimes? True, there have been some entirely improper acts, notably

Michael Flynn's failure to register as an agent of Turkey. But that is not the focus of the anger of the Democrats, whose primary concern in this affair seems to be to extinguish one of the few rays of light in the Trump performances, his indications of concern to reduce tensions with Russia that might well explode to terminal nuclear war. It's perhaps of some interest that one may turn to the leading establishment journal, *Foreign Affairs*, to find an informed analysis of the fierce liberal opposition to such sensible moves and its background.

An argument could be made that a major part of the explanation for Trump's apparent infatuation with Vladimir Putin is not only the fact that "The Donald" is naturally drawn to strongmen, but also that he sees Russia and the United States as the only stalwarts left that are able and willing to halt what they see as the "decline" of Western Christian civilization by targeting large numbers of Muslims, thereby preventing the alleged "Islamization" of the Western world. Do you see any validity behind this way of conceptualizing Trump's mindset?

As I said, I don't claim any particular insight into his thinking. The term "infatuation" seems to me too strong, at least on the basis of what I have seen, though he has expressed admiration for Putin, much like Marine Le Pen and other unsavory political figures who are rising in the West. If Trump's concern is "rolling back the Muslim hordes," he need go no further than Europe, where a majority of the population favors a complete ban on Muslim immigrants, including those fleeing from countries ravaged by Europe, in some cases for centuries. These are among the signs of the severe moral-cultural crisis of the West that is mislabeled a "refugee crisis."

NATO troops recently held a military exercise near the Norwegian-Russian border. This is clearly an act of provocation, so one wonders if Trump supported this move. Any thoughts on the matter?

Very clearly. These are among the provocations that increased under Obama-Clinton and apparently continue without change under Trump. I don't think he and his associates have had much to say about these provocations, which trace back to NATO expansion after the collapse of the Soviet

Union. The mounting provocations on both sides of the border underscore the wisdom of European historian Richard Sakwa's observation that NATO's prime mission today is "to manage the risks created by its existence." And it's worth remembering that it's the Russian border, not the Mexican border, and a border that is on the invasion route through which Russia was virtually destroyed twice by Germany alone in the past century.

In Trump's "America first" vision, military superiority over other nations includes the US being "on top of the pack" on nuclear weapons. Do you think we will see the end of Pax Americana under Donald Trump's presidency?

Trump's position on nuclear weapons is unclear, but many of his comments have been worrisome, in particular his dismissal of the New START treaty on mutual Russia-US reduction of nuclear weapons as a bad deal for the US, in a phone call with Putin. The treaty is a good deal not only for the US but for the world, even though partial. And it would be bad news indeed if Trump chooses not to renew it. In general, on nuclear programs he seems to have kept so far to Obama's dangerous modernization program. And being "on top of the pack" on nuclear weapons means little, since even a small number would be enough to destroy everything.

Trump has, of course, proposed sharp increases in the already bloated military budget, at the cost of social programs despised by the establishment Republicans who pretty much run the show. And he has relaxed conditions on use of force, removing oversight, decisions that have already led to several major atrocities.

As for Pax Americana, it has hardly been much of a Pax. It is not coming to an end, but it is continuing to decline, just as American power has declined since its peak at the end of World War II.

In this connection, however, it is important to bear in mind revealing insights developed in recent work by political economist Sean Starrs, exploring some significant consequences of the neoliberal globalization of the world economy. As he discusses, corporate ownership of the world's wealth is becoming a more realistic measure of global power than national wealth as the world departs more than before from the model of nationally discrete political economies.

The results of his investigations are quite striking. It turns out that in virtually every economic sector—manufacturing, finance, services, retail, and others—US corporations are well in the lead in ownership of the global economy. Overall, their ownership is close to 50 percent of the total, roughly the maximum figure of estimated US national wealth in 1945. This was the figure used by the revered figure of American diplomacy George Kennan, for example, when he advised in 1948 that our central policy goal must be to maintain the "position of disparity" that separated our enormous wealth from the poverty of others, referring specifically to Asia, though the import was more general. To achieve that goal, he advised, "We should cease to talk about vague and . . . unreal objectives, such as human rights, the raising of the living standards, and democratization," and must "deal in straight power concepts," not "hampered by idealistic slogans" about "altruism and world-benefaction."

Kennan was soon removed from the decision-making apparatus because he was considered too soft-hearted to deal with this harsh world. Much as today, there may then have been real opportunities for détente at the time, dismissed in favor of much harsher policies. These soon contributed to threats registered by the *Bulletin of Atomic Scientists* expert advisers, who moved the hands of the famous doomsday clock forward to two minutes to midnight in 1953 after the US and Russia exploded hydrogen bombs. That's the closest it has ever been to terminal disaster. It is hardly comforting to note that a few days into Trump's term, the clock was moved again to two and a half minutes to midnight, the closest to doom since 1953, advancing from an ominous three minutes to midnight during the two preceding years.

Returning to Pax Americana, American decline is real, in state power, while US ownership of the world economy is overwhelming. These changes in the nature of world order, commonly overlooked, are of no slight significance.

Trump ran on an "antiestablishment" platform, yet his budget cut proposals and overall economic policy agenda favor the rich and will make life for struggling Americans even more difficult. First, what are your thoughts on his budget cuts, and, second, do you think this will make his

supporters realize that he pulled the biggest trick on them in the history of US politics?

Trump's budget proposals are very clear: expand the military and lavish gifts on the rich and powerful, while the rest are somehow to fend for themselves, including his rural and working-class constituency. For the moment, they seem to be keeping to the faith that somehow Trump meant what he said and will bring back jobs. On this matter, we should recall that for a long time the word "jobs" in US political discourse has been the conventional way to pronounce an obscene seven-letter word—which I will not spell, out of concern for the thought police. It begins "p-r-o" and ends "f-i-t-s." The resort to the euphemism goes back many years. Some will remember George H. W. Bush's trip to Asia in order to gain "jobs, jobs, jobs," as he proclaimed. Others fall into line, including the media.

It will take creative propaganda initiatives to sustain the con game in Trump's case. Sooner or later, the veil will fall away, just as it did with Obama's "hope" and "change," at that time shifting working-class votes to their bitter class enemy. If that happens, we can expect that the Trump-Bannon crowd will seek to divert attention in one of the many familiar ways—perhaps conjuring up some threat to American security (or if there is one, exploiting it). Or, perhaps, scapegoating the most vulnerable: immigrants, Muslims, welfare recipients (one of Reagan's disgusting techniques), and other available targets. That could turn very ugly. It could lead to the "friendly Fascism" that sociologist Bertram Gross predicted thirty years ago. Or worse.

At the same time, there are very promising opportunities ahead. A serious program to heal the pathologies of the neoliberal era could attract very broad popular support. There already is popular support for progressive programs. One example I've already mentioned: most Americans continue to prefer a government health care program of the kind that functions far better than ours in other developed countries.

Another example was provided recently by Fox News. They conducted a poll asking who is the most popular political figure in the country. In the lead, by a very large margin, was Bernie Sanders—even more so among the young, the hope for the future.

The success of the Sanders campaign was quite remarkable, a sharp break from political history. For over a century, elections in the US have been mostly bought. But here was someone who was scarcely known, who had virtually no support from the wealthy or corporate sector and was dismissed by the media, and even used the scare word "socialism." He would very likely have won the Democratic nomination had it not been for the shenanigans of the Obama-Clinton clique that dominates the party—and that has almost ruined it at local and state levels in recent years. And he might very well have become president.

Sanders called for a "political revolution," and with the sharp rightward drift of the past thirty years of the neoliberal assault, the term may not be inappropriate. His basically New Deal proposals, however, would not have surprised Dwight Eisenhower. It is useful to recall the nature of conservatism at the outset of Eisenhower's term in 1952, when he said, for example, that he has no use for those—regardless of their political party—who hold some foolish dream of spinning the clock back to days when unorganized labor was a huddled, almost helpless mass. . . . Today in America unions have a secure place in our industrial life. Only a handful of unreconstructed reactionaries harbor the ugly thought of breaking unions. Only a fool would try to deprive working men and women of the right to join the union of their choice.

And more generally, Eisenhower held that those who question New Deal policies have no place in the US political system.

Such ideas are not far below the surface, even as the political class has shifted very far to the right, with Clinton Democrats becoming what used to be called "moderate Republicans," and Republicans mostly drifting off the spectrum. They can be revived. The Sanders campaign was a dramatic illustration—not the only one. And those are by no means the limits of legitimate aspirations.

It's easy to succumb to a sense of futility and despair, but objective circumstances provide no justification for that stance. There have been many gains over past years thanks to struggles undertaken under far harsher conditions than those of today. These gains provide us with a legacy that offers a great many opportunities to avoid the worst, and to move on to a much better future.

The Long History of US Meddling in Foreign Elections

C. J. POLYCHRONIOU: Noam, the US intelligence agencies have accused Russia of interference in the US presidential election in order to boost Trump's chances, and some leading Democrats have actually gone on record saying that the Kremlin's canny operatives changed the election outcome. What's your reaction to all this talk in Washington and among media pundits about Russian cyber and propaganda efforts to influence the outcome of the presidential election in Donald Trump's favor?

NOAM CHOMSKY: Much of the world must be astonished—if they are not collapsing in laughter—while watching the performances in high places and in media concerning Russian efforts to influence an American election, a familiar US government specialty as far back as we choose to trace the practice. There is, however, merit in the claim that this case is different in character: by US standards, the Russian efforts are so meager as to barely elicit notice.

Let's talk about the long history of US meddling in foreign political affairs, which has always been morally and politically justified as the spread of American style-democracy throughout the world.

The history of US foreign policy, especially after World War II, is pretty much defined by the subversion and overthrow of foreign regimes, including parliamentary regimes, and the resort to violence to destroy popular organizations that might offer the majority of the population opportunities to enter the political arena.

Following the Second World War, the United States was committed to restoring the traditional conservative order. To achieve this aim, it was necessary to destroy the anti-Fascist resistance, often in favor of Nazi and Fascist collaborators, to weaken unions and other popular organizations, and to block the threat of radical democracy and social reform, which were live options under the conditions of the time. These policies were pursued worldwide—in Asia, including South Korea, the Philippines, Thailand, Indochina, and crucially, Japan; in Europe, including Greece, Italy, France, and crucially, Germany; in Latin America, including what the CIA took to be the most severe threats at the time, "radical nationalism" in Guatemala and Bolivia.

Sometimes the task required considerable brutality. In South Korea, about 100,000 people were killed in the late 1940s by security forces installed and directed by the United States. This was before the Korean war, which Jon Halliday and Bruce Cumings describe as "in essence" a phase—marked by massive outside intervention—in "a civil war fought between two domestic forces: a revolutionary nationalist movement, which had its roots in tough anti-colonial struggle, and a conservative movement tied to the status quo, especially to an unequal land system," restored to power under the US occupation. In Greece in the same years, hundreds of thousands were killed, tortured, imprisoned or expelled in the course of a counterinsurgency operation, organized and directed by the United States, which restored traditional elites to power, including Nazi collaborators, and suppressed the peasant- and worker-based communist-led forces that had fought the Nazis. In the industrial societies, the same essential goals were realized, but by less violent means.

Yet it is true that there have been cases where the US was directly involved in organizing coups even in advanced industrial democracies, such as in Australia and Italy in the mid-1970s. Correct?

Yes, there is evidence of CIA involvement in a virtual coup that overturned the Whitlam Labor government in Australia in 1975, when it was feared that Whitlam might interfere with Washington's military and intelligence bases in Australia. Large-scale CIA interference in Italian politics has been public knowledge since the congressional Pike Report was leaked in 1976, citing a figure of over $65 million to approved political parties and affiliates from 1948 through the early 1970s. In 1976, the Aldo Moro government fell in Italy after revelations that the CIA had spent $6 million to support anti-communist candidates. At the time, the European communist parties were moving toward independence of action with pluralistic and democratic tendencies (Eurocommunism), a development that in fact pleased neither Washington nor Moscow. For such reasons, both superpowers opposed the legalization of the Communist Party of Spain and the rising influence of the Communist Party in Italy, and both preferred center-right governments in France. Secretary of State Henry Kissinger described the "major problem" in the Western alliance as "the domestic evolution in many European countries," which might make Western communist parties more attractive to the public, nurturing moves towards independence and threatening the NATO alliance.

US interventions in the political affairs of other nations have always been morally and politically justified as part of the faith in the doctrine of spreading American-style democracy, but the actual reason was of course the spread of capitalism and the dominance of business rule. Was faith in the spread of democracy ever tenable?

No belief concerning US foreign policy is more deeply entrenched than the one regarding the spread of American-style democracy. The thesis is commonly not even expressed, merely presupposed as the basis for reasonable discourse on the US role in the world.

The faith in this doctrine may seem surprising. Nevertheless, there is a sense in which the conventional doctrine is tenable. If by "American-style democracy," we mean a political system with regular elections but no serious challenge to business rule, then US policymakers doubtless yearn to see it established throughout the world. The doctrine is therefore not undermined by the fact that it is consistently violated under a different interpretation of democracy, a system where citizens may play meaningful parts in the management of public affairs.

So, what lessons can be drawn from all this about the concept of democracy as understood by US policy planners in their effort to create a New World Order?

One problem that arose as areas were liberated from Fascism [after World War II] was that traditional elites had been discredited, while prestige and influence had been gained by resistance movements, based largely on groups responsive to the working class and poor, and often committed to some version of radical democracy. The basic quandary was articulated by Churchill's trusted adviser, South African Prime Minister Jan Christiaan Smuts, in 1943, with regard to southern Europe: "With politics let loose among those peoples," he said, "we might have a wave of disorder and wholesale Communism."

Here the term "disorder" is understood as threat to the interests of the privileged, and "Communism," in accordance with usual convention, refers to failure to interpret "democracy" as elite dominance, whatever the other commitments of the "Communists" may be. With politics let loose, we face a "crisis of democracy," as privileged sectors have always understood.

In brief, at that moment in history, the United States faced the classic dilemma of Third World intervention in large parts of the industrial world as well. The US position was "politically weak," though militarily and economically strong. Tactical choices are determined by an assessment of strengths and weaknesses. The preference has, quite naturally, been for the arenas of force and economic warfare and strangulation, where the US has ruled supreme.

Wasn't the Marshall Plan a tool for consolidating capitalism and spreading business rule throughout Europe after World War II?

Very much so. For example, the extension of Marshall Plan aid in countries like France and Italy was strictly contingent on exclusion of communists—including major elements of the anti-Fascist resistance and labor—from the government; this is "democracy" in the usual sense. US aid was critically important in early years for suffering people in Europe and was therefore a powerful lever of control, a matter of much significance for US business interests and longer term planning. The fear in Washington was that the communist left would emerge victorious in Italy and France without massive financial assistance.

On the eve of the announcement of the Marshall Plan, ambassador to France Jefferson Caffery warned Secretary of State Marshall of grim consequences if the communists won the elections in France: "Soviet penetration of Western Europe, Africa, the Mediterranean, and the Middle East would be greatly facilitated" (May 12, 1947). The dominoes were ready to fall. During May, the US pressured political leaders in France and Italy to form coalition governments excluding the communists. It was made clear and explicit that aid was contingent on preventing an open political competition, in which left and labor might dominate. Through 1948, Secretary of State Marshall and others publicly emphasized that if communists were voted into power, US aid would be terminated. This was no small threat, given the state of Europe at the time.

In France, the postwar destitution was exploited to undermine the French labor movement, along with direct violence. Desperately needed food supplies were withheld to coerce obedience, and gangsters were organized to provide goon squads and strike breakers, a matter that is described with some pride in semi-official US labor histories. They praise the AFL [American Federation of Labor] for its achievements in helping to save Europe by splitting and weakening the labor movement (thus frustrating alleged Soviet designs) and safeguarding the flow of arms to Indochina for the French war of reconquest, another prime goal of the US labor bureaucracy. The CIA reconstituted the Mafia for these purposes, in one of its early operations. The quid pro quo was restoration of the heroin trade. The US government connection to the drug boom continued for many decades.

US policies toward Italy basically picked up where they had been broken off by World War II. The United States had supported Mussolini's Fascism from the 1922 takeover through the 1930s. Mussolini's wartime alliance with Hitler terminated these friendly relations, but they were reconstituted as US forces liberated southern Italy in 1943, establishing the rule of Field Marshall [Pietro] Badoglio and the royal family that had collaborated with the Fascist government. As Allied forces drove toward the north, they dispersed the anti-Fascist resistance along with local governing bodies formed in its attempt to establish a new democratic state in the zones it had liberated from Germany. Eventually, a center-right government was established with neo-Fascist participation and the left soon excluded.

Here too, the plan was for the working classes and the poor to bear the burden of reconstruction, with lowered wages and extensive firing. Aid was contingent on removing communists and left socialists from office, because they defended workers' interests and thus posed a barrier to the intended style of recovery, in the view of the State Department. The Communist Party was collaborationist; its position "fundamentally meant the subordination of all reforms to the liberation of Italy and effectively discouraged any attempt in northern areas to introduce irreversible political changes as well as changes in the ownership of the industrial companies . . . disavowing and discouraging those workers' groups that wanted to expropriate some factories," as Gianfranco Pasquino put it.

But the party did try to defend jobs, wages, and living standards for the poor and thus "constituted a political and psychological barrier to a potential European recovery program," historian John Harper comments, reviewing the insistence of Kennan and others that communists be excluded from government though agreeing that it would be "desirable" to include representatives of what Harper calls the "democratic working class." The recovery, it was understood, was to be at the expense of the working class and the poor.

Because of its responsiveness to the needs of these social sectors, the Communist Party was labeled "extremist" and "undemocratic" by US propaganda, which also skillfully manipulated the alleged Soviet threat. Under US pressure, the Christian Democrats abandoned wartime promises about workplace democracy and the police, sometimes under the control of ex-Fascists, were encouraged to suppress labor activities. The Vatican announced that anyone who voted for the communists in the 1948 election would be denied sacraments, and backed the conservative Christian Democrats under the slogan: "*O con Cristo o contro Cristo*" ("Either with Christ or against Christ"). A year later, Pope Pius excommunicated all Italian communists.

A combination of violence, manipulation of aid, and other threats, and a huge propaganda campaign sufficed to determine the outcome of the critical 1948 election, essentially bought by US intervention and pressures.

The CIA operations to control the Italian elections, authorized by the National Security Council in December 1947, were the first major clandestine operation of the newly formed agency. CIA operations to subvert Italian democracy continued into the 1970s at a substantial scale.

In Italy, as well as elsewhere, US labor leaders, primarily from the AFL, played an active role in splitting and weakening the labor movement, and inducing workers to accept austerity measures while employers reaped rich profits. In France, the AFL had broken dock strikes by importing Italian scab labor paid by US businesses. The State Department called on the Federation's leadership to exercise their talents in union-busting in Italy as well, and they were happy to oblige. The business sector, formerly discredited by its association with Italian Fascism, undertook a vigorous class war with renewed confidence. The end result was the subordination of the working class and the poor to the traditional rulers.

Later commentators tend to see the US subversion of democracy in France and Italy as a defense of democracy. In a highly regarded study of the CIA and American democracy, Rhodri Jeffreys-Jones describes "the CIA's Italian venture," along with its similar efforts in France, as "a democracy-propping operation," though he concedes that "the selection of Italy for special attention . . . was by no means a matter of democratic principle alone." Our passion for democracy was reinforced by the strategic importance of the country. But it was a commitment to "democratic principle" that inspired the US government to impose the social and political regimes of its choice, using the enormous power at its command and exploiting the privation and distress of the victims of the war, who must be taught not to raise their heads if we are to have true democracy.

A more nuanced position is taken by James Miller in his monograph on US policies toward Italy. Summarizing the record, he concludes that "in retrospect, American involvement in the stabilization of Italy was a significant, if troubling, achievement. American power assured Italians the right to choose their future form of government and also was employed to ensure that they chose democracy. In defense of that democracy against real but probably overestimated foreign and domestic threats, the United States used undemocratic tactics that tended to undermine the legitimacy of the Italian state."

The "foreign threats," as he had already discussed, were hardly real; the Soviet Union watched from a distance as the US subverted the 1948 election and restored the traditional conservative order, keeping to its wartime agreement with Churchill that left Italy in the Western zone. The "domestic threat" was the threat of democracy.

The idea that US intervention provided Italians with freedom of choice while ensuring that they chose "democracy" (in our special sense of the term) is reminiscent of the attitude of the extreme doves toward Latin America: that its people should choose freely and independently—as long as doing so did not impact US interests adversely.

The democratic ideal, at home and abroad, is simple and straightforward: You are free to do what you want, as long as it is what we want you to do.

The US Health System Is an International Scandal

C. J. POLYCHRONIOU: **Trump and the Republicans are bent on doing away with Obamacare. Doesn't the 2010 Patient Protection and Affordable Care Act (ACA) represent an improvement over what existed before? And, what would the Republicans replace it with?**

NOAM CHOMSKY: I perhaps should say, to begin, that I have always felt a little uncomfortable about the term "Obamacare." Did anyone call Medicare "Johnsoncare?" Maybe wrongly, but it has seemed to me to have a tinge of Republican-style vulgar disparagement, maybe even of racism. But put that aside. . . . Yes, the ACA is a definite improvement over what came before—which is not a great compliment. The US health care system has long been an international scandal, with about twice the per capita expenses of other wealthy (OECD) countries and relatively poor outcomes. The ACA did, however, bring improvements, including insurance for tens of millions of people who lacked it, banning of refusal of insurance for people with prior disabilities, and other gains—and also, it appears to have led to a reduction in the increase of health care costs, though that is hard to determine precisely.

The House of Representatives, dominated by Republicans (with a minority of voters), has voted more than fifty times in the past six years to repeal or weaken Obamacare, but they have yet to come up with anything like a coherent alternative. That is not too surprising. Since Obama's election, the Republicans have been pretty much the party of NO. Chances are that they will now adopt a cynical [Paul] Ryan-style evasion, repeal, and delay, to pretend to be honoring their fervent pledges while avoiding at least for a time the consequences of a possible major collapse of the health system and ballooning costs. It's far from certain. It's conceivable that they might patch together some kind of plan, or that the ultraright and quite passionate "Freedom Caucus" may insist on instant repeal without a plan, damn the consequence for the budget, or, of course, for people.

One part of the health system that is likely to suffer is Medicaid, probably through block grants to states, which gives the Republican-run states opportunities to gut it. Medicaid only helps poor people who "don't matter" and don't vote Republican anyway. So [according to Republican logic], why should the rich pay taxes to maintain it?

Article 25 of the UN Universal Declaration on Human Rights (UDHR) states that the right to health care is indeed a human right. Yet, it is estimated that close to 30 million Americans remain uninsured even with the ACA in place. What are some of the key cultural, economic, and political factors that make the US an outlier in the provision of free health care?

First, it is important to remember that the US does not accept the Universal Declaration of Human Rights—though in fact the UDHR was largely the initiative of Eleanor Roosevelt, who chaired the commission that drafted its articles, with quite broad international participation.

The UDHR has three components, which are of equal status: civil-political, socioeconomic, and cultural rights. The US formally accepts the first of the three, though it has often violated its provisions. The US pretty much disregards the third. And to the point here, the US has officially and strongly condemned the second component, socioeconomic rights, including Article 25.

Opposition to Article 25 was particularly vehement in the Reagan and Bush I years. Paula Dobriansky, deputy assistant secretary of state for human rights and humanitarian affairs in these administrations, dismissed the "myth" that "'economic and social rights constitute human rights," as the UDHR declares. She was following the lead of Reagan's UN Ambassador Jeane Kirkpatrick, who ridiculed the myth as "little more than an empty vessel into which vague hopes and inchoate expectations can be poured." Kirkpatrick thus joined Soviet ambassador Andrei Vyshinsky, who agreed that it was a mere "collection of pious phrases." The concepts of Article 25 are "preposterous" and even a "dangerous incitement," according to Ambassador Morris Abram, the distinguished civil rights attorney who was US Representative to the UN Commission on Human Rights under Bush I, casting the sole veto of the UN Right to Development, which closely paraphrased Article 25 of the UDHR. The Bush II administration maintained the tradition by voting alone to reject a UN resolution on the right to food and the right to the highest attainable standard of physical and mental health (the resolution passed 52-1). Rejection of Article 25, then, is a matter of principle. And also a matter of practice. In the OECD [Organization for Economic Cooperation and Development] ranking of social justice, the US is in 27th place out of 31, right above Greece, Chile, Mexico, and Turkey. This is happening in the richest country in world history, with incomparable advantages. It was quite possibly already the richest region in the world in the 18th century.

In extenuation of the Reagan-Bush-Vyshinsky alliance on this matter, we should recognize that formal support for the UDHR is all too often divorced from practice.

US dismissal of the UDHR in principle and practice extends to other areas. Take labor rights. The US has failed to ratify the first principle of the International Labour Organization Convention, which endorses "Freedom of Association and Protection of the Right to Organise." An editorial comment in the American Journal of International Law refers to this provision of the International Labour Organization Convention as "the untouchable treaty in American politics." US rejection is guarded with such fervor, the report continues, that there has never even been any debate about the matter. The rejection of International Labour Organization Conventions contrasts dramatically with the fervor of Washington's dedication to the highly protectionist elements of the misnamed "free trade agreements," designed to guarantee monopoly pricing rights for corporations ("intellectual property rights"), on spurious grounds. In general, it would be more accurate to call these "investor rights agreements."

Comparison of the attitude toward elementary rights of labor and extraordinary rights of private power tells us a good deal about the nature of American society.

Furthermore, US labor history is unusually violent. Hundreds of US workers were being killed by private and state security forces in strike actions, practices unknown in similar countries. In her history of American labor, Patricia Sexton—noting that there are no serious studies—reports an estimate of 700 strikers killed and thousands injured from 1877 to 1968, a figure which, she concludes, may "grossly understate the total casualties." In comparison, one British striker was killed since 1911.

As struggles for freedom gained victories and violent means became less available, business turned to softer measures, such as the "scientific methods of strike breaking" that have become a leading industry. In much the same way, the overthrow of reformist governments by violence, once routine, has been displaced by "soft coups" such as the recent coup in Brazil, though the former options are still pursued when possible, as in Obama's support for the Honduran military coup in 2009, in near isolation. Labor remains relatively weak in the US in comparison to similar societies. It is constantly battling even for survival as a significant organized force in the society, under particularly harsh attack since the Reagan years.

All of this is part of the background for the US departure in health care from the norm of the OECD, and even less privileged societies. But there are deeper reasons why the US is an "outlier" in health care and social justice generally. These trace back to unusual features of American history. Unlike other developed state capitalist industrial democracies, the political economy and social structure of the United States developed in a kind of *tabula rasa*. The expulsion or mass killing of Indigenous nations cleared the ground for the invading settlers, who had enormous resources and ample fertile lands at their disposal, and extraordinary security for reasons of geography and power. That led to the rise of a society of individual farmers, and also, thanks to slavery, substantial control of the product that fueled the Industrial Revolution—cotton, the foundation of manufacturing, banking, commerce, retail for both the US and Britain, and less directly, other European societies. Also relevant is the fact that the country has actually been at war for five hundred years with little respite, a history that has created "the richest, most powerful, and ultimately most militarized nation in world history," as scholar Walter Hixson has documented.

For similar reasons, American society lacked the traditional social stratification and autocratic political structure of Europe, and the various measures of social support that developed unevenly and erratically. There has been ample state intervention in the economy from the outset—dramatically in recent years—but without general support systems.

As a result, US society is, to an unusual extent, business-run, with a highly class-conscious business community dedicated to "the everlasting battle for the minds of men." The business community is also set on containing or demolishing the "political power of the masses," which it deems as a serious "hazard to industrialists" (to sample some of the rhetoric of the business press during the New Deal years, when the threat to the overwhelming dominance of business power seemed real).

Here is yet another anomaly about US health care: according to data by the Organization for Economic Cooperation and Development, the US spends far more on health care than most other advanced nations, yet Americans have poor health outcomes and are plagued by chronic illnesses at higher rates than the citizens of other advanced nations. Why is that?

US health care costs are estimated to be about twice the OECD average, with rather poor outcomes by comparative standards. Infant mortality, for example, is higher in the US than in Cuba, Greece, and the EU generally, according to CIA figures.

As for reasons, we can return to the more general question of social justice comparisons, but there are special reasons in the health care domain. To an unusual extent, the US health care system is privatized and unregulated. Insurance companies are in the business of making money, not providing health care, and when they undertake the latter, it is likely not to be in the best interests of patients or to be efficient. Administrative costs are far greater in the private component of the health care system than in Medicare, which itself suffers by having to work through the private system.

Comparisons with other countries reveal much more bureaucracy and higher administrative costs in the US privatized system than elsewhere. One study of the US and Canada a decade ago, by medical researcher Steffie Woolhandler and associates, found enormous disparities, and concluded that "reducing US administrative costs to Canadian levels would save at least $209 billion annually, enough to fund universal coverage." Another anomalous feature of the US system is the law banning the government from negotiating drug prices, which leads to highly inflated prices in the US as compared with other countries. That effect is magnified considerably by the extreme patent rights accorded to the pharmaceutical industry in "trade agreements," enabling monopoly profits. In a profit-driven system, there are also incentives for expensive treatments rather than preventive care, as strikingly in Cuba, with remarkably efficient and effective health care.

Why aren't Americans demanding—not simply expressing a preference for in survey polls—access to a universal health care system?

They are indeed expressing a preference, over a long period. Just to give one telling illustration, in the late Reagan years 70 percent of the adult population thought that health care should be a constitutional guarantee, and 40 percent thought it already was in the Constitution since it is such an obviously legitimate right. Poll results depend on wording and nuance, but they have quite consistently, over the years, shown strong and often large majority support for universal health care—often called "Canadian-style," not because Canada necessarily has the best system, but because it is close by and observable. The early ACA proposals called for a "public option." It was supported by almost two-thirds of the population, but was dropped without serious consideration, presumably as part of a compact with financial institutions. The legislative bar to government negotiation of drug prices was opposed by 85 percent, also disregarded—again, presumably, to prevent opposition by the pharmaceutical giants. The preference for universal health care is particularly remarkable in light of the fact that there is almost no support or advocacy in sources that reach the general public and virtually no discussion in the public domain.

The facts about public support for universal health care receive occasional comment, in an interesting way. When running for president in 2004, Democrat John Kerry, *The New York Times* reported, "took pains . . . to say that his plan for expanding access to health insurance would not create a new government program," because "there is so little political support for government intervention in the health care market in the United

States." At the same time, polls in *The Wall Street Journal*, *Businessweek*, *The Washington Post* and other media found overwhelming public support for government guarantees to everyone of "the best and most advanced health care that technology can supply."

But that is only public support. The press reported correctly that there was little "political support" and that what the public wants is "politically impossible"—a polite way of saying that the financial and pharmaceutical industries will not tolerate it, and in American democracy, that's what counts.

Returning to your question, it raises a crucial question about American democracy: why isn't the population "demanding" what it strongly prefers? Why is it allowing concentrated private capital to undermine necessities of life in the interests of profit and power? The "demands" are hardly utopian. They are commonly satisfied elsewhere, even in sectors of the US system. Furthermore, the demands could readily be implemented even without significant legislative breakthroughs. For example, by steadily reducing the age for entry to Medicare.

The question directs our attention to a profound democratic deficit in an atomized society, lacking the kind of popular associations and organizations that enable the public to participate in a meaningful way in determining the course of political, social, and economic affairs. These would crucially include a strong and participatory labor movement and actual political parties growing from public deliberation and participation instead of the elite-run, candidate-producing groups that pass for political parties. What remains is a depoliticized society in which a majority of voters (barely half the population even in the super-hyped presidential elections, much less in others) are literally disenfranchised. Their representatives disregard their preferences, make decisions to benefit the corporate power and the wealthy, as study after study reveals.

The prevailing situation reminds us of the words of America's leading 20th-century social philosopher, John Dewey, whose work largely focused on democracy and its failures and promise. Dewey deplored the domination by "business for private profit through private control of banking, land, industry, reinforced by command of the press, press agents and other means of publicity and propaganda" and recognized that "power today resides in control of the means of production, exchange, publicity, transportation and communication. Whoever owns them rules the life of the country," even if democratic forms remain. Until those institutions are in the hands of the public, he continued, politics will remain "the shadow cast on society by big business."

This was not a voice from the marginalized far left, but from the mainstream of liberal thought.

Turning finally to your question again, a rather general answer, which applies in its specific way to contemporary Western democracies, was provided by David Hume over 250 years ago, in his classic study *Of the First Principles of Government*. Hume found

> nothing more surprising than to see the easiness with which the many are governed by the few; and to observe the implicit submission with which men resign their own sentiments and passions to those of their rulers. When we enquire by what means this wonder is brought about, we shall find, that as Force is always on the side of the governed, the governors have nothing to support them but opinion. 'Tis therefore, on opinion only that government is founded; and this maxim extends to the most despotic and most military governments, as well as to the most free and most popular.

Implicit submission is not imposed by laws of nature or political theory. It is a choice, at least in societies such as ours, which enjoys the legacy provided by the struggles of those who came before us. Here power is indeed "on the side of the governed," if they organize and act to gain and exercise it. That holds for health care and for much else.

Trump's America and the New World Order

C. J. POLYCHRONIOU: Noam, the president-elect's cabinet is being filled by financial and corporate bigwigs and military leaders. Such selections hardly reconcile with Trump's preelection promises to "drain the swamp," so what should we expect from this megalomaniac and phony populist insofar as the future of the Washington establishment is concerned?

NOAM CHOMSKY: In this respect—note the qualification—*Time* magazine put it fairly well (in a Dec. 26 column by Joe Klein): "While some supporters may balk, Trump's decision to embrace those who have wallowed in the Washington muck has spread a sense of relief among the capital's political class. 'It shows,' says one GOP consultant close to the President-elect's transition, 'that he's going to govern like a normal Republican.'"

There surely is some truth to this. Business and investors plainly think so. The stock market boomed right after the election, led by the financial companies that Trump denounced during his campaign, particularly the leading demon of his rhetoric, Goldman Sachs. According to Bloomberg News, "the firm's surging stock price," up 30 percent in the month after the election, "has been the largest driver behind the Dow Jones Industrial Average's climb toward 20,000." The stellar market performance of Goldman Sachs is based largely on Trump's reliance on the demon to run the economy, buttressed by the promised rollback in regulations, setting the stage for the next financial crisis (and taxpayer bailout).

Other big gainers are energy corporations, health insurers, and construction firms, all expecting huge profits from the administration's announced plans. These include a Paul Ryan–style fiscal program of tax cuts for the rich and corporations; increased military spending; turning the health care system over even more to insurance companies, with predictable consequences; taxpayer largesse for a privatized form of credit-based infrastructure development; and other "normal Republican" gifts to wealth and privilege at taxpayer expense. Rather plausibly, economist Larry Summers describes the fiscal program as "the most misguided set of tax changes in US history [which] will massively favor the top 1 per cent of income earners, threaten an explosive rise in federal debt, complicate the tax code and do little if anything to spur growth."

But, great news for those who matter.

There are, however, some losers in the corporate system. Since November 8, gun sales, which more than doubled under Obama, have been dropping sharply, perhaps because of lessened fears that the government will take away the assault rifles and other armaments we need to protect ourselves from the Feds. Sales rose through the year as polls showed Clinton in the lead, but after the election, the *Financial Times* reported, "Shares in gun makers such as Smith & Wesson and Sturm Ruger plunged." By mid-December, "the two companies had fallen 24 per cent and 17 per cent since the election, respectively." But all is not lost for the industry. As a spokesman explains, "To put it in perspective, US consumer sales of firearms are greater than the rest of the world combined. It's a pretty big market."

Normal Republicans cheer Trump's choice for Office of Management and Budget, Mick Mulvaney, one of the most extreme fiscal hawks, though a problem does arise—how will a fiscal hawk manage a budget designed to massively escalate the deficit? In a post-fact world, maybe that doesn't matter.

Also cheering to "normal Republicans" is the choice of the radically anti-labor Andy Puzder for secretary of labor, though here too a contradiction may lurk in the background. As an ultrarich CEO of restaurant chains, he relies on the most easily exploited nonunion labor, typically immigrants, for the dirty work; this doesn't comport well with the plans to deport them en masse. The same problem arises for the infrastructure programs, as the private firms set to profit from these initiatives rely heavily on the same labor source. Perhaps that problem can be finessed by redesigning the "beautiful wall" so that it will only keep out Muslims.

Is this to say then that Trump will be a "normal" Republican as America's 45th president?

In such respects as the ones mentioned above, Trump proved himself very quickly to be a normal Republican, if to the extremist side. But in other respects he may not be a normal Republican, if that means something like a mainstream establishment Republican—people like Mitt Romney, whom Trump went out of his way to humiliate in his familiar style, just as he did to McCain and others of this category. But it's not only his style that causes offense and concern. His actions do as well.

Take just the two most significant issues that we face, the most significant that humans have ever faced in their brief history on earth, issues that bear on species survival—nuclear war and global warming. Shivers went up the spine of many "normal Republicans," as of others who care about the fate of the species, when Trump tweeted that "the United States must greatly strengthen and expand its nuclear capability until such time as the world comes to its senses regarding nukes." Expanding nuclear capability means casting to the winds the treaties that have sharply reduced nuclear arsenals and that sane analysts hope may reduce them much further, in fact, to zero, as advocated by such normal Republicans as Henry Kissinger and Reagan secretary of state George Shultz, and by Reagan, in some of his moments. Concerns did not abate when Trump went on to tell the cohost of the TV show *Morning Joe*, "Let it be an arms race. We will outmatch them at every pass." And it wasn't too comforting when his White House team tried to explain that "The Donald" didn't say what he said.

Nor do concerns abate because Trump was presumably reacting to Putin's statement: "We need to strengthen the military potential of strategic nuclear forces, especially with missile complexes that can reliably penetrate any existing and prospective missile defense systems. We must carefully monitor any changes in the balance of power and in the political-military situation in the world, especially along Russian borders, and quickly adapt plans for neutralizing threats to our country."

Whatever one thinks of these words, they have a defensive cast, and as Putin has stressed, they are in large part a reaction to the highly provocative installation of a missile defense system on Russia's border on the pretext of defense against nonexistent Iranian weapons. Trump's tweet intensifies fears about how he might react when crossed, for example, by unwillingness of some adversary to bow to his vaunted negotiating skills. If the past is any guide, he might, after all, find himself in a situation where he must decide within a few minutes whether to blow up the world.

The other crucial issue is environmental catastrophe. It cannot be stressed too strongly that Trump won two victories on November 8—the lesser one in the Electoral College and the greater one in Marrakech, where some two hundred countries were seeking to put teeth in the promises of the Paris negotiations on climate change. On Election Day, the conference heard a dire report on the state of the Anthropocene from the World Meteorological Organization. As the results of the election came in, the stunned participants virtually abandoned the proceedings, wondering if anything could survive the withdrawal of the most powerful state in world history. Nor can one stress too often the astonishing spectacle of the world placing its hopes for salvation in China, while the leader of the free world stands alone as a wrecking machine.

Although, amazingly, most ignored these astounding events, establishment circles did have some response. In *Foreign Affairs*, Varun Sivaram and Sagatom Saha warned of the costs to the US of "ceding climate leadership to China," and the dangers to the world because China "would lead on climate-change issues only insofar as doing so would advance its national interests"—unlike the altruistic United States, which supposedly labors selflessly only for the benefit of mankind.

Trump's determination to drive the world to the precipice was revealed by his appointments, including his choices of two militant climate change deniers, Myron Ebell and Scott Pruit, to take charge of dismantling the Environmental Protection Agency (established under Richard Nixon) with another denier slated to head the Department of Interior.

But that's only the beginning. The cabinet appointments would be comical if the implications were not so serious. For Department of Energy, a man who said it should be eliminated (when he could remember its name) and is perhaps unaware that its main concern is nuclear weapons. For Department of Education, another billionaire, Betsy DeVos, who is dedicated to undermining and perhaps eliminating the public school system and who, as Lawrence Krause reminds us in the *New Yorker*, is a fundamentalist Christian member of a Protestant denomination holding that "all scientific theories be subject to Scripture" and that "Humanity is created in the image of God; all theorizing that minimizes this fact and all theories of evolution that deny the creative activity of God are rejected." Perhaps the Department should request funding from Saudi sponsors of Wahhabi madrassas to help the process along.

DeVos's appointment is no doubt attractive to the evangelicals who flocked to Trump's standard and constitute a large part of the base of today's Republican Party. She should also be able to work amicably with Vice-President-elect Mike Pence, one of the "prized warriors [of] a cabal of vicious zealots who have long craved an extremist Christian theocracy," as Jeremy Scahill details in *The Intercept*, reviewing his shocking record on other matters as well.

And so it continues, case by case. But not to worry. As James Madison assured his colleagues as they were framing the Constitution, a national republic would "extract from the mass of the Society the purest and noblest characters which it contains."

What about the choice of Rex Tillerson as secretary of state?

One partial exception to the above is choice of ExxonMobil CEO Rex Tillerson for secretary of state, which has aroused some hope among those across the spectrum who are rightly concerned with the rising and extremely hazardous tensions with Russia. Tillerson, like Trump in some of his pronouncements, has called for diplomacy rather than confrontation, which is all to the good—until we remember the sable lining of the beam of sunshine. The motive is to allow ExxonMobil to exploit vast Siberian oil fields and so to accelerate the race to disaster to which Trump and associates, and the Republican Party rather generally, are committed.

And how about Trump's national security staff—do they fit the mold of "normal" Republicans, or are they also part of the extreme right?

Normal Republicans might be somewhat ambivalent about Trump's national security staff. It is led by National Security Advisor Gen. Michael Flynn, a radical Islamophobe who declares that Islam is not a religion but rather, a political ideology, like Fascism, which is at war with us. Thus, we must defend ourselves, presumably against the whole Muslim world—a fine recipe for generating terrorists, not to speak of far worse consequences. Like the Red Menace of earlier years, this Islamic ideology is penetrating deep into American society, Flynn claims. They are, he says, being helped by Democrats, who have voted to impose Sharia law in Florida, much as their predecessors served the Commies, as Joe McCarthy famously demonstrated. Indeed, there are "over 100 cases around the country," including Texas, Flynn warned in a speech in San Antonio. To ward off the imminent threat, Flynn is a board member of ACT!, which pushes state laws banning Sharia law, plainly an imminent threat in states like Oklahoma, where 70 percent of voters approved legislation to prevent the courts from applying this grim menace to the judicial system.

Second to Flynn in the national security apparatus is Secretary of Defense Gen. James "Mad Dog" Mattis, considered a relative moderate. Mad Dog has explained that "it's fun to shoot some people." He achieved his fame by leading the assault on Fallujah in November 2004, one of the most vicious crimes of the Iraq invasion. A man who is "just great," according to the president-elect: "the closest thing we have to Gen. George Patton."

In your view, is Trump bent on a collision course with China?

It's hard to say. Concerns were voiced about Trump's attitudes toward China, again full of contradictions, particularly his pronouncements on trade, which are almost meaningless in the current system of corporate globalization and complex international supply chains. Eyebrows were raised over his sharp departure from long-standing policy in his phone call with Taiwan's president, but even more by his implying that the US might reject China's concerns over Taiwan unless China accepts his trade proposals, thus linking trade policy "to an issue of great-power politics over which China may be willing to go to war," the business press warned.

What of Trump's views and stance on the Middle East? They seem to be in line with those of "normal" Republicans, right?

Unlike with China, normal Republicans did not seem dismayed by Trump's tweet foray into Middle East diplomacy. Breaking with standard protocol, they demanded that Obama veto UN Security Council resolution 2334, which reaffirmed "that the policy and practices of Israel in establishing settlements in the Palestinian and other Arab territories occupied since 1967 have no legal validity and constitute a serious obstruction to achieving a comprehensive, just and lasting peace in the Middle East [and] Calls once more upon Israel, as the occupying Power, to abide scrupulously by the 1949 Fourth Geneva Convention, to rescind its previous measures and to desist from taking any action which would result in changing the legal status and geographical nature and materially affecting the demographic composition of the Arab territories occupied since 1967, including Jerusalem, and, in particular, not to transfer parts of its own civilian population into the occupied Arab territories."

Nor did they object when he informed Israel that it can ignore the lame duck administration and just wait until January 20, when all will be in order. What kind of order? That remains to be seen. Trump's unpredictability serves as a word of caution.

What we know so far is Trump's enthusiasm for the religious ultraright in Israel and the settler movement generally. Among his largest charitable contributions are gifts to the West Bank settlement of Beth El in honor of David Friedman, his choice as ambassador to Israel. Friedman is president of American Friends of Beth El Institutions. The settlement, which is at the religious ultranationalist extreme of the settler movement, is also a favorite of the family of Jared Kushner, Trump's son-in-law, reported to be one of Trump's closest advisers. A lead beneficiary of the Kushner family's contributions, the Israeli press reports, "is a yeshiva headed by a militant rabbi who has urged Israeli soldiers to disobey orders to evacuate settlements and who has argued that homosexual tendencies arise from eating certain foods." Other beneficiaries include "a radical yeshiva in Yitzhar that has served as a base for violent attacks against Palestinian villages and Israeli security forces."

In isolation from the world, Friedman does not regard Israeli settlement activity as illegal and opposes a ban on construction for Jewish settlers in the West Bank and East Jerusalem. In fact, he appears to favor Israel's annexation of the West Bank. That would not pose a problem for the Jewish state, Friedman explains, since the number of Palestinians living in the West Bank is exaggerated and therefore a large Jewish majority would remain after annexation. In a post-fact world, such pronouncements are legitimate, though they might become accurate in the boring world of fact after another mass expulsion. Jews who support the international consensus on a two-state settlement are not just wrong, Friedman says, they are "worse than kapos," the Jews who were controlling other inmates in service to their Nazi masters in the concentration camps—the ultimate insult.

On receiving the report of his nomination, Friedman said he looked forward to moving the US embassy to "Israel's eternal capital, Jerusalem," in accord with Trump's announced plans. In the past, such proposals were withdrawn, but today they might actually be fulfilled, perhaps advancing the prospects of a war with the Muslim world, as Trump's national security adviser appears to recommend.

Returning to UNSC 2334 and its interesting aftermath, it is important to recognize that the resolution is nothing new. The quote given above was not from UNSC 2334 but from UNSC Resolution 446, passed on March 12, 1979, reiterated in essence in UNSC 2334.

UNSC 446 passed 12-0 with the US abstaining, joined by the UK and Norway. Several resolutions followed, reaffirming 446. One resolution of particular interest was even stronger than 446-2334, calling on Israel "to dismantle the existing settlements" (UNSC Resolution 465, passed in March 1980). This resolution passed unanimously, no abstentions.

The government of Israel did not have to wait for the UN Security Council (and more recently, the World Court) to learn that its settlements are in gross violation of international law. In September 1967, only weeks after Israel's conquest of the occupied territories, in a Top Secret document, the government was informed by the legal adviser to [Israel's] Ministry of Foreign Affairs, the distinguished international lawyer Theodor Meron, that "civilian settlement in the administered territories [Israel's term for the occupied territories] contravenes explicit provisions of the Fourth Geneva Convention." Meron explained further that the prohibition against transfer of settlers to the occupied territories "is categorical and not conditional upon the motives for the transfer or its objectives. Its purpose is to prevent settlement in occupied territory of citizens of the occupying state." Meron therefore advised that "if it is decided to go ahead with Jewish settlement in the administered territories, it seems to me vital, therefore, that settlement is carried out by military and not civilian entities. It is also important, in my view, that such settlement is in the framework of camps and is, on the face of it, of a temporary rather than permanent nature."

Meron's advice was followed. Settlement has often been disguised by the subterfuge suggested, the "temporary military entities" turning out later to be civilian settlements. The device of military settlement also has the advantage of providing a means to expel Palestinians from their lands on the pretext that a military zone is being established. Deceit was scrupulously planned, beginning as soon as Meron's authoritative report was delivered to the government. As documented by Israeli scholar Avi Raz, in September 1967, on the day a second civilian settlement came into being in the West Bank, the government decided that "as a 'cover' for the purpose of [Israel's] diplomatic campaign," the new settlements should be presented as army settlements and the settlers should be given the necessary instructions in case they were asked about the nature of their settlement. The Foreign Ministry directed Israel's diplomatic missions to present the settlements in the occupied territories as military "strongpoints" and to emphasize their alleged security importance.

Similar practices continue to the present.

In response to the Security Council orders of 1979–80 to dismantle existing settlements and to establish no new ones, Israel undertook a rapid expansion of settlements with the cooperation of both of the major Israeli political blocs, Labor and Likud, always with lavish US material support.

The primary differences today are that the US is now alone against the whole world, and that it is a different world. Israel's flagrant violations of Security Council orders, and of international law, are by now far more extreme than they were thirty-five years ago, and are arousing far greater condemnation in much of the world. The contents of Resolutions 446-2334 are therefore taken more seriously. Hence, the revealing reactions to 2334 and to Secretary of State John Kerry's explanation of the US vote.

In the Arab world, the reactions seem to have been muted: We've been here before. In Europe they were generally supportive. In the US and Israel, in contrast, coverage and commentary were extensive, and there was considerable hysteria. These are further indications of the increasing isolation of the US on the world stage. Under Obama, that is. Under Trump US isolation will likely increase further and indeed, already did, even before he took office, as we have seen.

Why did Obama choose abstention from the UN vote on Israeli settlements at this juncture, i.e., only a month or so before the end of his presidency?

Just why Obama chose abstention rather than veto is an open question; we do not have direct evidence. But there are some plausible guesses. There had been some ripples of surprise (and ridicule) after Obama's February 2011 veto of a UNSC resolution calling for implementation of official US policy, and he may have felt that it would be too much to repeat it if he is to salvage anything of his tattered legacy among sectors of the population that have some concern for international law and human rights. It is also worth remembering that among liberal Democrats, if not Congress, and particularly among the young, opinion about Israel-Palestine has been moving toward criticism of Israeli policies in recent years, so much so that 60 percent of Democrats "support imposing sanctions or more serious action" in reaction to Israeli settlements, according to a December 2016 Brookings Institute poll. By now the core of support for Israeli policies in the US has shifted to the far right, including the evangelical base of the Republican Party. Perhaps these were factors in Obama's decision, with his legacy in mind.

The 2016 abstention aroused furor in Israel and in the US Congress as well, among both Republicans and leading Democrats, including proposals to defund the UN in retaliation for the world's crime. Israeli Prime Minister Netanyahu denounced Obama for his "underhanded, anti-Israel" actions. His office accused Obama of "colluding" behind the scenes with this "gang-up" by the Security Council, producing particles of "evidence" that hardly rise to the level of sick humor. A senior Israeli official added that the abstention "revealed the true face of the Obama administration," adding that "now we can understand what we have been dealing with for the past eight years."

Reality is rather different. Obama has, in fact, broken all records in support for Israel, both diplomatic and financial. The reality is described accurately by *Financial Times* Middle East specialist David Gardner: "Mr. Obama's personal dealings with Mr. Netanyahu may often have been poisonous, but he has been the most pro-Israel of presidents: the most prodigal with military aid and reliable in wielding the US veto at the Security Council. . . . The election of Donald Trump has so far brought little more than turbo-frothed tweets to bear on this and other geopolitical knots. But the auguries are ominous. An irredentist government in Israel tilted towards the ultraright is now joined by a national populist administration in Washington fire-breathing Islamophobia."

Public commentary on Obama's decision and Kerry's justification was split. Supporters generally agreed with Thomas Friedman that "Israel is clearly now on a path toward absorbing the West Bank's 2.8 million Palestinians . . . posing a demographic and democratic challenge." In a *New York Times* review of the state of the two-state solution defended by Obama-Kerry and threatened with extinction by Israeli policies, Max Fisher asks, "Are there other solutions?" He then turns to the possible alternatives, all of them "multiple versions of the so-called one-state solution" that poses a "demographic and democratic challenge": too many Arabs—perhaps soon a majority—in a "Jewish and democratic state."

In the conventional fashion, commentators assume that there are two alternatives: the two-state solution advocated by the world, or some version of the "one-state solution." Ignored consistently is a third alternative, the one that Israel has been implementing quite systematically since shortly after the 1967 war and that is now very clearly taking shape before our eyes: a Greater Israel, sooner or later incorporated into Israel proper, including a vastly expanded Jerusalem (already annexed in violation of Security Council orders) and any other territories that Israel finds valuable, while excluding areas of heavy Palestinian population concentration and slowly removing Palestinians within the areas scheduled for incorporation within

Greater Israel. As in neocolonies generally, Palestinian elites will be able to enjoy Western standards in Ramallah, with "90 per cent of the population of the West Bank living in 165 separate 'islands,' ostensibly under the control of the [Palestinian Authority]" but actual Israeli control, as reported by Nathan Thrall, senior analyst with the International Crisis Group. Gaza will remain under crushing siege, separated from the West Bank in violation of the Oslo Accords.

The third alternative is another piece of the "reality" described by David Gardner.

In an interesting and revealing comment, Netanyahu denounced the "gang-up" of the world as proof of "old-world bias against Israel," a phrase reminiscent of Donald Rumsfeld's Old Europe–New Europe distinction in 2003.

It will be recalled that the states of Old Europe were the bad guys, the major states of Europe, which dared to respect the opinions of the overwhelming majority of their populations and thus refused to join the US in the crime of the century, the invasion of Iraq. The states of New Europe were the good guys, which overruled an even larger majority and obeyed the master. The most honorable of the good guys was Spain's José María Aznar, who rejected virtually unanimous opposition to the war in Spain and was rewarded by being invited to join Bush and Blair in announcing the invasion.

This quite illuminating display of utter contempt for democracy, along with others like it at the same time, passed virtually unnoticed, understandably. The task at the time was to praise Washington for its passionate dedication to democracy, as illustrated by "democracy promotion" in Iraq, which suddenly became the party line after the "single question" (will Saddam give up his WMD?) was answered the wrong way.

Netanyahu is adopting much the same stance. The old world that is biased against Israel is the entire UN Security Council; more specifically, anyone in the world who has some lingering commitment to international law and human rights. Luckily for the Israeli far right, that excludes the US Congress and—very forcefully—the president-elect and his associates.

The Israeli government is, of course, cognizant of these developments. It is therefore seeking to shift its base of support to authoritarian states, such as Singapore, China, and Modi's right-wing Hindu nationalist India, now becoming a very natural ally with its drift toward ultranationalism, reactionary internal policies, and hatred of Islam. The reasons for Israel's looking in this direction for support are outlined by Mark Heller, principal research associate at Tel Aviv's Institution for National Security Studies. "Over the long term," he explains, "there are problems for Israel in its relations with Western Europe and with the US," while in contrast, the important Asian countries "don't seem to indicate much interest about how Israel gets along with the Palestinians, Arabs, or anyone else." In short, China, India, Singapore, and other favored allies are less influenced by the kinds of liberal and humane concerns that pose increasing threats to Israel.

Are we then in the midst of new trends and tendencies in world order?

I believe so, and the tendencies developing in world order merit some attention. As noted, the US is becoming even more isolated than it has been in recent years, when US-run polls—unreported in the US but surely known in Washington—revealed that world opinion regarded the US as by far the leading threat to world peace, no one else even close. Under Obama, the US is now alone in abstention on the illegal Israel settlements, against an otherwise unanimous Security Council. With President Trump joining his bipartisan congressional supporters on this issue, the US will be even more isolated in the world in support of Israeli crimes.

Since November 8, the US is isolated on the crucial matter of global warming, a threat to the survival of organized human life in anything like its present form. If Trump makes good on his promise to exit from the Iran deal, it is likely that the other participants will persist, leaving the US still more isolated from Europe.

The US is also much more isolated from its Latin American "backyard" than in the past, and will be even more isolated if Trump backs off from Obama's halting steps to normalize relations with Cuba, undertaken to ward off the likelihood that the US would be pretty much excluded from hemispheric organizations because of its continuing assault on Cuba, in international isolation.

Much the same is happening in Asia, as even close US allies (apart from Japan)—and even the UK—flock to the China-based Asian Infrastructure Investment Bank and the China-based Regional Comprehensive Economic

Partnership, in this case including Japan. The China-based Shanghai Cooperation Organization (SCO) incorporates the Central Asian states, Siberia with its rich resources, India, Pakistan, and soon, probably Iran, and perhaps Turkey. The SCO has rejected the US request for observer status and demanded that the US remove all military bases from the region.

Immediately after the Trump election, we witnessed the intriguing spectacle of German chancellor Angela Merkel taking the lead in lecturing Washington on liberal values and human rights. Meanwhile, since November 8, the world looks to China for leadership in saving the world from environmental catastrophe, while the US, in splendid isolation once again, devotes itself to undermining these efforts.

US isolation is not complete, of course. As was made very clear in the reaction to Trump's electoral victory, the US has the enthusiastic support of the xenophobic ultraright in Europe, including its neofascist elements. The return of the right in parts of Latin America offers the US opportunities for alliances there as well. And the US retains its close alliance with the dictatorships of the Gulf and Egypt, and with Israel, which is also separating itself from more liberal and democratic sectors in Europe and linking with authoritarian regimes that are not concerned with Israel's violations of international law and harsh attacks on elementary human rights.

The developing picture suggests the emergence of a New World Order, one that is rather different from the usual portrayals within the doctrinal system.

Trump and the Flawed Nature of US Democracy

C. J. POLYCHRONIOU: Noam, I want to start by asking you to reflect on the following: Trump won the presidential election even though he lost the popular vote. In this context, if "one person, one vote" is a fundamental principle behind every legitimate model of democracy, what type of democracy prevails in the US, and what will it take to undo the anachronism of the Electoral College?

NOAM CHOMSKY: The Electoral College was originally supposed to be a deliberative body drawn from educated and privileged elites. It would not necessarily respond to public opinion, which was not highly regarded by the founders, to put it mildly. "The mass of people . . . seldom judge or determine right," as Alexander Hamilton put it during the framing of the Constitution, expressing a common elite view. Furthermore, the infamous 3/5th clause ensured the slave states an extra boost, a very significant issue considering their prominent role in the political and economic institutions.

As the party system took shape in the 19th century, the Electoral College became a mirror of the state votes, which can give a result quite different from the popular vote because of the first-past-the-post rule—as it did once again in this election. Eliminating the Electoral College would be a good idea, but it's virtually impossible as the political system is now constituted. It is only one of many factors that contribute to the regressive character of the [US] political system, which, as Seth Ackerman observes in an interesting article in *Jacobin* magazine, would not pass muster by European standards.

Ackerman focuses on one severe flaw in the US system: the dominance of organizations that are not genuine political parties with public participation, but rather elite-run candidate-selection institutions often described, not unrealistically, as the two factions of the single business party that dominates the political system. They have protected themselves from competition by employing many devices that bar genuine political parties that grow out of free association of participants, as would be the case in a properly functioning democracy. Beyond that there is the overwhelming role of concentrated private and corporate wealth, not just in the presidential campaigns, as has been well documented, particularly by Thomas Ferguson, but also in Congress.

A recent study by Ferguson, Paul Jorgensen, and Jie Chen on "How Money Drives US Congressional Elections," reveals a remarkably close correlation between campaign expenditures and electoral outcomes in Congress over decades. And extensive work in academic political science—particularly by Martin Gilens, Benjamin Page, and Larry Bartlett—reveals that most of the population is effectively unrepresented, because their attitudes and opinions have little or no effect on decisions of the people they vote for. Instead, these decisions are pretty much determined by the very top of the income-wealth scale. In the light of such factors, the defects of the Electoral College, while real, are of lesser significance.

To what extent is this presidential election a defining moment for Republicans and Democrats alike?

For the eight years of the Obama presidency, the Republican organization has hardly qualified as a political party. A more accurate description was given by the respected political analysts Thomas Mann and Norman Ornstein of the conservative American Enterprise Institute: the party became an "insurgent outlier—ideologically extreme; contemptuous of the inherited social and economic policy regime; scornful of compromise; unpersuaded by conventional understanding of facts, evidence and science; and dismissive of the legitimacy of its political opposition."

Its guiding principle was: whatever Obama tries to do, we have to block it, but without providing some sensible alternative. The goal was to make the country ungovernable, so that the insurgency could take power. Its infantile antics on the Affordable Care Act are a good illustration: endless votes to repeal it in favor of—nothing. Meanwhile, the party has become split between the wealthy and privileged "establishment"—devoted to the interests of their class—and the popular base that was mobilized when establishment commitments to wealth and privilege became so extreme that it would be impossible to garner votes by presenting them accurately.

It was therefore necessary to mobilize sectors that had always existed, but not as an organized political force: a strange amalgam of Christian evangelicals—a huge sector of the American population—nativists, white supremacists, white working- and lower-middle-class victims of the neoliberal policies of the past generation, and others who are fearful and angry, cast aside in the neoliberal economy while they perceive their traditional culture as being under attack. In past primaries, the candidates who rose from the base—Michele Bachmann, Herman Cain, Rick Santorum, and the rest—were so extreme that they were anathema to the establishment, and they were able to use their ample resources, rid themselves of the plague, and choose their favored candidate. The difference in 2016 is that they were unable to do it.

Now the Republican Party faces the task of formulating policies other than "No." It must find a way to craft policies that will somehow pacify or marginalize the popular base, while serving the real constituency of the establishment. It is from this sector that Trump is picking his close associates and cabinet members: not exactly coal miners, iron and steel workers, small business owners, or representatives of the concerns and demands of much of his voting base.

Democrats have to face the fact that for forty years they have pretty much abandoned whatever commitment they had to working people. It's quite shocking that Democrats have drifted so far from their modern New Deal origins that some workers are now voting for their class enemy, not for the party of FDR. A return to some form of social democracy should not be impossible, as indicated by the remarkable success of the Sanders campaign, which departed radically from the norm of elections effectively bought by wealth and corporate power. It is important to bear in mind that his "political revolution," while quite appropriate for the times, would not have much surprised Dwight Eisenhower, another indication of the shift to the right during the neoliberal years.

If the Democratic Party is going to be a constructive force, it will have to develop and commit itself credibly to programs that address the valid concerns of the kind of people who voted for Obama, attracted by his message of "hope and change." When disillusioned by the disappearance of hope and the lack of change, they switched to the con man who declared that he would bring back what they have lost.

It will be necessary to face honestly the malaise of much of the country, including people like those in the Louisiana Bayou whom Arlie Hochschild studied with such sensitivity and insight, and surely including the former working-class constituencies of the Democrats. The malaise is revealed in many ways, not least by the astonishing fact that mortality has increased in the country, something unknown in modern industrial democracies apart from catastrophic events.

That's particularly true among middle-aged whites, mainly traceable to what are sometimes called "diseases of despair" (opioids, alcohol, suicide, etc.). A statistical analysis reported by the *Economist* found that these health metrics correlate with a remarkable 43 percent of the Republican Party's gains over the Democrats in the 2016 election, and remain significant and predictive even when controlling for race, education, age, gender, income, marital status, immigration, and employment. These are all signs of severe collapse of much of the society, particularly in rural and working-class areas. Furthermore, such initiatives have to be undertaken alongside of firm dedication to the rights and needs of those sectors of the population that have historically been denied rights and repressed, often in harsh and brutal ways.

No small task, but not beyond reach, if not by the Democrats, then by some political party replacing them, drawing from popular movements—and through the constant activism of these movements, quite apart from electoral politics.

Much of the rest of the world—with the notable exception of some of Europe's extreme nationalist and anti-immigrant political leaders—also seems to be rather anxious about Trump's aims and intents. Isn't that so?

Trump's victory was met in Europe with shock and disbelief. The general reaction was captured quite accurately, for instance, on the front cover of *Der Spiegel* [a major German weekly]. It depicted a caricature of Trump presented as a meteor hurtling toward Earth, mouth open, ready to swallow it up. And the lead headline read *"Das Ende Der Welt!"* ("The End of the World"). And in small letters below, "as we have known it." To be sure, there might be some truth to that concern, even if not exactly in the manner in which the artist and the authors who echoed that conception had in mind.

The Resurgence of Political Authoritarianism

C. J. POLYCHRONIOU: In 1992, Francis Fukuyama published an intellectually embarrassing book titled *The End of History and the Last Man*, in which he prophesied the "end of history" after the collapse of the communist bloc, arguing that liberal democracy would become the world's "final form of human government." However, what has happened in this decade in particular is that the institutions and values of liberal democracy have come under attack by scores of authoritarian leaders all over the world, and extreme nationalism, xenophobia, and "soft Fascist" tendencies have begun reshaping the political landscape in Europe and the United States. How do you explain the resurgence of political authoritarianism in the early part of the 21st century?

Noam Chomsky: The "political landscape" is indeed ominous. While today's political and social circumstances are much less dire, still they do call to mind Antonio Gramsci's warning from Mussolini's prison cells about the severe crisis of his day, which "consists precisely in the fact that the old is dying and the new cannot be born [and] in this interregnum a great variety of morbid symptoms appear."

One morbid symptom is the resurgence of political authoritarianism, a highly important matter that is properly receiving a great deal of attention in public debate. But "a great deal of public attention" should always be a warning sign: Does the shaping of the issues reflect power interests, which are diverting attention from what may be more significant factors behind the general concerns? In the present case, I think that is so, and before turning to the very significant question of the resurgence of political authoritarianism, I'd like to bring up related matters that do not seem to me to receive the attention they merit, and in fact are almost totally excluded from the extensive public attention.

It's entirely true that "the institutions and values of liberal democracy are under attack" to an unusual extent, but not only by authoritarian leaders, and not for the first time. I presume all would agree that primary among the values of liberal democracy is that governments should be responsive to voters. If that is not the case, "liberal democracy" is a farce.

It has been well established that it is not the case. Ample work in mainstream political science shows that a majority of voters are not represented by their own elected representatives, who listen to different voices—the voices of the donor class, great wealth, and the corporate sector (Martin Gilens, *Affluence and Influence: Economic Inequality and Political Power in America*, Princetoh University Press, 2014; Benjamin Page and Martin Gilens, *Democracy in America? What Has Gone Wrong and What We Can Do About It*, University of Chicago press, 2017; Larry Bartels, *Unequal Democracy: The Political Economy of the New Gilded Age*, 2nd ed., Princeton University Press, 2018, among others). Furthermore, the penetrating work of Thomas Ferguson reveals that for a long time, elections have been substantially bought, including Congress, continuing right to the present, 2016.

These facts alone show that the furor about alleged Russian interference with our pristine democratic process reveals profound indoctrination—in capitalist, not democratic, values.

Furthermore, those who find foreign interference to be especially troublesome despite its marginality should clearly be looking elsewhere. It is not even in question that Israel interferes massively in US elections and governance, proudly and ostentatiously. One recent case that was unusually brazen was in 2015, when Prime Minister Netanyahu addressed Congress without even informing President Obama in order to undermine his Iran program, a mere fragment of Israel's constant and far-reaching efforts to influence US politics.

Putting aside these secondary matters, the major attack on the institutions and values of liberal democracy is by the powerful business classes, intensifying since Reagan as both political parties have drifted toward greater subordination to their interests—the Republicans to such an extreme that by now they barely can be considered a political party. Anyone who finds this surprising must be uninformed about American society and how it functions.

By now, as business power has been unleashed by its servants in the Republican Party, the traditional business attack on "the institutions and values of liberal democracy" has reached levels not seen since the Gilded Age, if even then.

Of course, it is quite legal to buy elections, to send lobbyists to congressional offices to write legislation, and in other ways "to shape public policy in a way that serves [private power's] narrow interests"—indeed, these comprise "an essential, nonaccidental part of . . . business strategy," Zephyr Teachout writes in a valuable study. Investigation has shown, she adds, that a CEO's investment in changing laws to decrease corporate tax rates yields a vastly greater return than investment in reducing cost of production. Small wonder that all of this is normal business strategy.

Teachout cites a Supreme Court decision of 1874 which concluded that "if any of the great corporations of the country were to hire adventurers who make market of themselves [for] the promotion of their private interests, the moral sense of every right-minded man would instinctively denounce the employer and employed as steeped in corruption." That was, of course, before the ideology of business supremacy had risen to the level of "hegemonic common sense," in Gramscian terms. The sharp transition well illustrates the force of indoctrination in a society with a powerful and highly class-conscious business community.

The Reagan-Thatcher project of enhancing untrammeled business power, carried forward and extended by their successors, has been the political extension of a dedicated and coordinated campaign by the business classes to reverse the "crisis of democracy" of the 1960s; this period deeply troubled liberal international elites, who devoted the first major publication of the Trilateral Commission to this serious malady. Their prime concern was the increased engagement of popular classes in the political arena where they pressed their demands, imposing too much pressure on the state, and threatening (though this remains implicit) the dominance of the business world. As the American rapporteur, Harvard professor of government

Samuel Huntington, observed nostalgically, "Truman had been able to govern the country with the cooperation of a relatively small number of Wall Street lawyers and bankers," but those happy days were disappearing under the attack of the great majority, whose role in a liberal democracy is to be passive and acquiescent, a doctrine with a rich pedigree, which I've reviewed elsewhere.

That was the liberal end of the political spectrum. Toward the conservative end, at the same time, the influential "Powell Memorandum," directed to the Chamber of Commerce by corporate lawyer Lewis Powell (later appointed to the Supreme Court by Richard Nixon), called for open war by the business world to defend itself from a virtual takeover by the radical forces destroying "free enterprise" under the leadership of Ralph Nader, Herbert Marcuse, and other "dangerous extremists."

The messages are pretty much the same, but the rhetoric is quite different. The liberal rhetoric is largely reserved, while the business rhetoric reaches the frenzied pitch of a three-year-old who has all the toys and laments that one might be taken away.

The business world, of course, did not need reminders to dedicate resources to reverse democratic progress and the highly successful regulated capitalism of the postwar era that indeed infringed on business power, and crucially threatened profit, as political economist Robert Brenner has shown. The neoliberal counterattack substantially beat back these threats, sharply increasing private power and the wealth of a tiny segment of the population. Meanwhile, the majority of the population faced economic stagnation or decline, increasingly precarious lives, and the natural loss of political influence as concentrated private economic power gained even greater dominance.

All of this continues under the revival from the housing-financial crisis that proceeds under Obama and Trump. The latest report of the Department of Labor finds that "from May 2017 to May 2018, real average hourly earnings decreased 0.1 percent, seasonally adjusted. The decrease in real average hourly earnings combined with a 0.6-percent increase in the average workweek resulted in a 0.5-percent increase in real average weekly earnings over this period." Meanwhile, surging corporate profits are inflated still further by the tax scam that is the jewel in the crown of Trump's Republican Party, overwhelmingly used for buyouts and other devices to enrich the wealthy rather than productive investment that would benefit society and lift wages.

The other side of the coin is the Reagan-Thatcher assault on unions, now advanced by the authorization of right-to-scrounge laws (in Orwellian terminology, "right-to-work" laws) by the most reactionary Supreme Court in over a century. The mission is to create a world of isolated individuals at the mercy of concentrated private power, in accord with the Thatcherite doctrine that "there is no society." Thatcher unwittingly paraphrased Marx's bitter condemnation of authoritarian leaders who sought to turn society into a "sack of potatoes."

There are other sources for the malaise of the general population. The radical financialization of the economy and the prioritization of shareholder value during the neoliberal years, expedited by Reagan's "Chicago Boys," has shifted corporate behavior sharply from the retain-and-invest model of the great growth years of regimented capitalism. The "buyback economy" of the neoliberal reaction has been explored with much insight by William Lazonick.

Lazonick estimates that "trillions of dollars that could have been spent on productive investment have instead been used to buy back stock in order to boost share prices," enriching the rich but not providing meaningful and steady work or useful goods. Apple, the world's largest corporation in market value, was once devoted to product innovation and development. Under its new CEO, Tim Cook, it has become the "buyback king," enriching shareholders (and management). Others are doing much the same. The Republican tax scam of 2018 is having the same effects, all to the detriment of working people and the general population. The rapid increase in speculation has had similar consequences. The same is true of the repeated financial crises following deregulation, severely harming the poor and working people but not the culprits in the financial industry, who are bailed out by the public and emerge richer than before.

There are remedies, but their advocates remain for now at the fringes of the political economy. Though perhaps not for long.

These are, to be sure, generalities. Like most complex processes, the rise of authoritarian leaders and the concomitant antisocial tendencies are overdetermined. There are many more specific factors, but the essence, I think, is along the lines just outlined.

Today's most powerful authoritarian leaders—e.g., Vladimir Putin in Russia, Viktor Orbán in Hungary, Recep Tayyip Erdoğan in Turkey, Bibi Netanyahu in Israel, and Donald Trump in the US, to name just a few— are enjoying widespread popularity with the masses and happen, in fact, to have risen to power via democratic means. What's going on? Is something wrong with today's democracy?

Here specific causes intrude.

In the case of Western societies—Trump in the US, and throughout Western Europe—democracy is in decline, with attendant attacks on prospects for decent lives, and the increased control of political systems by concentrated private power and wealth. These are natural consequences of the neoliberal assault against the social democratic tendencies of the early postwar decades. It should be recalled that the Great Depression and World War II unleashed radical democratic forces throughout much of the world. Although the reaction of the business world was quick to come (e.g., Taft-Hartley in 1947), it was muted until the economic disruptions of the 1970s, which provided an opportunity for more vigorous class war.

It's also worth recalling the rather belated recognition in 1978 by United Auto Workers president Doug Fraser that businessmen had "chosen to wage a one-sided class war in this country, a war against working people, the unemployed, the poor, the minorities, the very young and the very old, and even many in the middle class of our society" and had "broken and discarded the fragile, unwritten compact previously existing during a period of growth and progress." In fact, the class war was already underway in the latter days of the prewar New Deal years, but it was not yet one-sided, since a vigorous labor movement existed—the target of bitter and increasingly one-sided class war in the postwar years.

In Europe, the attack on democracy is amplified by the strongly undemocratic institutions of the European Union. Major decisions over policy are made by the unelected Troika—European Commission, International Monetary Fund (IMF), European Central Bank—with the northern banks right at their shoulders. The population has little say, and knows it—a large reason for the general collapse of centrist parties that have governed the countries since World War II.

In a very revealing inquiry, economist Mark Weisbrot reviews the reports of the regular IMF consultations with member governments of the European Union. He discovered "a remarkably consistent and disturbing pattern." The financial crisis was exploited as an opportunity to lock in the neoliberal reforms: spending cuts in the public sector rather than tax increases, reduced benefits and public services, cuts in health care, undermining of collective bargaining, and in general, moves to create a society "with less bargaining power for labor and lower wages, more inequality and poverty, a smaller government and social safety nets, and measures that reduce growth and employment."

"The IMF papers," Weisbrot concludes, "detail the agenda of Europe's decision-makers, and they have accomplished quite a bit of it over the past five years." The agenda is quite familiar in the US and in fact, wherever the neoliberal assault has proceeded.

In England, Thatcher-Major and Blair's New Labour, followed by Tory austerity, had similar effects. The Corbyn movement is an encouraging reaction, bitterly opposed by the Labour establishment and most of the media.

The other cases mentioned have their own special features.

Putin seems to have been genuinely popular throughout his tenure. Crimeans, it appears, support the takeover by Russia. There seemed to be possibilities for social democratic developments in Russia after the collapse of the Soviet Union, possibly even for mutually supportive linkages to social democratic Europe. Such hopes were dashed by the harsh effects of the US-backed market reforms, which devastated the economy, led to millions of deaths, and opened the way for immense corruption as oligarchs took over state assets. Putin was seen by the public as a corrective to the neoliberal disaster and the decline of Russia on the world scene. Authoritarian no doubt, often brutal, but, it seems, popular.

In Israel, too, the right-wing nationalist-religious coalition is genuinely popular. Threats to Netanyahu are primarily from his right. This is quite a change from the time when Israel conquered Palestinian lands in the 1967, and soon set forth on its illegal settlement programs. The change was predicted early on by those who understood the natural dynamics of crushing people under your jackboot. One commentator who was particularly outspoken was the respected Israeli sage Yeshayahu Leibowitz. He condemned the occupation bitterly, not because of concern for the Palestinians, for whose fate he expressed only contempt, but because of the predictable effect on Jews, who, he warned, would become "Judeo-Nazis" as they carried out the tasks of repression and displacement.

The signs by now are dramatic, both in actions and in legislation, both with regard to the criminal acts in the occupied territories and the shift to unconcealed racism at home. The occupied territories include Gaza, despite Israel's claim to the contrary, which is not even accepted by its loyal US supporter. In the full knowledge that the home of 2 million people is likely to become literally "unlivable" within a few years, as international monitors have predicted, Israel maintains its stranglehold, designed officially to keep the population on a "diet" while the self-described "most moral army in the world" pounds away with atrocities that are appalling the world.

Turkey, too, is a special case, with a long and complex history since the current Turkish state took form after World War I. Keeping to recent times, in the '90s, Turkey was the scene of some of the worst atrocities of the period during the state terror campaign against the Kurds. Tens of thousands were killed, thousands of towns and villages were destroyed, hundreds of thousands—maybe millions—were driven from their homes, some now barely surviving in abandoned buildings in Istanbul. The main support for the state crimes was Washington: Clinton provided 80 percent of the arms in an increasing flow as atrocities increased. Little was reported even though the major press had bureaus in Turkey, of course. Much of the information available comes from the detailed reports of the outstanding researcher for Human Rights Watch, Jonathan Sugden; his work was so outstanding that he was finally expelled by the government. Particularly significant were a remarkable group of Turkish intellectuals —leading writers, artists, journalists, publishers, and others—who not only protested the crimes, but undertook civil disobedience, facing and sometimes enduring long and severe punishment. I know of no group like them anywhere.

By the turn of the century, the situation was improving, soon quite considerably, including the early Erdoğan years. But soon regression began under his leadership, and it has become extremely severe. Turkey held the worst record in the world for persecuting journalists, and the repression has extended to academics and many others. Vicious attacks on Kurdish areas have increased. The country is divided between a secular liberal-left sector and a deeply religious, mostly rural population. A dedicated Islamist, Erdoğan has rallied support among this sector and is relying on it to create a harsh and repressive authoritarian state with strong Islamist elements. What is happening is particularly painful to observe, not just because of the crimes, but because of the hopeful prospects that seemed ahead only a few years ago and the fact that Turkey could serve as a valuable cultural and economic bridge between West and East.

Hungary is another special case. It is a cultural/linguistic island, which has had remarkable cultural achievements and also an ugly record of Fascism and cooperation with the Nazis. From what I have read—I have no close knowledge—the country has long been obsessed with the fear of decline, even disappearance. These fears exacerbated by the passage of refugees through Hungary to Western Europe. The population is declining, partly from low fertility, partly from a large exodus to the West. Orbán has exploited these fears to construct an "illiberal democracy" dedicated to "saving Hungary" and "traditional values," with the usual xenophobic and racist elements of such appeals.

There's a good deal more to say about racism in Europe, not always visible when the populations are highly homogenous, but quickly apparent as soon as there is any "contamination" by those who are a bit different. And there is no need to comment on the history of the Jews, and of the Roma right to the present.

Speaking of authoritarian leaders, I've been dumbfounded by the US political establishment's reaction to Trump's handling of the Helsinki summit with Putin. What's wrong with the idea of the US and Russia working together to address major international issues facing the world today, including the threat of nuclear weapons? What's your own reaction to this matter? Was Trump wrong? Was he being "anti-American"?

There's surely nothing wrong with the US and Russia seeking rapprochement and cooperation on such issues. It is essential for hopes for a better future, even survival. Russia should not refuse to deal with the US nor (were it imaginable) impose sanctions on the US and UK because they invaded and devastated Iraq with all of the hideous regional consequences, or (with France) destroyed Libya with terrible effects from West Africa to the Levant, along with other crimes too numerous to mention. Or conversely (putting aside the scale of crimes).

There are numerous issues on which the countries must cooperate, and sometimes do, as in Syria to avoid clashes that could set off war. The needs are far greater at the Russian border, where, as a result of NATO expansion and buildup of forces, accidents with indescribable consequences could easily occur. There are many other cases where serious interchange is necessary. On nuclear issues, even more so. As we've discussed elsewhere, Obama's programs to modernize nuclear weapons increased "killing power" sufficiently to create "exactly what one would expect to see, if a nuclear-armed state were planning to have the capacity to fight and win a nuclear war by disarming enemies with a surprise first strike," as explained in an important study in the Bulletin of the Atomic Scientists. Trump's nuclear programs enhance the threat even beyond, with new and very dangerous weapons systems and severe lowering of the threshold for nuclear war—an existential threat to Russia, and the world; even the attacker would be devastated by a first-strike. Under George W. Bush, the US withdrew from the Anti-Ballistic Missile treaty, another serious threat to Russia. Russian weapons initiatives and reactions also enhance the threat of terminal destruction.

Turning to Trump, his actions make no sense at all if they are guided by some geopolitical strategy. On the one hand, he is talking politely with Putin (some say genuflecting) and calling for reduction of tensions, while on the other hand, he is significantly escalating tensions and threats. The nuclear program just mentioned is one very serious example. He is also sending arms to Ukraine and increasing NATO forces and operations on the Russian border—actions that any Russian leader would regard as a severe threat. Harsher sanctions have been imposed on Russia, which is by no means unaware of the increasing threats —how could they be? The business press, citing US Treasury reports, observes that Russia is "liquidating dollar assets at a record pace, selling four-fifths of its cache of US government debt, $81 billion worth, over a two-month period" in order to safeguard assets in case relations continue to deteriorate.

While Trump's policies make no sense from a geostrategic perspective, they fall into place on the assumption that he is continuing to pursue his "Me First" agenda, damn the consequences for the world, matters we've discussed before. The agenda requires maintaining the loyalty of his base and ensuring that they will remain loyal if the Mueller investigation comes up with something that damages him. The centerpiece of his press conference with Putin, bitterly condemned by elite opinion, was his effort to discredit Mueller. The tactic is succeeding quite well. A large majority of Republicans approve of the way Trump dealt with Putin, and polls show that Mueller's public image is at an all-time low.

Meanwhile, the sharp escalation and threats satisfy the national security hawks.

The latter constitute a broad spectrum. While it is sometimes hard to believe, we cannot overlook the fact that the most highly regarded moderates firmly uphold doctrines that are, quite literally, too outlandish to discuss. For example, Richard Haass, a respected scholar and diplomat and long-time president of the influential Council on Foreign Relations, instructs us with a straight face that "International order for 4 centuries has been based on non-interference in the internal affairs of others and respect for sovereignty. Russia has violated this norm by seizing Crimea and by interfering in the 2016 US election. We must deal [with] Putin's Russia as the rogue state it is."

Words fail.

In Israel, a controversial bill about the "Jewish nation-state" was just passed that makes no mention of minority rights. Is there something new behind the passing of this bill that wasn't always a reality from Israel's standpoint of view?

Regrettably, within Israel itself, the new nationality law of July 2018 was not very controversial, though it has appalled liberal opinion throughout the world. Rather typical is what is happening in the US, which since the 1967 war, has been Israel's leading supporter. For a long period, Israel was the darling of liberal and progressive opinion. By today, that has changed considerably. "According to a Pew Research Center survey in April [2018], self-described liberal Democrats were twice as likely to sympathize with

Palestinians over Israel than they were only two years ago. Forty percent of liberals sympathized more with Palestinians, the most since 2001, while 33 percent sympathized more with Israel."

Support for Israel has shifted to the ultranationalist right and Christian evangelicals—many of whom combine passionate support for Israel with the doctrine that the Second Coming, perhaps very soon, will consign all Jews to the torments of eternal perdition apart from a very few who will find Christ in time—a level of anti-Semitism unmatched even in Nazi Germany.

Israel is well aware that it is losing support among sectors of world opinion that have at least some concern for human and civil rights. It is therefore seeking to expand its base of support to the East, primarily to China and India, the latter becoming a very natural ally for a number of reasons, including the drift in both societies toward ultranationalism, reactionary internal policies, and hatred of Islam. It is also firming up what have been tacit alliances with the most reactionary and brutal Arab states, Saudi Arabia and the UAE, joined now by Egypt under the current harsh military dictatorship.

The new nationality law declares Israel to be the nation-state of the Jewish people, downgrades the status of Arabic and formally authorizes Jewish-only communities. It does break some new ground, but not very much. What is new is primarily the elevation of these racist principles to the Basic Law—constitutional status. Long ago, Israel's highest court determined that Israel is "the sovereign state of the Jewish people" . . . but not the state of its 20 percent non-Jewish citizens, essentially the same doctrine.

One of the few articulate critics of the new law, the fine Israeli writer Yitzhak Laor, reminds us that in debates on the Land Law of 1960, Zerach Warhaftig, a founder of the National Religious Party and a signer of the Declaration of Independence, declared that, "We wish it to be clear that the land of Israel belongs to the nation of Israel. *Nation of Israel* is a wider concept than the nation that lives in Zion, because the nation of Israel is found in the entire world. . . . [In this new law] there is a very great judicial novelty: we are giving a legal cover to the regulations of the Keren Kayemet LeIsrael [Jewish National Fund, or JNF]" (translated from Hebrew).

The JNF regulations in turn obligate the organization to work for the benefit of "persons of Jewish race, religion, or origin." It may be added that these radical violations of civil rights are funded by American taxpayers thanks to the tax-free status of the JNF as a charitable organization.

Warhaftig was quite right almost sixty years ago. An array of legal and administrative rules was established to ensure that the JNF would have authority over all state lands—93 percent of the territory of the country—hence, authority to ensure that lands would be reserved for Jews alone, with minor and derisory exceptions. Details are spelled out and documented in my *Towards a New Cold War* (1982).

Laor reminds us that since the law was established, "700 settlements were established, all for Jews, apart from a few cities for [displaced] Bedouins (which merit ridicule)." Meanwhile, the 20 percent non-Jewish minority has been restricted to the 2 percent of the land allotted to them when the state was established seventy years ago.

In 2000, the racist land administration arrangements finally reached Israel's High Court. It issued a narrow ruling that granted the petitioners, a professional Arab couple, the right to move to the all-Jewish town of Katzir. Very soon, arrangements began to be contrived to get around the law, but now it is no longer necessary, since segregation is legally authorized by the Basic Law.

Much of this should be familiar to Americans. New Deal public housing projects were restricted to whites by laws that remained in effect until the late 1960s, when it was too late to help African Americans because the postwar years of rapid and egalitarian growth, which offered them some opportunities, were coming to an end, and the neoliberal assault was soon to come, imposing stagnation. Another grim chapter in the history of racism in America.

Also familiar to Americans is US isolation in support of such measures (with the attractive exceptions noted earlier), now reaching new levels in the Trump administration. In the last days of the Apartheid regime in South Africa, Reagan was alone in the world in supporting it, even denying the existence of Apartheid, even after Thatcher and Israel had abandoned the sinking ship. We might also recall that during the last throes of Apartheid, in 1988, the Reagan administration declared Nelson Mandela's African National Congress to be "one of the more notorious terrorist groups" in the world. While greatly honored internationally, Mandela remained on the US terrorist list until 2008, when at last a congressional resolution allowed him to enter the "land of the free" without special dispensation.

Often, there is indeed little new under the sun.

The World Bank continues to support authoritarian regimes throughout the Global South by providing funds and bailouts. How can the UN and Western democratic governments tolerate such a stance on the part of the World Bank?

Unfortunately, the answer is all too clear. As their own practice consistently illustrates, the "Western democratic governments" pursue similar policies with enthusiasm. It should be superfluous to illustrate, but since we live in an atmosphere of self-celebration, it might be useful to consider at least one example. Take the Congo, which should be one of the richest and most advanced countries of the world, with huge resources and no threats—from its neighbors, that is. When Europe was despoiling Africa, the Congo was the domain of King Leopold of Belgium, whose hideous crimes surpassed even the normal standards of the "enlightened" West. He didn't pass without censure. In the famous 11th edition of the *Britannica*, the article on the monarch lauds his achievements, but does add a phrase at the end saying that he treated his subjects harshly —slaughtering millions and ordering atrocious tortures to gain more rubber for his overflowing coffers.

"The horror, the horror" finally came to end in 1960, when Congo declared independence. Its leading figure was the young charismatic Patrice Lumumba, who might have extricated Congo from the misery of colonialism. But it was not to be. The CIA was assigned the task of murdering him, but the Belgians got there first, and together with other liberal democracies, helped plunge Congo back to terror and destruction under the leadership of the Western favorite, the murderous kleptomaniac Mobutu, who ensured that the riches of the Congo would flow in the right direction. Fast forwarding to today, all of those who enjoy smart phones and other technical delights benefit from the rich minerals of Eastern Congo, handed over to the multinationals hovering nearby by warring militias and marauders from US-backed Rwanda while the death toll mounts to many millions.

That Western democracies should tolerate support for authoritarian regimes is not much of a mystery.

What do you think it will take to halt the spread of political authoritarianism across the globe?

The familiar advice, easy to state, hard to follow, but if there's another way, it's been kept a dark secret: honest, dedicated, courageous, and persistent engagement, ranging from education and organization to direct activism, carefully honed for effectiveness under prevailing circumstances. Hard work, necessary work, the kind that has succeeded in the past and can again.

The Anatomy of Trumpocracy

C. J. POLYCHRONIOU: Noam, while many in the country and the world at large watch aghast as Donald Trump's nightmare of white supremacy continues to unravel the United States, it still remains something of a puzzle as to what propelled Trumpism to political prominence. For starters, why did voters turn to Trump? Who are the people that make up his hard-core base, and how do we explain the fact that he has essentially taken over the Republican Party without any serious opposition?

NOAM CHOMSKY: Part of the solution to the puzzle is Obama's performance in office. Many were seduced by the rhetoric of "hope" and "change," and deeply disillusioned by the very early discovery that the words had little substance. I don't usually agree with Sarah Palin, but she had a point when she ridiculed this hopey-changey stuff. A fair number of Obama voters, mostly working people, switched to Trump. These developments were already clear by the time of the 2010 special election in Massachusetts to fill the seat of Senator Kennedy —the liberal lion. Virtually unknown Scott Brown won the election, the first Republican elected to the Senate in [more than] forty years in this liberal state. Analysis of the vote showed that even union members hardly supported his liberal opponent because of anger at Obama: the way he handled the housing-financial crisis (bailing out the rich, including the perpetrators, while letting their victims hang out to dry) and much else, including provisions of his health care proposal that working people saw, with justice, as an attack on health programs that they had won in contract negotiations.

Quite apart from Obama's disappointing policies, he and the [Democratic] Party were victims of the intense racism that is deeply rooted in large parts of American society. The visceral hatred of Obama cannot be explained in other terms.

But there is far more than that. For some time, candidates for Republican primaries who emerged from the base have been far off the traditional spectrum. The establishment was able to suppress them and gain their own candidate, but that didn't change the basis for their support. For years, both parties have drifted to the right—the Republicans off the spectrum of normal parliamentary politics. Their dedication to wealth and corporate power is so extreme that they cannot get votes on their actual policies—which are now being revealed to us daily—and so have had to mobilize a voting base on issues unrelated to their service to their actual constituency. These include religious fundamentalism—a major phenomenon in the US unlike other developed societies—white supremacy, xenophobia, and other latent antisocial attitudes that tend to break through to the surface during periods of disillusionment and distress. This is partly a matter of a "search for scapegoats," the actual sources concealed in the usual manner of propaganda; thus, the public vastly exaggerates the number of immigrants, even more than in Europe. In the current period, these malignant tendencies are natural consequences of the harsh neoliberal policies that we have discussed before. We see much the same in Europe, for similar reasons.

Trump has had overwhelming support among whites and less educated sectors, but for the most part, his mass voting base is relatively affluent and privileged. A recent Pew poll of Trump approvers found two-thirds are either college graduates, women, or nonwhite, the last group apparently not many.

Trump's roughly 90 percent support among Republicans is actually not unusual for an incumbent party at this stage in office—about the same as Obama among Democrats, though the fervor and passion are different, presumably reflecting the general atmosphere of anger, hatred, and fear. And frightening. Recognizing the great differences, I still can't repress childhood memories of hearing Hitler's Nuremberg rallies on the radio, not understanding the words, though the mood was unmistakable.

For the actual Republican constituency of wealth and corporate power, these are glory days, so why object, even if his antics sometimes cause some grimaces? The core constituency of evangelicals is solidly in Trump's pocket, thanks to the crumbs thrown their way. Many working people maintain the illusion that Trump cares about them and will bring back lost days of steady jobs in mining and manufacturing. Even those realistic enough to dismiss this act at least see someone who is standing up to the "foreign devils" who have been "robbing us," and in particular, the cultural elites that regard them and their values with contempt, just "deplorables." Mostly farce, but [also] much successful propaganda, with enough elements of truth to be persuasive—for a while at least.

It's revealing to take a closer look at attitudes of the huge evangelical community. According to a study by the Public Religion Research Institute, "In 2011, only 30 percent believed that personal immorality was consistent with an ethical performance of official duties. Today, 72 percent of white evangelicals—up an astounding 42 points—believe that the two can go together."

No comment needed, but instructive.

Trump himself seems to be having the time of his life. He's constantly in the limelight, his loyal base worships his every move, he's free to defy convention, to insult anyone he chooses, to disrupt the international economic and political order at will—whatever comes to mind next, knowing that he's the biggest thug on the block and can probably get away with it—again, for a while, at least.

I don't think it's quite fair, however, to call him a liar. Lying presupposes having a concept of truth, and being in a situation where telling the truth matters. We don't say that three-year-olds are lying if they say they saw a dragon outside, or an actor in a play. It's also not clear that it's tactically useful to tot up the random falsehoods that pepper his tweets and orations. That just fires up his worshipful base, providing more evidence that the hated liberal elites are trying to destroy the one guy in the political arena who is dedicated to defending the common folk—whom he is shafting, with delight, at every opportunity.

It's an intriguing spectacle, and not a little worrisome.

Trump loves to present himself as an "art-of-the-deal" president. Exactly what kind of deals has he made so far that can justify his claim to being a master negotiator?

There are no deals with others of any note, but there are real accomplishments. The most heralded one is the tax bill, a very welcome gift to the actual [corporate] constituency, with the side benefit of expanding the deficit and thus offering the opportunity to dismantle the limited social programs, which are [deemed] a nuisance, dispensable, since they raise the taxes of the actual constituency and do not benefit them. Steps are already underway to weaken these programs further. That includes the steady dismantling of protections provided by the hated "Obamacare." I've often wondered whether the term itself might have caught on because of implicit racism; we didn't call Medicare "Johnsoncare."

A scathing report of the [UN] "Special Rapporteur [Philip Alston] on extreme poverty and human rights" on his mission to the United States of America, recently released, was well-timed—and may have been the immediate reason for the US withdrawal from the UN Human Rights Council, which discredited itself by revealing improper truths about ourselves, just as the World Court discredited itself—and was roundly condemned by elite opinion—for daring to condemn the US for international terrorism ("unlawful use of force") in the murderous Reaganite attack on Nicaragua.

Other gifts to the actual constituency are being offered regularly. Elizabeth Warren's Consumer Financial Protection Bureau is being rendered toothless. Betsy DeVos is making it easier for the for-profit colleges she cherishes to cheat students, part of the concerted corporate-led campaign to dismantle public education, one of the real contributions of the US to contemporary civilization. The Department of Labor's fiduciary rule, designed to ensure that financial advisers act in the best interest of clients, has been sent to the ashcan, along with Dodd-Frank restrictions on the actions of banks, which are already enjoying record profits with more to come as the effects of the tax scam are felt. Bulging profits were heralded as a spur to investment, of which there is scarcely a trace as they are used to enrich the rich still further.

In general, things are proceeding quite well for "those who matter," though they have some concerns that Trump's erratic trade policies might infringe on the interests of the investor class.

I've skipped foreign policy, and have omitted so far, the most important accomplishments—astonishingly, commonly ignored by the opposition party and media commentary. Pride of place goes to the quite successful efforts to escalate the very severe and not remote threat of global warming. Expansion and modernization of the huge military system and provocative actions at the Russian border are not far behind.

In brief, there are no meaningful deals, though there surely are impressive accomplishments.

How do we explain the fact that Trump continues to cause chaos on all fronts, both domestically and internationally, and yet his popularity remains at quite high levels?

As I mentioned, Trump's popularity among Republicans is unusually fervent and high, though not uniquely so. The affluent are doing fine. The economy is continuing the slow growth under Obama, though wages are barely rising and job security is low. Apart from the business world, concerned that the wrench thrown into the global trading system might harm profits, the elements of his constituency that I ran through above for the most part apparently don't care much about the chaos, or even seem to enjoy seeing their leader offending elites and the damned foreigners.

Midterm elections are rapidly approaching. Do you see a "blue wave" coming? And if it happens, will it be sufficient to move Trumpism to the dustbin of history?

If the Democrats could get their act together, overcoming the schism between the donor-oriented New Democrat Party management and the increasingly activist and social democratic base, they would have a decent chance to take over Congress. That seems questionable, at the moment, though they should make some gains. But whatever gains there might be would not rid us of Trumpism, or its European counterparts. These have grown out of a mixture of authentic grievances and social pathologies—the latter surfacing in part because of the grievances. These are rooted in socioeconomic policies and bitter and so far, quite successful one-sided class struggle. None of this can easily be cast to the dustbin of history.

In some ways, as you have previously pointed out yourself, the most impressive aspect about recent developments on the US political landscape was the Bernie Sanders phenomenon, which represented a clear indication that the base of the Democratic Party had moved unmistakably to the left. Is the Sanders phenomenon—or at least the elements that gave rise to it—over? And how difficult is it for a new political party to emerge that advocates a progressive economic, social, and foreign policy agenda?

The Sanders phenomenon was striking in two ways. One, as you mention, is the sign that the popular base of the party has moved to the left and gave impressive support to a candidate with social democratic, New Deal–style commitments—a breath of fresh air in the current state of affairs. The second was the sharp break from a long political history of pretty much bought elections. The phenomenon is by no means over. Sanders emerged as the most popular political figure in the country. In a functioning democracy, his voice—which continues to be loud and clear—would reach a wide public through mainstream media. Not here, where it is scarcely heard. Nevertheless, the offshoots of his campaign, Our Revolution, are doing important work, joining others in creating what might become stable and effective popular movements.

The barriers are not insuperable, but to overcome them will require large-scale and effective organization based on popular mass movements. A lot has to be done to overcome the demolition of unions and atomization of society during the neoliberal years under the Thatcherite slogan "You know, there's no such thing as society"—unwittingly echoing Marx's bitter condemnation of authoritarian rulers who want to turn society into "a sack of potatoes," isolated individuals incapable of confronting concentrated economic and political power. The US political system has serious flaws, among them very high structural barriers for forming a new party. The last political party to have reached the mainstream is the Republican Party, but those were very different days. Where there is proportional representation, new parties can find a place in the political system, and have a chance to become major players—the British Labour Party, for example. In the US, even formal balloting procedures, run by state legislatures, virtually restrict participation to the two parties. Furthermore, the political parties are not membership organizations; rather, they are candidate-producing machines.

There are serious tasks ahead for those who aspire to a livable world.

Fascism, Showmanship, and Democrats' Hypocrisy in the Trump Era

C. J. POLYCHRONIOU: Noam, I want to start by asking for your reading of what took place at the Singapore summit, and the way this event was covered in the US media.

NOAM CHOMSKY: It's reminiscent of Sherlock Holmes and the dog that didn't bark. What was important was what *didn't* happen. Unlike his predecessors, Trump did not undermine the prospects for moving forward. Specifically, he did not disrupt the process initiated by the two Koreas in their historic April 27, 2018, [Panmunjom] Declaration, in which they "affirmed the principle of determining the destiny of the Korean nation on their own accord" (repeat: *on their own accord*), and for the first time presented a detailed program as to how to proceed. It is to Trump's credit that he did not undermine these efforts, and in fact made a move toward facilitating them by cancelling the US–South Korean war games, which, as he correctly said, are "very provocative." We would certainly not tolerate anything of the sort on our borders—or anywhere on the planet—even if they were not run by a superpower which not long before had utterly devastated our country with the flimsiest of pretexts after the war was effectively over, glorying in the major war crimes it had committed, like bombing major dams, after there was nothing else to bomb.

Beyond the achievement of letting matters proceed, which was not slight, no "diplomatic skills" were involved in Trump's triumph.

The coverage has been quite instructive, in part because of the efforts of the Democrats to outflank Trump from the right. Beyond that, the coverage across the spectrum illustrates quite well two distinct kinds of deceit: lying and not telling relevant truths. Each merits comment.

Trump is famous for the former, and his echo chamber is as well. Liberal commentators exult in totting up and refuting Trump's innumerable lies and distortions, much to his satisfaction since it provides the opportunity for him to fire up his loyal—by now almost worshipful—base with more evidence of how the hated "Establishment" is using every possible under-handed means to prevent their heroic leader from working tirelessly to de-fend them from a host of enemies.

A canny politician, Trump surely understands well that the base on which he relies, by now almost the entire Republican Party, has drifted to a surreal world, in part under his influence. Take the major Trump-Ryan legislative achievement, the tax scam—"The US Donor Relief Act of 2017," as Joseph Stiglitz termed it. It had two transparent aims: to enrich the very wealthy and the corporate sector while slamming everyone else, and to create a huge deficit. The latter achievement—as the main architect of the scam Paul Ryan helpfully explained—provides the opportunity to realize the cherished goal of reducing benefits that serve the general population, already very weak by comparative standards, but still an unacceptable in-fringement on the prerogatives of the 1 percent. The congressional Joint Committee on Taxation estimates that the law will add $1 trillion to deficits over the next decade. Virtually every economist generally agrees. But not 80 percent of Republican voters, of whom half believe that the deficit will be *reduced* by the gift their leader has lavished upon them.

Or consider something vastly more significant, attitudes toward global warming (apologies for the obscenity: climate change), which poses a severe threat to organized human life, and not in the distant future.

Half of Republicans believe that what is plainly happening is not happen-ing, bolstered by virtually the entire leadership of the party, as the Republican Primary debates graphically revealed. Of the half who concede that the real world exists, barely half think that humans play a role in the process.

Such destructive responses tend to break through the surface during periods of distress and fear, very widespread feelings today, for good reason: a generation of neoliberal policies has sharply concentrated wealth and power while leaving the rest to stagnate or decline, often joining the growing precariat. In the US, the richest country in history with unparalleled advantages, over 40 percent of the population don't earn enough to afford a monthly budget that includes housing, food, child care, health care, transportation, and a cell phone. And this is happening in what's called a "booming economy."

Productivity has risen through the neoliberal period, even if not as much as before, but wages have stagnated or declined as wealth is funneled to a few bulging pockets. Distress is so severe that among white middle-aged Americans, mortality is actually increasing, something unheard of in functioning societies apart from war or pestilence. There are similar phenomena in Europe under the "business first" ("neoliberal"/"austerity") assault.

Returning to forms of deceit, one technique is simply lying, honed to a high art by the Maestro. Another technique is not telling parts of the "whole story" that matter.

To illustrate, consider the analysis of "Trump's claims about the North Korea deal" by the expert and highly competent fact-checker of the *Washington Post*, Glenn Kessler. His article originally ran under the title of "Not the Whole Story," with the title presented in extra-large letters to emphasize the ignominy. Kessler's acid (and accurate) critique of Trump's distortions and inventions opens by declaring (again correctly) that "North Korea has a long history of making agreements and then not living up to its obligations," citing the most crucial case, the September 2005 US–North Korea agreement (under six-power auspices), in which, in the official wording, "The DPRK [North Korea] committed to abandoning all nuclear weapons and existing nuclear programs and returning, at an early date, to the Treaty on the Nonproliferation of Nuclear Weapons and to IAEA [International Atomic Energy Agency] safeguards."

As Kessler points out, the North Koreans did not live up to these promises, and in fact, soon returned to producing nuclear weapons. Obviously, they can't be trusted.

But this is "Not the Whole Story." There is a rather significant omission: before the ink was dry on the agreement, the US undermined it. To repeat the unwanted facts from our earlier discussion of the matter, "the

Bush administration broke the agreement. It renewed the threat of force, froze North Korean funds in foreign banks and disbanded the consortium that was to provide North Korea with a light-water reactor. Bruce Cumings, the leading US Korea scholar, writes that 'the sanctions were specifically designed to destroy the September pledges [and] to head off an accommodation between Washington and Pyongyang.'" The whole story is well known to scholarship, but somehow doesn't reach the public domain.

Kessler is a fine and careful journalist. His evasion of "the whole story" appears to be close to exceptionless in the media. Every article on the matter by the *New York Times* security and foreign policy experts is the same, as far as I've seen. The practice is so uniform that it is almost unfair to pick out examples. To choose only one, again from a fine journalist, *Washington Post* specialist on Korea Anna Fifield writes that North Korea "signed a denuclearization agreement" in 2005, but didn't stick to the agreement (omitting the fact that this was a response to Washington's breaking the agreement). "So perhaps the wisest course of action," she continues, "would be to bet that it won't abide by this one, either." And to complete the picture with a banned phrase, "So perhaps the wisest course of action would be to bet that [Washington] won't abide by this one, either."

There are endless laments about the deceitfulness and unreliability of the North Koreans; many are cited in Gareth Porter's review of media coverage. But it would be hard to find a word about the rest of the story. This is only one case.

I don't incidentally suggest that the deceit is conscious. Much more likely, it's just the enormous power of conformity to convention, to what Gramsci called hegemonic "common sense." Some ideas are not even rejected; they are unthinkable. Like the idea that US aggression is aggression; it can only be "a mistake," "a tragic error," "a strategic blunder." I also don't want to suggest this is "American exceptionalism." It's hard to find an exception to the practice in the history of imperialism.

So far, at least, Trump has kept from disrupting the agreement of the two Koreas. Of course, all of this is accompanied by boasts about his amazing deal-making abilities, and the brilliance of his skillful tactics of threatening "fire and fury" in order to bring the dictator to the negotiating table. There are many accolades by others across the spectrum for this triumph—which is about on a par with the standard claims that Obama's harsh sanctions forced Iran to capitulate by signing the joint agreement on nuclear weapons, claims effectively refuted by Trita Parsi (*Losing an Enemy*). Whatever the factual basis, such claims are necessary to justify harsh measures against official enemies and to reinforce the general principle that what we do is *right* (with occasional tragic errors).

In the present case too, there is good evidence that the truth is almost the opposite of the standard claims, and that the harsh US stance has impeded progress toward peaceful settlement. There have been many opportunities in addition to the 2005 agreement. In 2013, in a meeting with senior US diplomats, North Korean officials outlined steps toward denuclearization. One of those who attended the meeting, former US official and Stimson Center senior fellow Joel Wit reports that, "Not surprisingly, for the North Koreans, the key to denuclearization was that the United States had to end its 'hostile policy.'"

While the US maintains its threatening stance, the North Korean leadership—"not surprisingly"—has sought "to develop a nuclear arsenal as a shield to deter the US while they moved to develop the economy." The North Korean government, in June 2013, "issued an important new pronouncement that it was open to negotiations on denuclearization," Wit writes, adding that "the Obama administration dismissed it at the time as propaganda." He adds further that "the North Koreans have given a great deal of thought to denuclearization and almost certainly have a concrete plan of action for the upcoming [Singapore] summit, whether the White House does or not." In fact, at the 2013 meetings, "the North Korean officials actually laid out a concrete plan to achieve denuclearization," Wit reports.

Not the only case. China's "double freeze" proposal, supported by Russia, Germany, and others, has been on the table for years, rejected by Washington—until the Singapore summit.

Trump's diplomacy, such as it is, has been subjected to withering attack, especially by liberal opinion: *How could the US president agree to meet on friendly terms with a brutal dictator? How could he fail to demand that North Korea end its human rights violations, which are indeed horrendous?*

Willingness to look at "the whole story" suggests some other questions, of course unasked—in fact, unthinkable: *How could Kim agree to meet on friendly terms with the head of the state that world opinion overwhelmingly regards as the greatest threat to peace? How could North Korea fail to demand that the US end its human rights violations, also horrendous? Has North Korea done anything remotely like invading Iraq, the worst crime of this century? Or destroying Libya? Has it been condemned by the ICJ [International Court of Justice] for international terrorism ("unlawful use of force")?* And a lot more that is easy enough to reel off.

It made perfect sense for North Korea not to bring up US crimes as a condition for moving forward. The proper goal of the meeting was to expedite the efforts of the two Koreas to pursue the directions outlined in their April 27 Declaration. And the argument cuts both ways.

Interestingly enough, while Trump seeks to appease his political doppelgänger in Pyongyang, he has succeeded in alienating most of the US's major Western allies, including Canada, France, and Germany. Is this the consequence of his alleged foreign policy doctrine "We are America, bitch"?

There are extensive efforts to try to discern some coherent doctrine that guides Trump's behavior, but I suspect it's a fool's errand. A very good predictor of Trump policy is [his fixation on] . . . reversing anything associated with the despised "Kenyan Muslim" he replaced: in foreign policy, tearing up the successful Iran deal and accepting the long-standing possibilities for addressing the serious North Korea crisis (proclaiming to have created an astonishing breakthrough). Much the same is true of other actions that look like random shots when the driving forces are ignored.

All of this has to be done while satisfying the usual Republican constituencies: primarily the business world and the rich. For Trump, that also means unleashing the more brutal wing of the Republican Party so that they can dedicate themselves even beyond the norm to the interest of private wealth and corporate power. Here the technique is to capture the media with attention-grabbing antics, which can be solemnly exposed while the game goes on—so far, quite effectively.

Then comes the task of controlling the so-called "populist" base: the angry, frightened, disillusioned white population, primarily males. Since there is no way for Trumpism to deal with their economic concerns, which are actually being exacerbated by current policy formation, it's necessary to posture heroically as "standing up" for them against "malevolent forces" and to cater to the antisocial impulses that tend to surface when people are left to face difficult circumstances alone, without institutions and organizations to support them in their struggles. That's also being done effectively for the time being.

The "We are America, bitch" posture appeals to chauvinistic instincts and the white supremacy that is a deeply rooted feature of American culture and is now exacerbated by concern that whites might even become a minority. The posture can also delude working people into believing that their tough-guy protector will bring back the world they've lost. Such propaganda exercises cannot, of course, target those actually responsible for the plight of the victims of neoliberal globalization. On the contrary, attention has to be diverted away from corporate managers who largely shape state policy while establishing complex global supply chains to maximize profit at the expense of working people. More appropriate targets are desperate people fleeing horrors for which we are largely responsible: "foreigners" who have been "robbing us" with the connivance of "treacherous liberals" and other assorted devils that can be conjured up in periods of social breakdown.

Allies, friends, who cares? There is no need for policies that are "coherent" in any traditional sense. Consequences don't matter as long as the primary goals are met.

After months of harsh rhetoric against China's trade practices, Trump has decided to impose tariffs of $50 billion on Chinese imports, prompting Beijing, subsequently, to declare that the US has embarked on a trade war and to announce in turn that it will retaliate with similar measures against US imports. First, isn't it true that China is merely practicing today the same sort of mercantilist policies that the US and Great Britain practiced in the past on their way to global ascendancy? Second, is the targeting of tariffs expected to have any impact either on China's economy or on the size of the US trade deficit? And lastly, if a new era of protectionism is about to take off, what could the consequences of such development be for the reign of global neoliberalism?

Several questions arise. First, what is Trump's motive? If it were concern about China's economic management and trade policies, he wouldn't be going out of his way to alienate allies with tariffs and insults but would be joining with them to confront China on the issues of concern. If, however, the driving force is what I discussed earlier, then targeting both China and allies with abuse and tariffs has a certain logic: it may play well in the Rust Belt, contributing to the delusion that our hero is fighting to ensure jobs for working people—though it's a tricky strategy, because it harms other parts of his loyal base, mainly farmers, and also, though more subtly, because it imposes a new tax on consumption, which is what tariffs amount to.

As for China's economic policies, yes, they are similar to those that have been used by developed societies generally, beginning with Britain and then its former North American colony. Similar, but more limited. China lacks the means available to its predecessors. Britain stole superior technology from India, the Low Countries, Ireland, and by force and severe protectionism, undermined the Indian economy, then the world's most advanced along with China. The US, under the Hamiltonian system, resorted to high tariffs to bar superior British goods, and also took British technology in ways barred by the current US-initiated global trading system. Economic historian Paul Bairoch describes the US as "the mother country and bastion of protectionism" into the 1920s, well after it had become far and away the richest country in the world.

The general practice is called "kicking away the ladder" by economic historians: first use the practices to develop, then bar others from following.

Earlier, Britain's economic development relied on large-scale piracy, now considered by its former practitioner to be the most heinous of crimes. Keynes wrote that the booty of English pirates, like the famed and admired Sir Francis Drake, "may fairly be considered the fountain and origin of British foreign investments." Piracy was also a standard practice in the American colonies. Both British and US economies also relied crucially on the most hideous system of slavery in human history. Cotton was the oil of the Industrial Revolution, providing the basis for manufacturing, finance, commerce, retail. Such practices are not available to China.

Like Britain before it, the US called for "free trade" when it recognized that the playing field was tilted properly in its direction. After World War II, when the US had incomparable power, it promoted the "liberal world order" that has been an enormous boon to the US corporate system, which now owns about half of the global economy, an astonishing policy success.

Again, following the British model, the US hedged its commitment to "free trade" for the benefit of domestic private power. The British-dominated "free trade" system kept India as a largely closed protectorate. The US-dominated system imposes an extreme patent system ("intellectual property") that provides virtual monopoly power to major US industries. The US government also provides huge subsidies to energy industries, agribusiness and financial institutions. While the US complains about Chinese industrial policy, the modern high-tech industry has relied crucially on research and development in the publicly subsidized sector of the economy, to such an extent that the economy might fairly be regarded as a system of public subsidy, private profit. And there are many other devices to subsidize industry. Procurement, for example, has been shown to be a significant device. In fact, the enormous military system alone, through procurement, provides a huge state subsidy to industry. These comments only skim the surface.

Britain abandoned laissez-faire when it could no longer cope with Japanese competition, part of the background for World War II in the Pacific. Some in the US are having similar qualms today, concerns that Trump is cynically exploiting. But not the powerful corporate sector that relies crucially on the US-designed global economic order.

The corporate sector relies so extensively on the global economy it has designed that it is sure to use its enormous power to try to head off a major trade war. The Trump tariffs and the retaliation might escalate, but it's likely that the threat will be contained. Trump is quite right, however, in proclaiming that the US would "win" a limited trade war, given the scale of the US economy, the huge domestic market, and unique advantages in other respects. The "We are America, bitch" doctrine is a powerful weapon of intimidation.

The Trump administration is moving full speed ahead with its intent on cracking down on unauthorized entries to the country by separating immigrant children from their parents. More than two thousand children have been separated from their parents during the last seven weeks,

and Attorney General Jeff Sessions sought recently to justify Trump's immigration policy by citing a verse from the Bible. What can one say about an advanced Western society in which religion continues to crowd out reason in shaping public policy and public attitudes? And didn't the Nazis, although they were no believers, also use Christianity to justify their immoral and criminal acts?

The immigration policy, always grotesque, has descended to levels so revolting that even many of those who foster and exploit xenophobia are running for cover—like Trump, who is desperately trying to blame it on the Democrats, and like the first lady, who is appealing to "both sides of the aisle" to come together to stop the obscenity. We should, however, not overlook the fact that Europe is crawling through much the same gutters.

One can quote scripture for almost any purpose one likes. Sessions doubtless knows that "all the law" hangs on two commandments: loving God and "Thou shalt love thy neighbor as thyself." But that is not the appropriate thought for the occasion.

It is true, however, that the US is unique among developed societies in the role of religion in social life, ever since the Puritans landed.

Recently, Trump stated that he had the absolute right to pardon himself (after he had already said that he could shoot someone on New York's 5th Avenue and not lose any support), while his lawyer, former New York City mayor Rudy Giuliani, said the president could even commit murder in the Oval Office and still not be prosecuted for it. Your thoughts?

After praising Kim [Jong Un] effusively as a strong leader who "speaks and his people sit up at attention," Trump added: "I want my people to do the same." When the predictable reaction followed, he said he was kidding. Maybe. I hope we don't have an opportunity to find out.

While it is clear that the country is well on its way to becoming a pariah nation, the Democrats continue to focus their attention primarily on Trump's alleged collusion with Russia and unethical behavior, all the while trying to outflank the president on the jingoist front, adopting new restrictions for the 2020 elections so they can keep away the likes of

Bernie Sanders, and of course, playing masterfully the fundraising game that works in a plutocracy. With all this in mind, how would you describe the nature of contemporary US politics?

Much as in Europe, the centrist political institutions in the United States, which have long been in the driver's seat, are in decline. The reasons are not obscure. People who have endured the rigors of the neoliberal assault—austerity in the recent European version—recognize that the institutions are working for others, not for them. In the US, people do not have to read academic political science to know that a large majority, those who are not near the top of the income scale, are effectively disenfranchised, in that their own representatives pay little attention to their views, hearkening rather to the voices of the rich, the donor class. As previously noted, in Europe, anyone can see that basic decisions are made by the unelected Troika, in Brussels, with the northern banks peering over their shoulders.

In the US, respect for Congress has long been hovering in single digits. In recent Republican primaries, when candidates emerged from the base, the Establishment was able to beat them down and obtain their own candidate. In 2016, that failed for the first time. True, it's not far from the norm for a billionaire with enormous media support and almost $1 billion in campaign funding to win an election, but Trump was hardly the choice of the Republican elites. The most spectacular result of the election was not the Trump phenomenon. Rather, it was the remarkable success of Bernie Sanders, breaking sharply with US political history. With no support from big business or the media, Sanders might well have won the Democratic nomination had it not been for the machinations of Obama-Clinton party managers. Similar processes are apparent in recent European elections.

Like it or not, Trump is doing quite well. He has the support of 83 percent of Republicans, which is without precedent apart from rare moments. Whatever their feelings may be, Republicans dare not cross him openly. His general support in the low 40s is not far from the norm, about the same as Obama's going into his first midterm. He is lavishing gifts on the business world and the wealthy, the authentic constituency of the Republicans (with the Democrat leadership not far behind). He has thrown enough crumbs to keep the evangelicals happy and has struck the right chords for racist/white supremacy elements. And he has, so far, managed to convince coal miners and steel workers that he is one of them. In fact, his support among union members has increased to 51 percent.

It is hardly in doubt that Trump cares almost nothing about the fate of the country or the world. What matters is *me*. That's clear enough from his attitude toward global warming. He is perfectly well aware of the dire threat—to his properties. His application for a seawall to protect his Irish golf course is based explicitly on the threat of global warming. But pursuit of power impels him to lead the race to destruction, quite happily, as is evident from his performances. The same holds of other serious, if lesser, threats, among them the threat that the country may be isolated, despised, declining—with dues to pay after it's no longer his concern.

The Democrats are now torn between a popular base that is largely social democratic and a New Democrat leadership that panders to the donor class. Under Obama, the party was reduced to shambles at the local and state level, a particularly serious matter because the 2020 elections will determine redistricting, offering opportunities for gerrymandering even beyond today's scandalous situation.

The bankruptcy of the Democratic elite is well illustrated by the obsession with alleged Russian meddling with our sacred elections. Whatever it might amount to—apparently very little—it cannot begin to compare with the "meddling" of campaign funding, which largely determines electoral outcomes, as extensive research has shown, particularly the careful work of Thomas Ferguson, which he and his colleagues have now extended to the 2016 elections. As Ferguson points out, when Republican elites realized that it was going to be Trump or Clinton, they responded with a huge wave of last-minute money that not only led to Clinton's late October decline but also had the same effect on Democratic candidates for Senate, "virtually in lock step." It is "outlandish," Ferguson observes, that former FBI Director James Comey or the Russians "could be responsible for both collapses" in the final stage of the campaign: "For the first time in the entire history of the United States, the partisan outcome of Senate races coincided perfectly with the results of every state's presidential balloting." The outcome conforms very well to Ferguson's well-supported "investment theory of party competition."

But facts and logic matter little. The Democrats are bent on revenge for their 2016 failure, having run such a rotten campaign that what looked like a "sure thing" collapsed. Evidently, Trump's severe assault against the common good is a lesser matter, at least to the party elite.

It's sometimes been noted that the US not only regularly meddles in foreign elections, including Russian ones, but also proceeds to subvert and sometimes overthrow governments it doesn't like. Horrifying consequences abound, to the present, from Central America to the Middle East. Guatemala has been a horror story since a US-backed coup overthrew its elected reformist government in 1954. Gaza, declining in misery, may become unlivable by 2020, the UN predicts, not by acts of God. In 2006, Palestinians committed a grave crime: they ran the first free election in the Arab world, and made the "wrong" choice, handing power to Hamas. Israel reacted by escalating violence and a brutal siege. The US reverted to standard operating procedure and prepared a military coup, preempted by Hamas. In punishment for this new crime, US-Israeli torture of Gaza sharply increased, not only with strangulation but also regular murderous and destructive US-backed Israeli invasions, on pretexts that quickly collapse on examination. Elections that come out the wrong way plainly cannot be tolerated under our policy of "democracy promotion."

In recent European elections, there has been much concern about possible Russian meddling. That was particularly true of the 2017 German elections, when the far-right party Alternative für Deutschland (AfD) did surprisingly well, winning ninety-four seats in the Bundestag, the first time it had won seats. One can easily imagine the reaction had Russian meddling been detected behind these frightening results. It turns out that there was indeed foreign meddling, but not from Russia. AfD hired a Texas media firm (Harris Media) known for support of right-wing nationalist candidates (Trump, Le Pen, Netanyahu). The firm enlisted the cooperation of the Berlin office of Facebook, which provided it with detailed information about potential voters for use in microtargeting those who might be receptive to AfD's message. It may have worked. The story seems to have been ignored, apart from the business press.

If the Democratic Party cannot overcome its deep internal problems and the slow expansion of the economy under Obama and Trump continues without disruption or disaster, the Republican wrecking ball may be swinging away at the foundations of a decent society, and at the prospects for survival, for a long time.

Donald Trump and the "Me First" Doctrine

C. J. POLYCHRONIOU: Noam, Donald Trump rose to power with "America First" as the key slogan of his election campaign. However, looking at what his administration has done so far on both the domestic and international front, it is hard to see how his policies are contributing to the well-being and security of the United States. With that in mind, can you decode for us what Trump's "America First" policy may be about with regard to international relations?

NOAM CHOMSKY: It is only natural to expect that policies will be designed for the benefit of the designers and their actual—not pretended—constituency, and that the well-being and security of the society will be incidental. And that is what we commonly discover. We might recall, for example, the frank comments on the Monroe Doctrine by Woodrow Wilson's secretary of state, Robert Lansing: "In its advocacy of the Monroe Doctrine the United States considers its own interests. The integrity of other American nations is an incident, not an end. While this may seem based on selfishness alone, the author of the Doctrine had no higher or more generous motive in its declaration." The observation generalizes in international affairs, and much the same logic holds within the society.

There is nothing essentially new about "America First," and "America" does not mean America, but rather the designers and their actual constituency.

A typical illustration is the policy achievement of which the Trump-Ryan-McConnell administration is most proud: the tax bill—what Joseph

Stiglitz accurately called "The US Donor Relief Act of 2017." It contributes very directly to the well-being of their actual constituency: private wealth and corporate power. It benefits the actual constituency indirectly by the standard Republican technique (since Reagan) of blowing up the deficit as a pretext for undermining social programs, which are the Republicans' next targets. The bill is thus of real benefit to its actual constituency and severely harms the general population.

Turning to international affairs, in Trumpian lingo, "America First" means "me first" and damn the consequences for the country or the world. The "me first" doctrine has an immediate corollary—it's necessary to keep the base in line with fake promises and fiery rhetoric, while not alienating the actual constituency. It also follows that it's important to do the opposite of whatever was done by Obama. Trump is often called "unpredictable," but his actions are highly predictable on these simple principles.

His most important decision, by far, was to pull out of the Paris negotiations on climate change and to tear to shreds efforts to prevent environmental catastrophe—a threat that is extremely severe, and not remote. All completely predictable on the basic principles just mentioned.

The decision benefits the actual constituency: the energy corporations, the automotive industry (most of it), and others who pursue the imperative of short-term profit. Consider perhaps the most-respected and "moderate" member of the Trump team, former ExxonMobil CEO Rex Tillerson, kicked out because he was too soft-hearted. We now know that ExxonMobil scientists were in the lead in the 1970s in recognizing the dire threat of global warming—facts surely known to the CEO, who presided over efforts to maximize the threat and to fund denialism of what the management knew was true—all to fill some overstuffed pockets with more dollars before we say "goodbye" to organized human life, not in the distant future.

It's hard to find a word in the language to describe such behavior.

The decision also appeals to the pretended constituency: the voting base. Half of Republicans deny that global warming is taking place, and of the rest, a bare majority think that humans may have a role in it. It's doubtful that anything comparable exists elsewhere.

And, of course, the decision reverses an Obama initiative, thus keeping to high principles.

One cannot overemphasize the astonishing fact that the most powerful country in world history refuses to join the world in doing at least something—in some cases a lot—about this existential threat to organized human life (and to the species that are disappearing as the Sixth Extinction proceeds on its lethal course). And beyond that, is devoting its efforts to accelerating the race to disaster. And no less astonishing is the failure to highlight, even to discuss this extraordinary situation. Considering what is at stake, it is hard to find a historical parallel.

The same holds pretty much on other policies, though sometimes with more elite opposition. Take Obama's Iran deal—the Joint Comprehensive Plan of Action (JCPOA). That, of course, has to go, on pretexts too ludicrous to discuss, and always ignoring the fact that while Iran has been adhering to the agreement, the US has been violating it all along by acting to block Iran's reintegration into the global economy, particularly the global financial system, and to undermine "the normalisation of trade and economic relations with Iran." All in violation of the JCPOA, but of no concern, on the prevailing tacit assumption that "the indispensable nation" stands above the law.

A considerable majority of Republicans have always opposed the deal, though in this case, Republican elites are often more realistic. The business world does not appear to have supported even the earlier sanctions regime—one of those interesting cases where state policy diverges from the interests of the actual constituency, much like Cuba policy. The decision harms the welfare and security of the general population, and might have truly horrendous consequences, but that is scarcely a consideration.

The Trump team is working hard to maximize the likely disastrous effects. Secretary of State Mike Pompeo made his first major speech at the ultra-reactionary Heritage Foundation, focusing on Iran, with demands so extreme that the goal must be to ensure that they are instantly rejected. Among them, that Iran withdraw its forces from Syria and end its support for Hezbollah and Hamas, and more generally, end its campaign "to dominate the Middle East"—newspeak for Iran's unwillingness to retreat into a shell and allow the US its traditional right to dominate the Middle East (and any other place it can) by force, with no impediments. Pompeo also warned the Europeans to join the US jihad, or else.

There is some merit in Trump's posturing about how the JCPOA should be improved. It definitely can be. In particular, it can be extended to establishing a nuclear-weapon-freezone (NWFZ) in the Middle East, with serious inspections, which would eliminate any alleged threat of eventual Iranian nuclear programs. To achieve that goal should be quite straightforward. There is no need to obtain Iran's acquiescence. Iran has long been in the forefront of those calling for establishment of an NWFZ, particularly as the spokesperson for G-77—the former nonaligned countries—which strongly advocates this development. The Arab states, with Egypt in the lead, initiated this proposal and have strongly urged that it be implemented. There is overwhelming international support. The matter regularly comes up in the review sessions of the Non-Proliferation Treaty, with full agreement— almost. One country regularly blocks the effort, most recently Obama in 2015. The reason is not obscure—as discussed earlier, Israel's nuclear weapons systems must not be subject even to inspection, let alone steps toward dismantlement.

It is important to add that the US and UK have a special responsibility to work to establish a Middle East NWFZ. They are committed to this goal by Security Council Resolution 687—a commitment that takes on even greater force because they appealed to this resolution when seeking desperately to create legal pretext for their 2003 criminal invasion of Iraq.

But all of this is unmentionable, so we can put it aside.

The Trump decision has infuriated much of the world, with the usual exceptions. In particular, it has infuriated European allies. Whether they will be willing to stand up against the global bully is unclear; it is a frightening prospect. If Europe does not proceed with the JCPOA, as the Trump wreckers hope, that might encourage Iranian hardliners to develop "nuclear capability"—a capacity to produce nuclear weapons if they ever decide to, which many non-nuclear states have. That might provide a green light for those who have been itching to bomb Iran for a long time, among them the new national security adviser John Bolton and Israeli Prime Minister Benjamin Netanyahu.

Case by case, we find much the same, sometimes with further complexities.

Trump's view of world affairs seems to assign very little role to diplomacy, as evidenced by the desolation of the State Department under his administration. What's your own understanding and explanation for Trump's aversion to diplomacy?

His position makes good sense. In confronting adversaries—for Trump, most of the world, apart from a few favored dictatorships (and the increasingly reactionary Israeli client)—it is only reasonable to play one's strong card. The US is militarily strong—in fact, overwhelming in military strength. Trump's *increase* in the vastly inflated military budget amounts to about 80 percent of the total Russian military budget, which is declining. But increasingly under Trump, the US is diplomatically weak and isolated. So why bother with diplomacy?

Incidentally, this is by no means a completely new departure. As its global power declined from its peak in the 1940s, the US has increasingly disregarded international institutions. During the years of its overwhelming global dominance, when the UN could be counted on to stay in line and serve as a weapon against adversaries, the UN was highly respected by elite opinion and Russia was berated for constantly saying "no." As other industrial countries reconstructed from wartime devastation and decolonization proceeded on its agonizing course, the UN lost its allure. By the 1980s, respected intellectuals were pondering the strange cultural-psychological defect that was causing the world to be out of step. The US cast its first Security Council veto in 1970, and quickly gained the lead in doing so. It is the only country to have gone so far as to veto a Security Council resolution calling on all states to observe international law—mentioning no one, but it was understood that it was a response to Washington's rejection of World Court orders to end its "unlawful use of force" (aka international terrorism) against Nicaragua and to pay substantial reparations. The US rarely ratifies international conventions, and when it does, it is typically with crucial reservations, effectively exempting itself: the genocide and torture conventions, and many others.

Rather generally, while Trump is carrying defiance of world opinion to new extremes, he can claim predecessors.

Trump's decision to move the US embassy to Jerusalem (something which many of his predecessors had actually promised of doing but never carried out when in office) has created havoc in the Middle East, just as expected, although the administration has justified this decision as part of the need to "secure peace" in the region. First, what were the motives behind this decision? Second, can this move be regarded as legal according to norms and principles of international law? And, thirdly, can this decision be undone by future US presidents?

The motive was hardly concealed, and follows from the usual Trump principles. The move is strongly supported by Trump's evangelical base—by now, the major popular support for Israel as more liberal sectors, as elsewhere in the world, are coming to oppose Israel's violence, repression, and flagrant violations of international law. The move is also a gift to major Republican Party donors like Sheldon Adelson and Paul Singer. This decision, too, isolates the US in the world scene, harming the country in the longer term, but that is irrelevant. The US vetoed an otherwise unanimous Security Council resolution condemning the move, which is in violation of numerous [UN Security Council] resolutions on Jerusalem since 1968. The decision can be reversed.

The Gaza massacre in the aftermath of the Trump administration decision to move the US embassy to Jerusalem exposed not only the historical insensitivity of the Trump gang to the plight of the Palestinian people under Israeli occupation (as well as its unconscionable ignorance of Muslim culture and history), but also the brutality of the Israeli state and, equally important, the cowardice, once again, of the so-called international community. Your thoughts or reactions to all of the above?

All correct, except that reference to the "Trump gang" is too narrow. Few are aware of the extent of Israeli brutality. Just to take one pertinent example, few are aware that just as the recent nonviolent demonstrations were beginning, leading to the Gaza massacre when Israel responded with military force, Hamas leadership approached Israel with a call for a long-term ceasefire ("hudna"). Israel, of course, rejected it, as it invariably does, rarely even giving reasons, though after the murderous Operation Protective Edge in

2014, an Israeli defense official explained that Israel did not respond "because there was no reason to conduct a dialogue with a bruised and beaten movement." In short: *We have overwhelming military force, you are defenseless, we can smash your society to bits any time we like, so why on earth should we call for an end to violence, abandoning our virtual monopoly?*

The North Korea nuclear saga has become a key global issue featuring the "rocket man" and America's "dotard." Do you see any prospects for a lasting peace between North and South Korea?

One possibility, advanced by China with broad international support, including North Korea intermittently, has been a double freeze: North Korea would freeze its development of nuclear weapons and missiles, and the US would cease its threatening military maneuvers on North Korea's borders, including menacing flights by the most advanced nuclear capable bombers—no laughing matter in a country that was flattened by merciless US bombing, even destruction of major dams (a serious war crime), within easy memory. The option has been rejected by the US.

As previously noted double freeze could have opened the way to further negotiations, perhaps reaching as far as what was achieved in 2005. Under international pressure, the Bush administration turned to negotiations, which achieved substantial success. North Korea agreed to abandon "all nuclear weapons and existing nuclear programs" and allow international inspections—phrases worth rereading in the light of constant misrepresentation. In return, the US was to provide a light-water reactor for medical use, issue a nonaggression pledge, and join in an agreement that the two sides would "respect each other's sovereignty, exist peacefully together, and take steps to normalize relations."

At once, the Bush administration broke the agreement. It renewed the threat of force, froze North Korean funds in foreign banks and disbanded the consortium that was to provide North Korea with a light-water reactor. Bruce Cumings, the leading US Korea scholar, writes that "the sanctions were specifically designed to destroy the September pledges [and] to head off an accommodation between Washington and Pyongyang."

That path could be pursued again.

On April 27, 2018, North and South Korea signed a historic document, the Panmunjom Declaration for Peace, Prosperity, and Unification of the Korean Peninsula. It's worth reading carefully. In the declaration, the two Koreas "affirmed the principle of determining the destiny of the Korean nation on their own accord [repeat: *on their own accord*] . . . to completely cease all hostile acts against each other in every domain [to] . . . actively cooperate to establish a permanent and solid peace regime on the Korean Peninsula . . . to carry out disarmament in a phased manner, [in order to achieve] the common goal of realizing, through complete denuclearization, a nuclear-free Korean Peninsula…to strengthen the positive momentum towards continuous advancement of inter-Korean relations as well as peace, prosperity and unification of the Korean Peninsula." They also "agreed to actively seek the support and cooperation of the [international] community [meaning, the US] for the denuclearization of the Korean Peninsula."

Moreover, as Korea specialist Chung-in Moon reviews in *Foreign Affairs*, the two sides did not just make high-level commitments. They also laid out specific timetables for implementing them and took concrete steps that would have immediate effects in facilitating cooperation and preventing conflict—something quite new and very significant.

The import of the declaration is clear. The US should back off and allow the two Koreas to achieve peace, disarmament, unification, and complete denuclearization. We should accept the call for support and cooperation in this endeavor by the two parts of the Korean nation to determine its destiny "on their own accord."

To put it more simply, the declaration is a polite letter saying, "Dear Mr. Trump, declare victory if you want to prance around in public, but please go away and let us move towards peace, disarmament and unification without disrupting the process."

US analysts have been clear and frank about the real nature of the North Korean threat. *New York Times* foreign affairs commentator Max Fisher writes that North Korea "has achieved what no country has since China developed its own program a half-century ago: a nuclear deterrent against the United States," and Trump's threats and sanctions have not succeeded "to stall or reverse those gains." Clearly, we must act to prevent anyone from deterring our resort to force and violence.

It's worth noting that Iran poses problems similar to North Korea. Specialists across the political spectrum would likely agree with the conclusion of the respected and properly conservative International Institute of Strategic Studies in 2010 that "Iran's nuclear program and its willingness to keep open the possibility of developing nuclear weapons is a central part of its deterrent strategy." US intelligence concurs. Again, that is intolerable to the two rogue states that demand the right to rampage freely in the region, as they regularly do.

If Trump and his advisers have any sense, they will seize the opportunity and accept the plea of the two Koreas.

Unfortunately, expecting some sense may be too hopeful. The egregious hawk John Bolton, who has been just as publicly eager to bomb North Korea as Iran, went out of his way to bring up a model that he surely knew would infuriate and antagonize North Korea—the "Libya model": *You give up your deterrent, and then we will destroy you, ending with a brutal murder applauded with a vulgar joke by Hillary Clinton.* Then Vice President Mike Pence chimed in saying it's not a mere threat but "more of a fact" that "this will only end like the Libyan model ended if Kim Jong Un doesn't make a deal."

Along with threatening military maneuvers at the North Korean borders, this is just the way to move negotiations forward. Predictably, there was a harsh verbal North Korean response, though coupled with some crucial actions: North Korea reported that it had just destroyed its key nuclear weapons testing site, setting off explosions to collapse underground tunnels. Trump responded a few hours later by cancelling the planned summit meeting in Singapore with Kim Jong Un.

This is not the end, however, and perhaps those who understand that Trump might register an ill-deserved triumph may prevail.

Israel's prime minister, the irrevocable Bibi Netanyahu, has been driven for years by the idea of "regime change" in Tehran. Do you think this is a realistic objective now that Tel Aviv has a "real friend" in the White House?

I don't think so, and I doubt that Israeli strategists do either. An invasion of Iran is most unlikely. If the US and Israel attack, it's likely to be from a safe distance—missiles mainly—and aimed at specific targets, though there might be Special Forces operations. We might recall that the US and Israel have already committed what the Pentagon describes as an "act of war" against Iran, justifying a military response from the target—namely, the cyberwar attack on Iranian nuclear facilities.

Europe's key leaders seem to be distancing themselves with ever greater frequency from Washington's policies on global affairs. Do you think we may be at the start of a new era between European and American relations? This is something that many had expected to happen from the time of Charles de Gaulle all the way up to the reign of Mikhail Gorbachev, but perhaps the time has finally come. So, your take on this? Is the era of US hegemony and obedience to Washington's dictates nearing its end?

From the early postwar years, there was considerable concern in planning circles in Washington that Europe might move to become a "third force" in global affairs, a neutralist bloc. De Gaulle was indeed the leading proponent of this conception, and a version was revived by Gorbachev in his call for a "Common European Home" of cooperation and interchange from the Atlantic to the Urals, in which both NATO and the Warsaw Pact would be dismantled in favor of a Pan-European security system. The idea was dismissed by the US in favor of expanding NATO, over the strong objections of George Kennan and other statesmen who warned, accurately enough, that this "policy error of historic proportions" would lead to rising and very ominous tensions on the Russian border. NATO's mission today, historian Richard Sakwa writes, is "to manage the risks created by its existence."

As to whether Europe today might move in an independent direction, I'm skeptical. Despite Trump's moves to diminish and isolate America, and to alienate allies, and despite the exit of America's major advocate (Britain) from the European Union, I suspect that Europe will be unwilling to pose a serious challenge to Washington. Europe faces too many internal problems, and despite Trump, the US still remains unmatched as a global power, with means of violence and coercion that it is not reluctant to use, as the world knows all too well.

But a lot remains uncertain. As the business press observes, the United States' "ability to impose financial sanctions around the world depends on the willingness of China and Europe to comply—and that may be waning." In the case of China, it has been waning rapidly. China has been moving to establish an international currency regime and trading system independent of the US. Trump's effort to destroy the Iran nuclear deal has infuriated the Europeans, who reacted at once by agreeing to invoke rules to shield European Union companies from US sanctions, to permit the European Investment Bank to finance business in Iran, and to encourage European countries to explore transfers to Iran's central bank, bypassing the US-dominated international financial system. These "blocking mechanisms" were last invoked in 1996, when Clinton sought to curb European investment in Cuba, Iran, and Libya. Clinton backed down. But the world has changed.

It's possible that Trump may succeed in creating a diminished America, hiding in fear behind walls, isolated and marginalized—though retaining plenty of guns to kill one another and a fearsome capacity to destroy at will.

"A Complete Disaster":
Trump and the Future of US Politics

C. J. POLYCHRONIOU: **Noam, it's been already fourteen months into Donald Trump's turbulent White House tenure, but sometimes we still need to pinch ourselves to make sure that it's not a nightmare that a racist, misogynist, homophobic man who apparently cares only about himself runs the world's most powerful nation. But, really, how bad is it having Trump in the White House?**

NOAM CHOMSKY: Very bad. As Trump began his second year in office, the Bulletin of Atomic Scientists advanced their Doomsday Clock to two minutes to midnight, citing increasing concerns about nuclear weapons and climate change. That's the closest it has been to terminal disaster since 1953, when the US and USSR exploded thermonuclear weapons. That was before the release of Trump's Nuclear Posture Review, which significantly increases the dangers by lowering the threshold for nuclear attack and by developing new weapons that increase the danger of terminal war.

On climate change, Trump is a complete disaster, along with the entire Republican leadership. Every candidate in the Republican primaries either denied that what is happening is happening or said . . . we shouldn't do anything about it. And these attitudes infect the Republican base. Half of Republicans deny that global warming is taking place, while 70 percent say that whether it is or not, humans are not responsible. Such figures would be shocking anywhere, but are remarkably so in a developed country with unparalleled resources and easy access to information.

It is hard to find words to describe the fact that the most powerful country in world history is not only withdrawing from global efforts to address a truly existential threat, but is also dedicating itself to accelerating the race to disaster, all to put more dollars in overstuffed pockets. No less astounding is the limited attention paid to the phenomenon.

When we turn to matters of great though lesser import, the conclusion is the same: disaster. While Trump's antics occupy the attention of the media, his associates in Congress have been working intensively to advance the interests of their actual constituency—extreme wealth and corporate power—while dismantling what is of value to the general population and future generations. With justice, the Republican leadership regard the tax bill as their greatest triumph. As noted, Joseph Stiglitz rightly describes the triumph as "The US Donor Relief Act of 2017," a vast giveaway to their actual constituency—and to themselves. As he points out, the Republican leaders "are stuffing themselves at the trough—Trump, Kushner and many others in his administration are among the biggest winners—thinking that this may be their last chance at such a feast." And "Après moi, le deluge"—literally in this case.

The grand triumph brings an extra advantage. It explodes the deficit (a trademark of Republicans since Reagan), which means that they can move on to cut away at entitlements, as the chief architect, Paul Ryan, announced happily at once. The US already ranks near the bottom of the [Organization for Economic Cooperation and Development] countries—the thirty-five richer and more developed countries—in social justice measures. The Republican triumph will sink it even lower. The tax scam is only the most prominent of the devices being implemented under the cover of Trump buffoonery to serve wealth and corporate power while harming the irrelevant population.

Many other policies are simply [unconscionable], such as Trump's initiative to have the Department of Homeland Security separate children, even infants, from their mothers in order to discourage immigration—seven hundred families have been split in this fashion since October, a *New York Times* investigation found. Many of these families are fleeing from the murderous consequences of US policies. Honduras has been the main source of refugee flight since the US, almost alone, endorsed the military coup that ousted the elected president and the fraudulent election that followed, initiating a reign of terror.

We also must endure the sight of Trump wailing in terror because a caravan of victims reached Mexico, most hoping to settle there. As mentioned, Trump's (tweeted?) suggestion that these victims threaten the security of the US is reminiscent of Reagan strapping on his cowboy boots and calling a national emergency because Nicaraguan troops were a two days' march from Texas, and about to overwhelm us. It's amazing that such performances do not evoke profound national embarrassment.

To the extent that politics is the art of the possible, would you say that Trump has been consistent so far with the promises he made to voters during the 2016 campaign?

In some cases, yes. He is fulfilling the wishes of the evangelicals who are a large part of his voting base. He is greatly increasing the military budget, as he promised. . . . Most of his promises are about as close to fulfillment as his commitment to "drain the swamp," which is now overflowing. [Scott] Pruitt's [Environmental Protection Agency] alone is a cesspool, though its dismantling of efforts to deal with the impact of climate change are far more serious than the wholesale robbery, which seems to be a Pruitt specialty from well before he was handed the wrecking ball.

On trade, though the policies, insofar as they are coherent, are generally harmful, the rhetoric is not completely false. Thus, it is true that China is using devices that violate World Trade Organization rules—devices that were critical to the growth of the rich societies, from England to the US and beyond, and are now banned by the investor rights agreements mislabeled "free trade agreements." As explained, this is a textbook illustration of what economic historians call "kicking away the ladder"—first we climb up, then we kick the ladder away so that you can't follow.

And Trump is right that the [North American Free Trade Agreement (NAFTA)] should be revised. Some sensible proposals have been put forth by the partners in NAFTA. For example, Canada has proposed that the revised NAFTA should ban harsh US anti-labor laws, like the right-to-scrounge laws called "right-to-work" in contemporary Newspeak. These laws are soon to become federal policy, it seems, under the reactionary

Roberts court, which was made more extreme by [Senate Majority Leader Mitch] McConnell's shameful parliamentary maneuvers to prevent even consideration of Obama's nomination, opening the way to the appointment of Neil Gorsuch—another gift to the far right.

The Canadian proposal was prominently reported in the major Canadian press, but, oddly, is missing from the discussions of NAFTA revision here, which keep to Trump proposals.

Allegations of collusion continue to haunt Donald Trump's presidency, primarily over his alleged ties to Russia and Putin, and former FBI director James Comey said in a recent interview with ABC News that Trump is "morally unfit" to be president. What's your take on all this, and what does Trump's disrespect for law and the fact that his base is refusing to abandon him tell us about the current state of American democracy and US politics in general?

We don't need Comey to tell us that Trump is morally unfit. He made that abundantly clear in the primaries, if not before. The fact that the Oval Office is coming to resemble a schoolyard on a bad day may be obnoxious, but it doesn't rank high among the misdeeds of the administration, in my opinion. . . . Same with his alleged ties to Russia and Putin. Much more serious is the clique that now surrounds him. It's a sad day when one has to hope that General [James] Mattis will keep the . . . [rest] in check. The [John] Bolton appointment in particular should send shivers up the spine of any person.

As for Trump's base, they are indeed quite loyal. Most Trump voters were relatively affluent and probably are fairly satisfied with the ultra-reactionary policies. Another important segment was non-college-educated whites, a group that voted overwhelmingly for Trump (a 40 percent advantage). There is a close analysis of this group in the current (Spring 2018) issue of the *Political Science Quarterly*. It found that racism and sexism were far more significant factors in their vote than economic issues. If so, this group has little reason to object to the scene that is unfolding, and the same with the white evangelicals who gave Trump 80 percent of their vote. Among justly angry, white, working-class Trump voters, many apparently enjoy watching him stick his thumb in the eyes of the hated elites even if he doesn't fulfill his promises to [working-class voters], which many never believed in the first place.

What all this tells us, yet again, is that the neoliberal programs that have concentrated wealth in a few hands while the majority stagnate or decline have also severely undermined functioning democracy by familiar mechanisms, leading to anger, contempt for the dominant centrist political forces and institutions, and often antisocial attitudes and behavior—alongside of very promising popular reactions, like the remarkable [Bernie] Sanders phenomenon, [Jeremy] Corbyn in England and positive developments elsewhere as well.

Ryan, an influential architect of the Republican economic platform, announced that he is stepping down from Congress. Do you think his decision was motivated by the fear that a "blue wave" may be coming in November as a result of a growing backlash against Trump and Trumpism?

There is much talk about how this "admirable" figure, who bedazzled the media with fraudulent spreadsheets, wants to spend time with his family. Much more likely, I think, is that he decided to leave Congress because he had achieved his long-standing goals, particularly with the "Donor Relief Act of 2017" and deficit cuts that open the way to sharp reduction of entitlements, including health, social security, pensions—whatever matters to the people beyond the very privileged. And perhaps he prefers to be out of town when it becomes too hard to conceal what's being done to the general population and someone will have to face the music.

With regard to foreign affairs, what do you consider to be the most menacing elements of Trump's handling of US foreign policy?

Trump inherited multiple crises. His own policies have been largely incoherent, but he has been consistent in some areas, primarily the Middle East. He has provided strong support for the Saudi war in Yemen, a major catastrophe, and is exulting in the huge arms sales to the dictatorship. Last December, UN agencies warned that the Saudi blockade of Yemen could lead to "one of the largest famines in modern times." Yemen already has the world's worst cholera outbreak, which is not under control. The Saudi blockade is hindering desperately needed imports of food, medicine, and fuel.

Apart from the human disaster it is creating, the Saudi dictatorship, always with firm US backing, seems intent on carrying forward the Taliban and ISIS projects of destroying precious antiquities. Reviewing the systematic Saudi destruction, the chair of Yemen's Organization of Antiquities and Museums charges that the attacks on sixty sites are "a conscious campaign to wreck Yemen's heritage and demoralize its citizens." Western experts agree that the destruction seems deliberate, using information provided by the [United Nations Educational, Scientific, and Cultural Organization] on cultural heritage sites to direct bombing attacks, with no military objective.

The US-led attack on ISIS in Raqqa, Syria, destroyed the city, and nothing is being done to reconstruct or help the victims. Under the influence of [US-UN Ambassador] Nikki Haley, one of the more sinister (and, it seems, ambitious) figures in the administration, Trump has sharply cut funding to the [United Nations Relief and Works Agency], which barely keeps millions of Palestinian refugees alive. In general, "make America great" means great at destroying, and that's where the greatness ends. It's by no means entirely new, but is now raised to a higher level and becoming a matter of principle.

In May, Trump will presumably refuse to renew sanctions relief for Iran, as required by the Iran nuclear deal (JCPOA). That does not constitute formal withdrawal, though that's the likely effect. Even if the European signers formally persist, the consequences will be severe because of central role of the US in the international financial system—not to speak of the danger that their persistence might arouse the ire of the unpredictable Trump, who can do great damage if crossed. Effective withdrawal might provide an opening for the new national security adviser, Bolton, a genuine war criminal who publicly calls for bombing Iran, presumably in collaboration with Israel and with tacit Saudi approval. Consequences could be horrendous.

There is much fevered debate as to whether Iran might have violated the JCPOA, contrary to the firm conclusion of [the International Atomic Energy Agency] director general Yukiya Amano on March 5, 2018, that "Iran is implementing its nuclear-related commitments." But we hear virtually nothing about US violations, though these have been clear enough. Thus, the JCPOA commits the signers to support the successful implementation of the agreement, including in their public statements, and to refrain from any adverse effects on trade and economic relations with Iran that conflict with their commitments to successful implementation of the JCPOA. The US has been in flat violation of all of these commitments; this has serious consequences.

Unmentionable as always is the obvious way to alleviate whatever threat Iranian nuclear programs are imagined to pose—establishing a nuclear-weapon-free zone in the region. The way is clear. The proposal is strongly supported by Iran, the Arab states, and the world generally. But there is an impediment. It has regularly been blocked by the US, for familiar reasons— Israel's nuclear weapons. Also ignored is that the US [and] UK have a special commitment to work for this goal, having committed themselves to it in the UN [Security Council] resolution they invoked in an effort to find some thread of justification for their invasion of Iraq.

There is more to say about this troubled region, but there are crises elsewhere as well. One involves North Korea, and here there might be some rays of light. Trump has so far accepted the moves of the two Koreas toward improving relations and has agreed to negotiations with North Korean dictator Kim Jong Un that so far look promising. If these initiatives succeed, they might go as far as the September 2005 agreement in which North Korea pledged to abandon "all nuclear weapons and existing weapons programs." Unfortunately, the Bush administration immediately violated all of its commitments under the agreement, and North Korea proceeded with its nuclear weapons programs. We may hope that Trump will be willing to accept success in denuclearizing the peninsula and in further steps toward accommodation. And if he wants to brag about the achievement as a demonstration of his brilliance as a dealmaker, just fine.

This by no means exhausts the foreign policy issues that should be seriously addressed—topics that would carry us far afield.

What's your overall sense about Trumpism? What is it really all about, and do you think Trumpism is showing us the future of right-wing politics in the US?

Trumpism is one of many manifestations of the effects of the neoliberal policies of the past generation. These have led to extreme concentration of wealth along with stagnation for the majority. There have been repeated crashes of the deregulated financial institutions, each worse than the last. Bursting bubbles have been followed by huge public bailouts for the perpetrators, while the victims have been abandoned. Globalization has been designed to set working people throughout the world in competition with one another while private capital is lavished with benefits. Democratic institutions have eroded. As already mentioned, all of this has led to anger, bitterness, and desperation.

One remarkable effect is the increasing mortality among middle-age whites discovered by Anne Case and Angus Deaton, analyzed as "deaths of despair," a phenomenon unknown in functioning societies. While there are variations from place to place, some features are common. One is the decline of the centrist parties that have long dominated political life, as we see in election after election. In the US, in recent years, whenever candidates arose from the base in the Republican primaries, the established powers were able to crush them and impose their own choice—Mitt Romney, most recently. In 2016, for the first time they were unable to do so, but they quickly rallied to the winning candidate, who proved quite willing to front for the more brutal wing of the traditional party. The real surprise in the election was the Sanders campaign, which broke with a long tradition of pretty much bought elections, and was stopped only by the machinations of the Obama-Clinton party managers. The Democratic Party is now split between the donor-oriented New Democrat managers and a growing activist social democratic base.

What all of this portends, worldwide, is far from clear. Though there are also significant signs of hope, some commentators have—with good reason—been quoting Gramsci's observation from his prison cell: "The crisis consists precisely in the fact that the old is dying and the new cannot be born; in this interregnum a great variety of morbid symptoms appear."

Imagining Our Way
beyond Neoliberalism

with Robert Pollin

C. J. POLYCHRONIOU: Noam, racism, inequality, mass incarceration, and gun violence are pathologies that run deep inside American society. How would a progressive government begin to address these problems if it found itself in a position of power in, say, the next decade or so?

NOAM CHOMSKY: Very serious problems, no doubt. In order to address them effectively, it's first necessary to understand them; not a simple matter. Let's take the four pathologies in turn.

Racism certainly runs deep. There is no need to elaborate. It's right before our eyes in innumerable ways, some with considerable historical resonance. Current anti-immigrant hysteria can hardly fail to recall the racist immigration laws that at first barred [Asians] and were extended in the 1920s to Italians and Jews (under a different guise). These laws, incidentally, helped to send many Jews to gas chambers, and after the war, they kept miserable survivors of the Holocaust from US shores.

Of course, the most extreme case for the past four hundred years is the bitter history of African Americans. Current circumstances are shameful enough, commonly held doctrines scarcely less so. The hatred of Obama and anything he touched surely reflects deep-rooted racism. Comparative studies by George Frederickson show that doctrines of white supremacy in the US have been even more rampant than in Apartheid South Africa.

The Nazis, when seeking precedents for the Nuremberg laws, turned to the United States, taking its anti-miscegenation laws as a model, though not entirely: [Certain] US laws were too harsh for the Nazis because of the "one drop of blood" doctrine. It was not until 1967, under the impact of the civil rights movement, that these abominations were struck down by the Supreme Court.

And it goes far back, taking many strange forms, including the weird Anglo-Saxon cult that has been prominent for centuries. Benjamin Franklin, the great American figure of the Enlightenment, pondered whether Germans and Swedes should be barred from the country because they are "too swarthy." Adopting familiar understanding, he observed that "the Saxons only [are] excepted" from this racial "defect"—and by some mysterious process, those who make it to the United States may become Anglo-Saxons, like those already accepted within the canon.

The national poet Walt Whitman, honored for his democratic spirit, justified the conquest of half of Mexico by asking, "What has miserable, inefficient Mexico . . . to do with the great mission of peopling the New World with a noble race? Be it ours, to achieve that mission!"—a mission accomplished by the most "wicked war" in history, in the judgment of General-President Ulysses Grant, who later regretted his service in it as a junior officer.

Coming to recent years, Henry Stimson, one of the most distinguished members of the FDR-Truman cabinets (and one of the few to oppose atomic bombing) "consistently maintained that Anglo-Saxons were superior to the 'lesser breeds,'" historian Sean Langdon Malloy observes in his book, *Atomic Tragedy: Henry L. Stimson and the Decision to Use the Bomb*—and again reflecting not uncommon views, asked to have one of his aides reassigned "on the slight possibility that he might be a Hebrew," in his own words.

The other three maladies that you mention are also striking features of US society—in some ways, even distinguishing features. But unlike racism, in all three cases, it is partially a contemporary phenomenon.

Take inequality. Through much of its history, the US did not have high inequality as compared with Europe. Less so, in fact. That began to change in the industrial age, reaching a peak in 1928, after the forceful destruction of the labor movement and crushing of independent thought. Largely as a result of labor mobilization, inequality declined during the Great Depression, a tendency continuing through the great growth period of regulated capitalism in the early postwar decades. The neoliberal era that followed reversed these trends, leading to extreme inequality that may even surpass the 1928 peak.

As noted previously, mass incarceration is also period-specific—in fact, the same period. It had reached high levels in the South in the post-Reconstruction years after an 1877 North-South compact gave the South free rein to institute "slavery by another name," as Douglas Blackmon calls the crime in his study of how the former slave-owning states devised techniques to incarcerate much of the Black population. By doing so, they created a renewed slave labor force for the Industrial Revolution of those years, this time with the state, rather than private capital, responsible for maintaining the slave labor force—a considerable benefit to the ownership class. Turning to more recent times, thirty years ago, US incarceration rates were within the range of developed societies, a little toward the high end. By now they are five to ten times as high, far beyond those of any country with credible statistics. Again, a phenomenon of the past three decades.

The gun cult is also not as deeply rooted as often supposed. Guns were, of course, needed to conduct the two greatest crimes of American history: controlling slaves and exterminating [Native Americans]. But the general public had little interest in weapons, a matter of much concern to the arms industry. The popular gun cult was cultivated by gun manufacturers in the 19th century in order to create a market beyond governments. Normal capitalism. Methods included concoction of "Wild West" mythology that later became iconic. Such efforts continue, vigorously, until the present. By now, in large sectors of the society, swaggering into a coffee shop with a gun shows that you are really somebody, maybe a Wyatt Earp clone. The outcomes are sobering. Gun homicides in the US are far beyond comparable countries. In Germany, for example, deaths from gun homicide are at the level of deaths in the US from "contact with a thrown or falling object." And even these shocking figures are misleading. Half of suicides in the US are with firearms, more than twenty thousand a year, amounting to two-thirds of all firearm deaths.

Turning to your question about the four "pathologies"—the four horse-men, one is tempted to say—the questions virtually answer themselves with a careful look at the history, particularly the history since World War II. There have been two phases during the postwar period: regulated capital-ism through the '50s and '60s, followed by the neoliberal period from the late '70s, sharply accelerating with Reagan and his successors. It is the latter period when the last three of four pathologies drove the US off the charts.

During the first postwar phase, there were some significant steps to counter endemic racism and its devastating impact on the victims. That was the great achievement of the mass civil rights movement, peaking in the mid-1960s, though with a very mixed record since. The achievements also had a major impact on the political system. The Democratic Party had been an uneasy coalition, including Southern Democrats, dedicated to racist policies and extremely influential because of seniority in one-party states. That's why New Deal measures [were] largely restricted to whites; for exam-ple, household and agricultural workers were barred from Social Security.

The alliance fell apart in the '60s with the fierce backlash against extend-ing minimal rights of citizenship to African Americans. The South shifted to Republican ranks, encouraged by Nixon's overtly racist "Southern strat-egy." The period since has hardly been encouraging for African Americans, apart from elite sectors.

Government policies could go some way toward ameliorating these so-cial pathologies, but a great deal more is needed. Such needs can only be ful-filled by dedicated mass popular activism and educational/organizational efforts. These can be facilitated by a more progressive government, but, just as in the case of the civil rights movement, that can be only a help, often a reluctant one.

On inequality, it was low (by comparative standards) during the period of regulated capitalism—the final era of "great compression" of income as it is sometimes called. Inequality began to increase rapidly with the advent of the neoliberal era, not only in the US, though the US is extreme among developed societies. During the tepid recovery from the Great Recession of 2008, virtually all gains went to the top few percent, mostly 1 percent or a fraction thereof. "For the United States overall, the top 1 percent captured 85.1 percent of total income growth between 2009 and 2013," an Economic

Policy Institute Study revealed. "In 2013 the top 1 percent of families nationally made 25.3 times as much as the bottom 99 percent."

And so, it continues. The latest Federal Reserve studies show that "the share of income received by the top 1 percent of families rose to 23.8 percent in 2016, up from 20.3 percent in 2013. The share of the bottom 90 percent of the distribution fell to 49.7 percent, the lowest on record in the survey's history." Other figures are grotesque. Thus, "average wealth holdings for white families in 2016 were about $933,700, compared with $191,200 for Hispanic families and $138,200 for black families," a product of deep-rooted racism exacerbating the neoliberal assault.

The gun culture, too, has expanded rapidly in recent decades. In 1975, the NRA formed a new lobbying arm—a few years later, a PAC—to channel funds to legislators. It soon became one of the most powerful interest-group lobbies, with often fervent popular participation. In 2008, the Supreme Court, in an intellectual triumph of "originalism," reversed the traditional interpretation of the Second Amendment, which had previously respected its explicit condition on the right to bear arms: the need for "a well regulated Militia, being necessary to the security of a free State . . ." That provision was understandable in 1790. There was almost no standing army. The world's most powerful state was still an enemy. The slave population had to be controlled. And the invasion of the rest of what became the national territory was about to be unleashed. Not exactly today's circumstances.

Since 2008, our "constitutional right to bear arms," as declared by the right-wing Roberts court, has become Holy Writ.

There are many contributing factors to the sharp break between the two postwar periods—neither [of] which began to approach what is surely possible in the richest society in world history, with incomparable advantages.

One leading factor is the financialization of the economy, creating a huge bloc of largely predatory institutions devoted to financial manipulations rather than to the real economy—a process by which "Wall Street destroyed Main Street," in the words of *Financial Times* editor Rana Foroohar. One of her many illustrations is the world's leading corporation, Apple. It has astronomical wealth, but to become even richer, has been shifting from devising more advanced marketable goods to finance. Its R&D as a percentage of sales has been falling since 2001, tendencies that extend widely among major corporations. In parallel, capital from financial institutions that financed business investments during the postwar growth period now largely "stays inside the financial system," Foroohar reports, "enriching financiers, corporate titans, and the wealthiest fraction of the population, which hold the vast majority of financial assets."

During the period of rapid growth of financial institutions since the '70s, there seem to have been few studies of their impact on the economy. Apparently, it was simply taken for granted that since it (sort of) accords with neoliberal market principles, it must be a Good Thing.

The failure of the profession to study these matters was noted by Nobel laureate in economics Robert Solow after the 2008 crash. His tentative judgment was that the general impact is probably negative: "The successes probably add little or nothing to the efficiency of the real economy, while the disasters transfer wealth from taxpayers to financiers." By now, there is substantially more evidence. A 2015 paper by two prominent economists found that productivity declines in markets with rapidly expanding financial sectors, impacting mostly the sector most critical for long-term growth and better jobs: advanced manufacturing. One reason, Foroohar observes, is that "finance would rather invest in areas like real estate and construction, which are far less productive but offer quicker, more reliable short-term gains" (hence also bigger bonuses for top management)—the Trump-style economy, palatial hotels and golf courses (along with massive debt and repeated bankruptcies).

In part for related reasons, though productivity has doubled since the late '70s when finance was beginning to take over the economy, wages have stalled—for male workers, declined. In 2007, before the crash, at the height of euphoria about the grand triumphs of neoliberalism, neoclassical economics and "the Great Moderation," real wages of American workers were lower than they had been in 1979, when the neoliberal experiment was just taking off. Another factor contributing to this outcome was explained to . Congress in 1997 by Fed Chair Alan Greenspan, when testifying on the healthy economy he was managing. In his own words, "Atypical restraint on compensation increases has been evident for a few years now and appears to be mainly the consequence of greater worker insecurity." Insecurity that was, as he noted, markedly increasing even as employment prospects improved. In short, with labor repressed and unions dismantled, workers were too intimidated to seek decent wages and benefits, a sure sign of the health of the economy.

The same happened to the minimum wage, which sets a floor for others; if it had continued to track productivity, it would now be close to $20 an hour. Crises have rapidly increased as deregulation took off, in accord with the "religion" that markets know best, deplored by another Nobel laureate, Joseph Stiglitz, in a World Bank publication twenty years ago, to no effect. Each crisis is worse than the last; each following recovery weaker than the last. None of this, incidentally, would have come as a surprise to Marxist economists, who pretty much disappeared from the scene in the United States.

Despite much lofty rhetoric about "free markets," like other major industries (energy, agribusiness, etc.), financial institutions benefit enormously from government subsidy and other interventions. An IMF study found that the profits of the major banks derive substantially from the implicit government insurance policy ("too big to fail"), which confers advantages far beyond the periodic bailouts when corrupt practices lead to a crash—something that did not happen during the earlier period, before bipartisan neoliberal doctrine fostered deregulation. Other benefits are real but immeasurable, like the incentive to undertake risky (hence profitable) transactions, with the understanding that if they crash, the hardy taxpayer will step in to repair the damage, probably leaving the institutions richer than before, as after the 2008 crash for which they were largely responsible.

Other factors include the accelerated attack on unions and the radical reduction in taxes for the wealthy, both natural concomitants of neoliberal ideology. Another is the particular form of neoliberal globalization, particularly since the '90s, designed in ways that offer very high protection and other advantages to corporations, investors, and privileged professionals, while setting working people in competition with one another worldwide, with obvious consequences.

Such measures have a mutually reinforcing effect. As wealth becomes more concentrated, so, automatically, does political power, which leads to government policies that carry the cycle forward.

A primary goal of the neoliberal reaction was to reverse the falling rate of profit that resulted, in part, from growing labor militancy. That goal has been achieved with impressive success. The professed goals, of course, were quite different. And as always, the reaction was buttressed by ideology. One staple has been the famous thesis of Simon Kuznets: while inequality increases in early economic development, it begins to decrease as the economy reaches a more advanced level. It follows, then, that there is no need for redistributive policies that interfere with the magic of the market. The Kuznets thesis soon became conventional wisdom among economists and planners.

There are a few problems, however. One, as [American University economics professor] Jon Wisman observes, is that it wasn't a thesis, but rather a conjecture, very cautiously advanced. As Kuznets explained, the conjecture was based on "perhaps 5 percent empirical information and 95 percent speculation, some of it possibly tainted by wishful thinking." This slight qualification in the article was overlooked in a manner not uncommon when there is doctrinal utility in so doing. Other justifications fare similarly.

One might almost define "neoliberalism"—a bit cruelly, but not entirely unfairly—as an ideology devoted to establishing more firmly a society based on the principle of "private affluence, public squalor"—John Kenneth Galbraith's condemnation of what he observed in 1958. Much worse was to come with the unleashing of natural tendencies of capitalism in the neoliberal years, now enhanced as its more [brutal] variants are given virtually free rein under Trump-Ryan-McConnell Republicanism.

All of this is under human control, and can be reversed. There are many realistic options, even without looking beyond short-term feasibility. A small financial transaction tax would sharply reduce the rapid trading that is a net loss to the society while benefiting a privileged few, and would also provide a progressive government with revenue for constructive purposes. It's common knowledge that the deterioration of infrastructure has reached grotesque proportions. Government programs can begin to address these serious problems. They can also be devoted to improving rather than undermining the deteriorating public education system. Living wage and green economy programs of the kind that Bob Pollin has developed could go a long way toward reducing inequality, and beyond that, creating a much more decent society. Another major contribution would be [an equitable] health care system. In fact, just eliminating the exorbitant patent protections that are a core part of the neoliberal "free trade agreements" would be a huge boon to the general economy—and the arguments for these highly protectionist measures are very weak, as economist Dean Baker has shown convincingly. Legislation to put an end to the "right to scrounge laws" (in Orwellian terminology, "right to work laws") that are designed to destroy unions could help revive the labor movement, by now with different constituencies, including service and part-time workers. That could reverse the growth of the new "precariat," another matter of fundamental importance. And it could restore the labor movement to its historic role as the leading force in the struggle for basic human rights.

There are other paths toward reviving a vital and progressive labor movement. The expansion of worker-owned and managed enterprises, now underway in many places, is a promising development, and need not be limited to a small scale. A few years ago, after the crash, Obama virtually nationalized a large part of the auto industry, then returned it to private ownership. Another possibility would have been to turn the industry over to the workforce, or to stakeholders more broadly (workers and community), who might, furthermore, have chosen to redirect its production to what the country sorely needs: efficient public transportation. That could have happened had there been mass popular support and a receptive government. Recent work by Gar Alperovitz and David Ellerman approaches these matters in highly informative ways. Conversion of military industry along similar lines is also quite conceivable—matters discussed years ago by Seymour Melman. [These are all] options under progressive initiatives.

The "right to work" legislation that is a darling of the far right will probably soon be established solidly by the Roberts court now that Neil Gorsuch is in place, thanks to some of Mitch McConnell's more sordid chicanery in barring Obama's nominee. The legislation has an interesting pedigree. It traces back to the Southern Christian American Association, an extreme racist and anti-Semitic organization that was bitterly opposed to unions, which its leaders condemned as a devilish contrivance in which "white women and white men will be forced into organizations with black African apes." Another enemy was "Jewish Marxism," the "Talmudists" who were planning to Sovietize the world and were already doing so in the US through the "Jew Deal," known elsewhere as the "New Deal."

An immediate objective of moderately progressive policy should be to sharply cut the huge military budget, well over half of discretionary spending and now expanding under the Republican project of dismantling government, apart from service to their wealthy/corporate constituency. One of many good reasons to trim the military budget is that it is extremely dangerous to our own security. A striking illustration is the Obama-Trump nuclear weapons modernization program, which has sharply increased "killing power," a very important study in the *Bulletin of Atomic Scientists* reported last March. Thereby, the program "creates exactly what one would expect to see, if a nuclear-armed state were planning to have the capacity to fight and win a nuclear war by disarming enemies with a surprise first strike." These developments, surely known to Russian planners, significantly increase the likelihood that they might resort to a preemptive strike—which means the end—in case of false alarms or very tense moments, of which there are all too many. And here, too, the funds released could be devoted to badly needed objectives, like quickly weaning ourselves from the curse of fossil fuels.

This is a bare sample. There's a long list.

C. J. POLYCHRONIOU: The United States spends more money on health care than any other nation in the world, yet its health care system is highly inefficient and leaves out millions from even basic coverage. What would a socialized health care system look like in the US, and how can the opposition from the private insurance sector, Big Pharma, and the medical industries in general be overcome?

NOAM CHOMSKY: The facts are startling. It's an international scandal, and not unknown. A recent study by the US-based Commonwealth Fund, a nonpartisan health policy research group, found that once again, as repeatedly in the past, the US health care system is the most expensive in the world, far higher than comparable countries, and that it ranks last in performance among these countries. To have combined these two results is a real triumph of the market. The roots of the achievement are not obscure. The US is alone in relying on largely unregulated private insurance companies. Their commitment is to profit, not health, and they produce huge waste in administrative costs, advertising, profit, and executive compensation. The government-run component of the health system (Medicare) is far more efficient, but suffers from the need to work through the private institutions. The US is also alone in legislation barring the government from negotiating drug prices, which, not surprisingly, are far above comparable countries.

These policies do not reflect popular will. Poll results vary, depending on how questions are formulated, but over time, they show considerable, often majority support for a public health system of the kind found elsewhere. Usually, Canada is the model because so little is known about the rest of the world, though it is not ranked as the best. That prize has regularly been won by the British National Health Service, though it, too, is reeling under the neoliberal assault. When Obama's [Affordable Care Act] was introduced, it included a public option, supported by almost two-thirds of the population. It was unceremoniously deleted. Popular opinion is particularly striking in that [it] receives so little mainstream support, even articulation; and if even brought up, is usually condemned. The main argument against the far more successful systems elsewhere is that adopting their framework would raise taxes. [However, single-payer usually results in] cutting expenses considerably more and benefiting the large majority—so the experience of other countries indicates, [as does] US Medicare.

The tide may be turning finally. Sanders has received considerable support, even within the political system, for his call for universal health care to be achieved step-by-step in his plan, by gradual extension of Medicare and other means. The temporary collapse of the fanatic seven-year Republican campaign to destroy "Obamacare" may provide openings as well—temporary collapse, because the extremist organization in power has means to undermine health care and are likely to use it in their passionate dedication to destroying anything connected to the reviled Black president. . . . Nevertheless, there are new openings for some degree of [reason], which could greatly enhance people's welfare, as well as improving the general economy.

To be sure, there will be massive opposition from private power, which has extraordinary influence in our limited class-based democracy. But it can be overcome. The historical record shows that economic-political elites respond to militant popular action—and the threat of more—by endorsing ameliorative measures that leave their basic dominance of the society in place. New Deal measures of social reform are one of many illustrations.

C. J. POLYCHRONIOU: Bob, you produced recently an economic analysis for the backing of a single-payer bill in California (SB-562) and worked on Bernie Sanders's proposal for universal health care, so what are your own views on the previous question?

ROBERT POLLIN: A socialized health care system for the US—whether we call it "single-payer," Medicare for All or something else—should include two basic features. The first is that every resident . . . should be guaranteed access to decent health care. The second is that the system achieves significant overall savings relative to our existing system through lowering administrative costs, controlling the prices of prescription drugs and fees for physicians and hospitals, reducing unnecessary treatments, and expanding preventive care.

In our study analyzing the California single-payer proposal, we estimated that providing decent coverage for all state residents—including, in particular, the roughly 40 to 45 percent of the state's population who are presently either uninsured or who have inadequate coverage—would increase total costs by about 10 percent under the existing system. But we also estimated that operating the single-payer system could achieve overall savings in the range of 18 percent relative to the existing system in the areas of administration, drug prices, fees for providers, and cutting back on wasteful service delivery. Overall then, we found that total health care spending in California would fall by about 8 percent, even with the single-payer system delivering decent care for everyone. My work on the Sanders's Medicare for All bill is ongoing as of now, so I will hold off on providing estimates of its overall impact.

Let's consider how transformative the California-type outcomes would be. Under single-payer in California, decent health care would be established as a basic human right, as it already is in almost all other advanced countries. Nobody would have to forego receiving needed treatments because they didn't have insurance or they couldn't afford high insurance premiums and copays. Nobody would have to fear a financial disaster because they faced a health care crisis in their family. Virtually all families would end up financially better off, and most businesses would also experience cost savings under single-payer relative to what they pay now to cover their employees.

How can the opposition from the private health insurance sector, Big Pharma, and the medical industries in general be overcome? It obviously will not be easy. Health care in the US is a $3 trillion business. Profits of the private companies are in the hundreds of billions, even while most of the funding for our existing health care system comes from the federal, state, and local government budgets. As one example of how to respond to this political reality, we can learn from the work of the California Nurses Association/National Nurses United. The nurses' union has been fighting for single-payer for over twenty years. They bring enormous credibility to the issue, because their members see firsthand how the health and financial well-being of especially nonwealthy people in the US suffer under our current system.

There is no secret as to how the nurses' union fights on behalf of single-payer. They believe in their cause and are highly effective in the ways they organize and advance their position. The basics are as simple as that.

Breaking through the Political Barriers to Free Education

with Robert Pollin

C. J. POLYCHRONIOU: Noam, higher education in the US is a terribly expensive affair, and hundreds of billions are owed in student loans. First, do you think that a system of free higher education can coexist alongside tuition-charging universities? Secondly, what could and should be done about student debt?

NOAM CHOMSKY: The educational system was a highly predictable victim of the neoliberal reaction, guided, as noted earlier, by the maxim of "private affluence and public squalor." Funding for public education has sharply declined. Tuition has exploded, leading to a plague of unpayable student debt. As higher education is driven to a business model in accord with neoliberal doctrine, administrative bureaucracy has sharply increased at the expense of faculty and students, developments reviewed well by sociologist Benjamin Ginsburg. Cost-cutting dictated by the revered market principles naturally leads to hyper exploitation of the more vulnerable, creating a new precariat of graduate students and adjuncts surviving on a bare pittance, replacing tenured faculty. All of this happens to be a good disciplinary technique, for obvious reasons.

For those with eyes open, much of what has happened was anticipated by the early '70s, at the point of transition from regulated capitalism to incipient neoliberalism. At the time, there was mounting elite concern about the dangers posed by the democratizing and civilizing effects of 1960s activism, and particularly the role of young people during "the time of troubles." The concerns were forcefully expressed at both ends of the political spectrum.

At the right end of the spectrum, the "Powell Memorandum" sent by corporate lobbyist (later Supreme Court Justice) Lewis Powell to the Chamber of Commerce called upon the business community to rise up to defend itself against the assault on freedom led by Ralph Nader, Herbert Marcuse, and other miscreants who had taken over the universities, the media, and the government. The picture was, of course, ludicrous but it did reflect the perceptions of Powell's audience, desperate about the slight diminution in their overwhelming power. The rhetoric is as interesting as the message, reminiscent of a spoiled three-year-old who has a piece of candy taken away. The memorandum was influential in circles that matter for policy formation.

At the other end of the spectrum, at about the same time, the liberal internationalists of the Trilateral Commission published their lament over "The Crisis of Democracy" that arose in the "terrible" '60s, when previously apathetic and marginalized parts of the population—the great majority—began to try to enter the political arena to pursue their interests. That posed an intolerable burden on the state. Accordingly, the Trilateral scholars called for more "moderation in democracy," a return to passivity and obedience. The American rapporteur, Harvard professor Samuel Huntington, reminisced nostalgically about the time when "Truman had been able to govern the country with the cooperation of a relatively small number of Wall Street lawyers and bankers," so that true democracy flourished.

A particular concern of the Trilateral scholars was the failure of the institutions responsible for "the indoctrination of the young," including the schools and universities. These had to be brought under control, along with the irresponsible media that were (occasionally) departing from subordination to "proper authority"—a precursor of concerns of the far-right Republican Party today.

The right-liberal spectrum of concerns provided a good indication of what was to come.

The underfunding of public education, from K-12 through colleges and universities, has no plausible economic rationale, and in fact is harmful to the economy because of the losses that ensue. In other countries, rich and poor, education remains substantially free, with educational standards that rank high in global comparisons. Even in the US, higher education was almost free during the economically successful years before the neoliberal reaction—and it was, of course, a much poorer country then. The GI bill provided free education to huge numbers of people—white men overwhelmingly—who would probably never have gone to college, a great benefit to them personally and to the whole society. Tuition at private colleges was far below today's exorbitant costs.

Student debt is structured to be a burden for life. The indebted cannot easily declare bankruptcy, unlike Trump. Current student debt is estimated to be over $1.45 trillion, [more than] $600 billion more than total credit card debt. Most is unpayable, and should be rescinded. There are ample resources for that simply from waste, including the bloated military and the enormous concentrated private wealth that has accumulated in the financial and general corporate sector under neoliberal policies.

There is no economic reason why free education cannot flourish from schools through colleges and university. The barriers are not economic but rather political decisions, skewed in the predictable direction under conditions of highly unequal wealth and power. Barriers that can be overcome, as often in the past.

C. J. POLYCHRONIOU: Bob, what's your own response to the question I posed above?

ROBERT POLLIN: Student debt in the US has exploded in the past decade. In 2007, total student debt was $112 billion, equal to 0.8 percent of GDP. As of 2016, total student debt was [more than] $1 trillion, equal to 5.6 percent of GDP. Thus, as a share of GDP, student debt has risen approximately seven-fold. As of 2012, nearly 70 percent of students left college carrying student loans, and these loans averaged $26,300.

The rise in student debt reflects a combination of factors. The first is that the private costs of attending college have risen sharply, with public higher education funding having been cut sharply. Average public funding per student was 15 percent lower in 2015 than in 2008, and 20 percent lower than in 1990. The burden of the public funding cuts [has] been worsened by the stagnation of average family incomes. Thus, in 1990, average tuition, fees, room and board amounted to about 18 percent of the median household income. By 2014, this figure had nearly doubled, to 35 percent of median household income.

Despite these sharply rising costs, college enrollments have continued to rise. There are many good reasons for young people to go off to college, open their minds, develop their skills, and enjoy themselves. But probably the major attraction is the fact that income disparities have increased sharply between those who go to college versus those who do not. This pattern corresponds with the stagnation of average wages since the early 1970s that we discussed [previously]. The reality under neoliberalism has been that, if you want to have a decent shot at a good-paying job with a chance for promotions and raises over time, the most important first step is to get a college education. The pressures to go to college would be much less intense if working-class jobs provided good pay and opportunities to advance, as was the pattern prior to the onset of neoliberalism.

Virtually all student debt in the US is now held by the federal government. It would therefore be a relatively simple matter to forgive some, if not all of it. This would enable young people to transition much more easily into creating their own households and families. At the same time, if the government is going to enact a major program of student debt forgiveness, it should be at least equally committed to relieving the heavy mortgage debt burdens still carried by tens of millions of nonaffluent households in the aftermath of the 2007–09 financial crash and Great Recession. Similarly, the government should also be at least equally committed to both lowering the costs of college education in the first place, and [supporting] better wages and work opportunities for people who do not attend college.

C. J. POLYCHRONIOU: The blueprint for a progressive US that the two of you have sketched out requires that a certain course of political action be carried out . . . which includes educating the masses in getting from here to there. How is this to be done, especially given not only the

peculiarities of American political culture, but also the balkanization of progressive and left forces in the country?

NOAM CHOMSKY: The answer is both easy and hard. Easy to formulate (and familiar), and hard to execute (also familiar). The answer is education, organization, [and] activism as appropriate to circumstances. Not easy, but often successful, and there's no reason why it cannot be now. Popular engagement, though scattered, is at quite a high level, as is enthusiasm and concern. There are also important elements of unity, like the Left Forum, novel and promising. And the movements we've already mentioned. Significant efforts are underway, such as those alluded to briefly [before], and there's no reason why they cannot be extended. While the left is famous for constant splits and internal disputes, I don't think that's more so now than in the past. And the general mood, particularly among young people, seems to me conducive to quite positive changes.

I don't feel that there is anything deep in the political culture that prevents "educating the masses." I'm old enough to recall vividly the high level of culture, general and political, among first-generation working people during the Great Depression. Workers' education was lively and effective, union-based—mostly the vigorous rising labor movement, reviving from the ashes of the 1920s. I've often seen independent and quite impressive initiatives in working-class and poor and deprived communities today. And there's a long earlier history of lively working-class culture, from the early days of the Industrial Revolution. The most important radical democratic movement in American history, the populist movement (not today's "populism"), was initiated and led by farmers in Texas and the Midwest, who may have had little formal education but understood very well the nature of their plight at the hands of the powerful banking and commercial sectors, and devised effective means to counter it. . . .

I've been fortunate enough to have seen remarkable examples elsewhere. I recall vividly a visit to an extremely poor, almost inaccessible rural village in southern Colombia, in an area under attack from all sides, where I attended a village meeting that was concerned with protecting their resources, including irreplaceable water supplies, from predatory international mining corporations. And in particular. a young man, with very little formal education, who led a thoughtful and very informed discussion of sophisticated development plans that they intended to implement. I've seen the same in poor villages in West Bengal, with a handful of books in the tiny schoolroom, areas liberated from landlord rule by Communist Party militancy. The opportunities and, of course, resources are vastly greater in rich societies like ours.

I don't think it is idle romanticism to recognize the potential that can be awakened, or arise independently, in communities that free themselves from indoctrination and passive subordination. The opportunities I think are there, to be grasped and carried forward.

ROBERT POLLIN: I think it is inevitable that leftist forces in the US would be divided, if not balkanized, to some extent. Among the full range of people who are committed to social and economic equality and ecological [justice]—i.e., to some variant of a leftist vision of a decent society—it will always be the case that some will be more focused on egalitarian economic issues, others around the environment and climate change, others on US imperialism, militarism and foreign policy, others on race and gender equality, and still others on sexual identity.

I certainly do not have the formula for how to most effectively knit all these groups together. But I do think we can learn a lot from the major successes out there. The 2016 Bernie Sanders presidential campaign is a first obvious example. Another is the California Nurses Association/National Nurses United (CNA/NNU) that I mentioned [before]. This is a union, fighting first for the well-being of its members, who are overwhelmingly women, with a high proportion being women of color. At the same time, CNA/NNU has been in the forefront of campaigns for single-payer health care and even the Robin Hood Tax on speculative Wall Street trading.

There are other progressive organizations that have proven track records of success. One is the Los Angeles Alliance for a New Economy (LAANE), which has long been active around both living wage and other worker rights issues, as well as community economic development and environmental justice. A more recently formed coalition is NY Renews, which is comprised of 126 organizations in New York State who have come together to advance a serious program in the state to both dramatically reduce greenhouse gas emissions and expand good job opportunities. The Washington State Labor

Council—part of the AFL-CIO—has also been committed and innovative in bringing together coalitions of labor and environmental groups. The US left needs to learn and build from the achievements and ongoing work of these and similar groups. In fact, as Margaret Thatcher used to say, "there is no alternative"—if we are serious about successfully advancing a left alternative to the disasters caused by forty years of neoliberal hegemony.

Blueprint for a Progressive United States

with Robert Pollin

C. J. POLYCHRONIOU: Noam, the rise of Donald Trump has unleashed a rather unprecedented wave of social resistance in the US. Do you think the conditions are ripe for a mass progressive/socialist movement in this country that can begin to reframe the major policy issues affecting the majority of people, and perhaps even challenge and potentially change the fundamental structures of the US political economy?

NOAM CHOMSKY: There is indeed a wave of social resistance, more significant than in the recent past—though I'd hesitate about calling it "unprecedented." Nevertheless, we cannot overlook the fact that in the domain of policy formation and implementation, the right is ascendant, in fact, some of its harshest and most destructive elements [are rising].

Nor should we overlook a crucial fact that has been evident for some time. The figure in charge, though often ridiculed, has succeeded brilliantly in his goal of occupying media and public attention while mobilizing a very loyal popular base—and one with sinister features, sometimes smacking of totalitarianism, including adoration of The Leader. That goes beyond the core of loyal Trump supporters. . . . [A majority of Republicans] favor shutting down or at least fining the press if it presents "biased" or "false news"—terms that mean information rejected by The Leader, so we learn from polls showing that by overwhelming margins, Republicans not only believe Trump far more than the hated mainstream media, but even far more than their own media organ, the extreme right Fox News. And half of Republicans would back postponing the 2020 election if Trump calls for it. It is also worth bearing in mind that among a significant part of his worshipful base, Trump is regarded as a "wavering moderate" who cannot be fully trusted to hold fast to the true faith of fierce White Christian identity politics. A recent illustration is the primary victory of the incredible Roy Moore in Alabama despite Trump's opposition. ("Mr. President, I love you but you are wrong," as the banners read). The victory of this Bible-thumping fanatic has led senior party strategists to [conclude] "that the conservative base now loathes its leaders in Washington the same way it detested President Barack Obama"—referring to leaders who are already so far right that one needs a powerful telescope to locate them at the outer fringe of any tolerable political spectrum.

The potential power of the ultraright attack on the far right is [illustrated] by the fact that Moore spent about $200,000, in contrast to his Trump-backed opponent, the merely far-right Luther Strange, who received more than $10 million from the national GOP and other far-right sources. The ultraright is spearheaded by Steve Bannon, one of the most dangerous figures in the shiver-inducing array that has come to the fore in recent years. It has the huge financial support of the Mercer family, along with ample media outreach through Breitbart News, talk radio, and the rest of the toxic bubble in which loyalists trap themselves.

In the most powerful state in history, the current Republican Party is ominous enough. What is not far on the horizon is even more menacing.

Much has been said about how Trump has pulled the cork out of the bottle and legitimized neo-Nazism, rabid white supremacy, misogyny, and other pathologies that had been festering beneath the surface. But it goes much beyond even that.

I do not want to suggest that adoration of the Dear Leader is something new in American politics, or confined to the vulgar masses. The veneration of Reagan that has been diligently fostered has some of the same character, in intellectual circles as well. Thus, in publications of the conservative Hoover Institution at Stanford University, we learn that Reagan's "spirit seems to stride the country, watching us like a warm and friendly ghost." Lucky us, protected from harm by a demi-god.

Whether by design, or simply inertia, the Republican wrecking ball has been following a two-level strategy. Trump keeps the spotlight on himself with one act after another, assuming (correctly) that yesterday's antics will be swept aside by today's. And at the same time, often beneath the radar, the "respectable" Republican establishment chips away at government programs that might be of benefit to the general population, but not to their constituency of extreme wealth and corporate power. They are systematically pursuing what *Financial Times* economic correspondent Martin Wolf calls "pluto-populism," a doctrine that imposes "policies that benefit plutocrats, justified by populist rhetoric." An amalgam that has registered unpleasant successes in the past as well.

Meanwhile, the Democrats and centrist media help out by focusing their energy and attention on whether someone in the Trump team talked to Russians, or [whether] the Russians tried to influence our "pristine" elections—though at most in ways that are undetectable in comparison with the impact of campaign funding, let alone other inducements that are the prerogative of extreme wealth and corporate power and are hardly without impact.

The Russian saboteurs of democracy seem to be everywhere. There was great anxiety about Russian intervention in the recent German elections, perhaps contributing to the frightening surge of support for the right-wing nationalist, if not neofascist, "Alternative for Germany" [AfD]. AfD did indeed have outside help, it turns out, but not from the insidious Putin. "The Russian meddling that German state security had been anticipating apparently never materialized," according to Bloomberg News. "Instead, the foreign influence came from America." More specifically, from Harris Media, whose clients include Marine Le Pen's National Front in France, Benjamin Netanyahu in Israel, and our own Donald Trump. With the valuable assistance of the Berlin office of Facebook, which created a population model and provided the needed data, Harris's experts micro-targeted Germans in categories deemed susceptible to AfD's message—with some success, it appears. The firm is now planning to move on to coming European races, it has announced.

Nevertheless, all is not bleak by any means. The most spectacular feature of the 2016 elections was not the election of a billionaire who spent almost as much as his lavishly funded opponent and enjoyed fervent media backing. Far more striking was the remarkable success of the Sanders campaign, breaking with over a century of mostly bought elections. The campaign relied on small contributions and had no media support, to put it mildly. Though lacking any of the trappings that yield electoral success in our semiplutocracy, Sanders probably would have won the Democratic Party nomination, perhaps the presidency, if it hadn't been for the machinations of party managers. His popularity undimmed, he is now a leading voice for progressive measures and is amassing considerable support for his moderate social democratic proposals, reminiscent of the New Deal—proposals that would not have surprised President Eisenhower, but are considered practically revolutionary today as both parties have shifted well to the right [with] Republicans virtually off the spectrum of normal parliamentary politics.

Offshoots of the Sanders campaign are doing valuable work on many issues, including electoral politics at the local and state level, which had been pretty much abandoned to the Republican right, particularly during the Obama years, to very harmful effect. There is also extensive and effective mobilization against racist and white supremacist pathologies, often spearheaded by the dynamic Black Lives Matter movement. Defying Trumpian and general Republican denialism, a powerful popular environmental movement is working hard to address the existential crisis of global warming. These, along with significant efforts on other fronts, face very difficult barriers, which can and must be overcome.

C. J. POLYCHRONIOU: Bob, it is clear by now that Trump has no plan for creating new jobs, and even his reckless stance toward the environment will have no effect on the creation of new jobs. What would a progressive policy for job creation look like that will also take into account concerns about the environment and climate change?

ROBERT POLLIN: A centerpiece for any kind of progressive social and economic program needs to be full employment with decent wages and working conditions. The reasons are straightforward, starting with money. Does someone in your family have a job and, if so, how much does it pay?

For the overwhelming majority of the world's population, how one answers these two questions determines, more than anything else, what one's living standard will be. But beyond just money, your job is also crucial for establishing your sense of security and self-worth, your health and safety, your ability to raise a family, and your chances to participate in the life of your community.

How do we get to full employment, and how do we stay there? For any economy, there are two basic factors determining how many jobs are available at any given time. The first is the overall level of activity—with GDP as a rough, if inadequate measure of overall activity—and the second is what share of GDP goes to employing people. In terms of our current situation, after the Great Recession hit in full in 2008, US GDP has grown at an anemic average rate of 1.3 percent per year, as opposed to the historic average rate from 1950 until 2007 of 3.3 percent. If the economy had grown over the past decade at something even approaching the historic average rate, the economy would have produced more than enough jobs to employ all 13 million people who are currently either unemployed or underemployed by the official government statistics, plus the nearly 9 million people who have dropped out of the labor force since 2007.

In terms of focusing on activities where job creation is strong, let's consider two important sets of economic sectors. First, spending $1 million on education will generate a total of about twenty-six jobs within the US economy, more than double the eleven jobs that would be created by spending the same $1 million on the US military. Similarly, spending $1 million on investments in renewable energy and energy efficiency will create over sixteen jobs within the US, while spending the same $1 million on our existing fossil fuel infrastructure will generate about 5.3 jobs—i.e., building a green economy in the US generates roughly three times more jobs per dollar than maintaining our fossil fuel dependency. So full employment policies should focus on accelerating economic growth and on changing our priorities for growth. We should expand educational opportunities across the board and build a green economy, while contracting the military and the fossil fuel economy.

A full employment program also obviously needs to focus on the conditions of work, starting with wages. The most straightforward measure of what neoliberal capitalism has meant for the US working class is that the average wage for nonsupervisory workers in 2016 was about *4 percent lower than in 1973.* This is while average labor productivity—the amount each worker produces over the course of a year—has more than doubled over this same forty-three-year period. *All of the gains* from productivity doubling under neoliberalism have therefore been pocketed by either supervisory workers, or even more so, by business owners and corporate shareholders seeing their profits rise. The only solution here is to fight to increase worker bargaining power. We need stronger unions and worker protections, including a $15 federal minimum wage. Such initiatives need to be combined with policies to expand the overall number of job opportunities out there. A fundamental premise of neoliberalism from day one has been to dismantle labor protections. We are seeing an especially aggressive variant of this approach today under the so-called "centrist" policies of the new French President Emmanuel Macron.

What about climate change and jobs? A view that has long been touted, most vociferously by Trump over the last two years, is that policies to protect the environment and to fight climate change are bad for jobs and therefore need to be junked. But this claim is simply false. In fact, as the evidence I have cited above shows, building a green economy is good for jobs overall, much better than maintaining our existing fossil-fuel based energy infrastructure, which also happens to be the most significant force driving the planet toward ecological disaster.

It is true that building a green economy will not be good for everyone's jobs. Notably, people working in the fossil fuel industry will face major job losses. The communities in which these jobs are concentrated will also face significant losses. But the solution here is straightforward: Just Transition policies for the workers, families, and communities who will be hurt as the coal, oil, and natural gas industries necessarily contract to zero over roughly the next thirty years. Working with Jeannette Wicks-Lim, Heidi Garrett-Peltier, and Brian Callaci at [the Political Economy Research Institute], and in conjunction with labor, environmental, and community groups in both the states of New York and Washington, we have developed what I think are quite reasonable and workable Just Transition programs. They include solid pension protections, reemployment guarantees, as well as retraining and relocation support for individual workers, and community support initiatives for impacted communities.

The single most important factor that makes all such initiatives work-able is that the total number of affected workers is relatively small. For example, in the whole United States today, there are a total of about 65,000 people employed directly in the coal industry. This represents less than 0.05 percent of the 147 million people employed in the US. Considered within the context of the overall US economy, it would only require a minimum level of commitment to provide a just transition to these workers as well as their families and communities.

Finally, I think it is important to address one of the major positions on climate stabilization that has been advanced in recent years on the left, which is to oppose economic growth altogether, or to support "de-growth." The concerns of de-growth proponents—that economic growth under neoliberal capitalism is both grossly unjust and ecologically unsustainable—are real. But de-growth is not a viable solution. Consider a very simple example—that under a de-growth program, global GDP contracts by 10 percent. This level of GDP contraction would be five times larger than what occurred at the lowest point of the 2007–09 Great Recession, when the unemployment rate more than doubled in the United States.

But even still, this 10 percent contraction in global GDP would have the effect, on its own, of reducing carbon dioxide (CO_2) emissions by precisely 10 percent. At a minimum, we would still need to cut emissions by another 30 percent within fifteen years, and another 80 percent within thirty years to have even a fighting chance of stabilizing the climate. As such, the only viable climate stabilization program is to invest massively in clean renew-able and high-energy-efficiency systems so that clean energy completely supplants our existing fossil-fuel dependent system within the next thirty years, and to enact comparable transformations in agricultural production processes.

C. J. POLYCHRONIOU: The "masters of the universe" have made a huge comeback since the last financial crisis, and while Trump's big-capital-friendly policies are going to make the rich get richer, they could also spark the next financial crisis. So, Bob, what type of progressive policies can and should be enforced to contain the destructive tendencies of finance capital?

ROBERT POLLIN: The classic book *Manias, Panics, and Crashes* by the late MIT economist Charles Kindleberger makes clear that, throughout the history of capitalism, unregulated financial markets have persistently produced instability and crises. The only deviation from this long-term pattern occurred in the first thirty years after World War II, roughly from 1946–1975. The reason US and global financial markets were much more stable over this thirty-year period is that the markets were heavily regulated then, through the Glass-Steagall regulatory system in the US, and the Bretton Woods system globally. These regulatory systems were enacted only in response to the disastrous Great Depression of the 1930s, which began with the 1929 Wall Street crash and which then brought global capitalism to its knees.

Of course, the big Wall Street players always hated being regulated and fought persistently, first to evade the regulations and then to dismantle them. They were largely successful through the 1980s and 1990s. But the full, official demise of the 1930s regulatory system came only in 1999, under the Democratic President Bill Clinton. At the time, virtually all leading mainstream economists—including liberals, such as Larry Summers, who was treasury secretary when Glass-Steagall was repealed—argued that financial regulations were an unnecessary vestige of the bygone 1930s. All kinds of fancy papers were written "demonstrating" that the big players on Wall Street are very smart people who know what's best for themselves and everyone else—and therefore, didn't need government regulators telling them what they could or could not do. It then took less than eight years for hyperspeculation on Wall Street to once again bring global capitalism to its knees. The only thing that saved capitalism in 2008–09 from a repeat of the 1930s Great Depression was the unprecedented government interventions to prop up the system, and the equally massive bailout of Wall Street.

By 2010, the US Congress and President Obama enacted a new set of financial regulations, the Dodd-Frank system. Overall, Dodd-Frank amounts to a fairly weak set of measures aiming to dampen hyperspeculation on Wall Street. A large part of the problem is that Dodd-Frank included many opportunities for Wall Street players to delay enactment of laws they didn't like, and for clever lawyers to figure out ways to evade the ones on the books. That said, the Trump administration, led by two former Goldman Sachs executives on economic policy matters, is committed to dismantling Dodd-Frank altogether, and allowing Wall Street to once again operate free of any significant regulatory constraints. I have little doubt that, free of regulations, the already ongoing trend of rising speculation—with, for example, the stock market already at a historic high—will once again accelerate.

What is needed to build something like a financial system that is both stable and supports a full-employment, ecologically sustainable growth framework? A major problem over time with the old Glass-Steagall system were the large differences in the degrees that commercial banks, investment banks, stock brokerages, insurance companies, and mortgage lenders were regulated, thereby inviting clever financial engineers to invent ways to exploit these differences. An effective regulatory system today should therefore be guided by a few basic premises that can be applied flexibly, but also universally. The regulations need to apply across the board, regardless of whether you call your business a bank, an insurance company, a hedge fund, a private equity fund, a vulture fund, or some other term that most of us haven't yet heard about.

One measure for promoting both stability and fairness across financial market segments is a small sales tax on all financial transactions—what has come to be known as a Robin Hood Tax. This tax would raise the costs of short-term speculative trading and therefore discourage speculation. At the same time, the tax will not discourage "patient" investors who intend to hold their assets for longer time periods, since, unlike the speculators, they will be trading infrequently. A bill called the Inclusive Prosperity Act was first introduced into the House of Representatives by Rep. Keith Ellison in 2012, and then in the Senate by Bernie Sanders in 2015, [and] is exactly the type of measure that is needed here.

Another important initiative would be to implement what are called asset-based reserve requirements. These are regulations that require financial institutions to maintain a supply of cash as a reserve fund in proportion to the other, riskier assets they hold in their portfolios. Such requirements can serve to discourage financial market investors from holding an excessive amount of risky assets, and as a cash cushion for investors to draw upon when market downturns occur.

This policy instrument can also be used to push financial institutions to channel credit to projects that advance social welfare, for example, promoting investments in renewable energy and energy efficiency. The policy could stipulate that, say, at least 5 percent of banks' loan portfolios should be channeled into clean-energy investments. If the banks fail to reach this 5 percent quota of loans for clean energy, they would then be required to hold this same amount of their total assets in cash.

Finally, both in the US and throughout the world, there needs to be a growing presence of public development banks. These banks would make loans based on social welfare criteria—including advancing a full-employment, climate-stabilization agenda—as opposed to scouring the globe for the largest profit opportunities regardless of social costs.... Public development banks have always played a central role in supporting the successful economic development paths in the East Asian economies.

Myths of Globalization

with Ha-Joon Chang

C. J. POLYCHRONIOU: Globalization is usually referred to as a process of interaction and integration among the economies and people of the world through international trade and foreign investment with the aid of information technology. Is globalization then simply a neutral, inevitable process of economic, social, and technological interlinkages, or something of a more political nature in which state action produces global transformations (state-led globalization)?

HA-JOON CHANG: The biggest myth about globalization is that it is a process driven by technological progress. This has allowed the defenders of globalization to brand the critics as "modern Luddites" who are trying to turn back the clock against the relentless progress of science and technology.

However, if technology is what determines the degree of globalization, how can you explain that the world was far more globalized in the late 19th and the early 20th century than in the mid-20th century? During the first Liberal era, roughly between 1870 and 1914, we relied upon steamships and wired telegraphy, but the world economy was on almost all accounts more globalized than during the far less liberal period in the mid-20th century (roughly between 1945 and 1973), when we had all the technologies of transportation and communications that we have today, except for the internet and cellular phones, albeit in less efficient forms.

The reason why the world was much less globalized in the latter period is that, during the period, most countries imposed rather significant restrictions on the movements of goods, services, capital, and people, and liberalized them only gradually. What is notable is that, despite [its] lower degree of globalization . . . this period is when capitalism has done the best: the fastest growth, the lowest degree of inequality, the highest degree of financial stability, and—in the case of the advanced capitalist economies—the lowest level of unemployment in the 250-year history of capitalism. This is why the period is often called "the Golden Age of Capitalism."

Technology only sets the outer boundary of globalization—it was impossible for the world to reach a high degree of globalization with only sail ships. It is economic policy (or politics, if you like) that determines exactly how much globalization is achieved in what areas.

The current form of market-oriented and corporate-driven globalization is not the only—not to speak of being the best—possible form of globalization. A more equitable, more dynamic and more sustainable form of globalization is possible.

C. J. POLYCHRONIOU: We know that globalization properly began in the 15th century, and that there have been different stages of globalization since, with each stage reflecting the underlying impact of imperial state power and of the transformations that were taking place in institutional forms, such as firms and the emergence of new technologies and communications. What distinguishes the current stage of globalization (1973–present) from previous ones?

HA-JOON CHANG: The current stage of globalization is different from the previous ones in two important ways.

The first difference is that there is less open imperialism.

Before 1945, the advanced capitalist countries practiced [overt] imperialism. They colonized weaker countries or imposed "unequal treaties" on them, which made them virtual colonies—for example, they occupied parts of territories through "leasing," deprived them of the right to set tariffs, etc.

Since 1945, we have seen the emergence of a global system that rejects such naked imperialism. There has been a continuous process of decolonialization and, once you get sovereignty, you became a member of the United Nations, which is based upon the principle of one country, one vote.

Of course, the practice has been different—the permanent members of the Security Council of the UN have a veto and many international economic organizations (the International Monetary Fund, the World Bank) are run on the principle of one dollar, one vote (voting rights are linked to paid-in capital). However, even so, the post-1945 world order was immeasurably better than the one that came before it.

Unfortunately, starting in the 1980s, but accelerating from the mid-1990s, there has been a rollback of the sovereignty that the post-colonial countries had been enjoying. The birth of the WTO (World Trade Organization) in 1995 has shrunk the "policy space" for developing countries. The shrinkage was intensified by subsequent series of bilateral and regional trade and investment agreements between rich countries and developing ones, like Free Trade Agreements with the US and Economic Partnership agreements with the European Union.

The second thing that distinguishes the post-1973 globalization is that it has been driven by transnational corporations far more than before. Transnational corporations existed even from the late 19th century, but their economic importance has vastly increased since the 1980s.

They have also influenced the shaping of the global rules in a way that enhances their power. Most importantly, they have inserted the investor-state dispute settlement (ISDS) mechanism into many international agreements. Through this mechanism, transnational corporations can take governments to a tribunal of three adjudicators, drawn from a pool of largely pro-corporate international commercial lawyers, for having reduced their profits through regulations. This is an unprecedented extension of corporate power.

C. J. POLYCHRONIOU: Noam, are globalization and capitalism different?

NOAM CHOMSKY: If by "globalization" we mean international integration, then it long predates capitalism. The silk roads dating back to the pre-Christian era were an extensive form of globalization. The rise of industrial state capitalism has changed the scale and character of globalization, and there have been further changes along the way as the global economy has been reshaped by those whom Adam Smith called the "masters of mankind," pursuing their "vile maxim": "All for ourselves, and nothing for other people."

There have been quite substantial changes during the recent period of neoliberal globalization, since the late 1970s, with Reagan and Thatcher the iconic figures—though the policies vary only slightly as administrations change. Transnational corporations are the driving force, and their political power largely shapes state policy in their interests.

During these years, supported by the policies of the states they largely dominate, transnational corporations have increasingly constructed global value chains (GVCs) in which the "lead firm" outsources production through intricate global networks that it establishes and controls. A standard illustration is Apple, the world's biggest company. Its iPhone is designed in the US. Parts from many suppliers in the US and East Asia are assembled mostly in China in factories owned by the huge Taiwanese firm Foxconn. Apple's profit is estimated to be about ten times that of Foxconn, while value added and profit in China, where workers toil under miserable conditions, is slight. Apple then sets up an office in Ireland so as to evade US taxes—and has recently been fined $14 billion by the EU in back taxes.

Reviewing the "GVC world" in the British journal *International Affairs*, Nicola Phillips writes that production for Apple involves thousands of firms and enterprises that have no formal relationship with Apple, and at the lower tiers may be entirely unaware of the destination of what they are producing. This is a situation that generalizes.

The immense scale of this new globalized system is revealed in the 2013 World Investment Report of the United Nations Commission on Trade and Development. It estimates that some 80 percent of global trade is internal to the global value chains established and run by transnational corporations, accounting for perhaps 20 percent of jobs worldwide.

Ownership of this globalized economy has been studied by political economist Sean Starrs. He points out that the conventional estimates of national wealth in terms of GDP are misleading in the era of neoliberal globalization. With complex integrated supply chains, subcontracting, and other such devices, corporate ownership of the world's wealth is becoming a more realistic measure of global power than national wealth, as the world departs more than before from the model of nationally discrete political economies.

Investigating corporate ownership, Starrs finds that in virtually every economic sector —manufacturing, finance, services, retail, and others— US corporations are well in the lead in ownership of the global economy. Overall, their ownership is close to 50 percent of the total. That is roughly the maximum estimate of US national wealth in 1945, at the historical peak of US power. National wealth by conventional measures has declined from 1945 to the present, to maybe 20 percent. But US corporate ownership of the globalized economy has exploded.

C. J. POLYCHRONIOU: The standard line of mainstream politicians is that globalization benefits everyone. Yet, globalization produces winners and losers, as Branko Milanovic's book *Global Inequality* has shown, so the question is this: Is success in globalization a matter of skills?

HA-JOON CHANG: The assumption that globalization benefits everyone is based on mainstream economic theories that assume that workers can be costlessly redeployed, if international trade or cross-border investments make certain industries unviable.

In this view, if the US signs NAFTA with Mexico, some autoworkers in the US may lose their jobs, but they will not lose out, as they can retrain themselves and get jobs in industries that are expanding, thanks to NAFTA, such as software or investment banking.

You will immediately see the absurdity of the argument—how many US autoworkers do you know who have retrained themselves as software engineers or investment bankers in the last couple of decades? Typically, ex-autoworkers fired from their jobs have ended up working as night-shift janitors in a warehouse or stacking shelves in supermarkets, drawing much lower wages than before.

The point is that, even if the country gains overall from globalization, there will always be losers, especially (although not exclusively) workers who have skills that are not valued anymore. And unless these losers are compensated, you cannot say that the change is a good thing for "everyone." . . .

Of course, most rich countries have mechanisms through which the winners from the globalization process (or any economic change, really) compensate the losers. The basic mechanism for this is the welfare state, but there are also publicly financed retraining and job-search mechanisms—the

Scandinavians do this particularly well—as well as sector-specific schemes to compensate the "losers" (e.g., temporary protection for firms to promote restructuring, money for severance payments for the workers). These mechanisms are better in some countries than others, but nowhere are they perfect, and, unfortunately, some countries have been running them down. (The recent shrinkage of the welfare state in the UK is a good example.)

C. J. POLYCHRONIOU: In your view, Ha-Joon Chang, is the convergence of globalization and technology likely to produce more or less inequality?

HA-JOON CHANG: As I have argued above, technology and globalization are not destiny.

The fact that income inequality actually fell in Switzerland between 1990 and 2000 and the fact that income inequality has hardly increased in Canada and the Netherlands during the neoliberal period show that countries can choose what income inequality they have, even though they are all faced with the same technologies and same trends in the global economy.

There is actually a lot that countries can do to influence income inequality. Many European countries, including Germany, France, Sweden, and Belgium are as unequal as (or occasionally even more so than) the US, before they redistribute income through progressive tax and the welfare state. Because they redistribute so much, the resulting inequalities in those countries are much lower.

C. J. POLYCHRONIOU: Noam, in what ways does globalization increase capitalism's inherent tendencies toward economic dependence, inequality, and exploitation?

NOAM CHOMSKY: Globalization during the era of industrial capitalism has always enhanced dependence, inequality, and exploitation, often to horrendous extremes. To take a classic example, the early Industrial Revolution relied crucially on cotton, produced mainly in the American South in the most vicious system of slavery in human history—which took new forms after the Civil War with the criminalization of Black life and sharecropping. Today's version of globalization includes not only super-exploitation at the lower tiers of the global value chains system but also virtual genocide, notably in Eastern Congo where millions have been slaughtered in recent years while critical minerals find their way to high-tech devices produced in the global value chains.

But even apart from such hideous elements of globalization . . . pursuit of the "vile maxim" quite naturally yields such consequences. The Phillips study I mentioned is a rare example of inquiry into "how inequalities are produced and reproduced in a [global value chains] world [through] asymmetries of market power, asymmetries of social power, and asymmetries of political power." As Phillips shows, "the consolidation and mobilization of these market asymmetries rests on securing a structure of production in which a small number of very large firms at the top, in many cases the branded retailers, occupy oligopolistic positions—that is, positions of market dominance, and in which the lower tiers of production are characterized by densely populated and intensely competitive markets. . . . The consequence across the world has been the explosive growth of precarious, insecure, and exploitative work in global production, performed by a workforce significantly made up of informal, migrant, contract, and female workers, and extending at the end of the spectrum to the purposeful use of forced labour."

These consequences are enhanced by deliberate trade and fiscal policies, a matter discussed particularly by Dean Baker. As he points out, in the US, "from December 1970 to December of 2000, manufacturing employment was virtually unchanged, apart from cyclical ups and downs. In the next seven years, from December of 2000 to December of 2007, manufacturing employment fell by more than 3.4 million, a drop of almost 20 percent. This plunge in employment was due to the explosion of the trade deficit over this period, not automation. There was plenty of automation (a.k.a. productivity growth) in the three decades from 1970 to 2000, but higher productivity was offset by an increase in demand, leaving total employment little changed. This was no longer true when the trade deficit exploded to almost 6 percent of GDP in 2005 and 2006 (more than $1.1 trillion in today's economy)."

These were substantially consequences of the high-dollar policy and the investor-rights agreements masquerading as "free trade"—among the political choices in the interests of the masters, not the results of economic laws.

C. J. POLYCHRONIOU: Ha-Joon Chang, progressives aim to develop strategies to counter the adverse effects of globalization, but there is little agreement on the most effective and realistic way to do so. In this context, the responses vary from alternative forms of globalization to localization? What's your take on this matter?

HA-JOON CHANG: In short, my preferred option would be a more controlled form of globalization, based on far more restrictions on global flows of capital and more restrictions on the flows of goods and services. Moreover, even with these restrictions, there will inevitably be winners and losers, and you need a stronger (not weaker) welfare state and other mechanisms through which the losers from the process get compensated. Politically, such a policy combination will require stronger voices for workers and citizens.

I don't think localization is a solution, although the feasibility of localization will depend on what the locality is and what issues we are talking about. If the locality in question is one village or a neighborhood in an urban area, you will immediately see that there are very few things that can be "localised." If you are talking about a German land (state) or US state, I can see how it can try to grow more of its own food or produce some currently imported manufactured products for itself. However, for most things, it is simply not viable to have the majority of things supplied locally. It would be unwise to have every country, not to speak of every American state, manufacture its own airplanes, mobile phones, or even all of its food.

Having said that, I am not against all forms of localization. There are certainly things that can be more locally provided, like certain food items or health care.

C. J. POLYCHRONIOU: One final question: The idea of a universal basic income is slowly but gradually gaining ground as a policy tool in order to address the problem of poverty and concerns over automation. In fact, companies like Google and Facebook are strong advocates of a universal basic income, although it will be societies bearing the cost of this policy while most multinational firms move increasingly to using robots and other computer-assisted techniques for performing tasks traditionally

done by labor. Should progressives and opponents of capitalist global-ization in general support the idea of a universal basic income?

HA-JOON CHANG: Universal basic income (UBI) has many different versions, but it is a libertarian idea in the sense that it puts emphasis on maximizing individual freedom rather than on collective identity and solidarity. All citizens in countries at more than middle-income level have some entitlements to a basic amount of resources. (In the poorer countries, there are virtually none.) They have access to some health care, education, pension, water, and other "basic" things in life. The idea behind UBI is that the resource entitlements should be provided to individuals in cash (rather than in kind) as much as possible, so that they can exercise maximum choice.

The right-wing version of UBI, supported by Friedrich von Hayek and Milton Friedman, the gurus of neoliberalism, is that the government should provide its citizens with a basic income at the subsistence level, while providing no (or little) further goods and services. As far as I can see, this is the version of UBI supported by the Silicon Valley companies. I am totally against this.

There are left-wing libertarians who support UBI, who would set its level quite high, which would require quite a high degree of income redistribution. But they too believe that collective provision of "basic" goods and services through the welfare state should be minimized (although their "minimum" would be considerably larger than the neoliberal one). This version is more acceptable to me, but I am not convinced by it.

First, if the members of a society are collectively provisioning some goods and services, they have the collective right to influence how people use their basic entitlements.

Second, provision through a citizenship-based universal welfare state makes social services like health, education, child care, unemployment insurance, and pensions much cheaper through bulk purchases and pooling of risk. The fact that the US spends at least 50 percent more on health care than other rich countries do (17 percent of GDP in the US compared to at most 11.5 percent of GDP in Switzerland) but has the worst health indicators is very suggestive of the potential problems that we could have in a system of UBI combined with private provision of basic social services, even if the level of UBI is high.

NOAM CHOMSKY: The answer, I think, is: "it all depends"—namely, on the socioeconomic and political context in which the idea is advanced. The society to which we should aspire, I think, would respect the concept "*jedem nach seinen Bedürfnissen*": to each according to their needs. Among the primary needs for most people is a life of dignity and fulfillment. That translates in particular as work undertaken under their own control, typically in solidarity and interaction with others, creative and of value to the society at large. Such work can take many forms: building a beautiful and needed bridge, the challenging task of teaching-and-learning with young children, solving an outstanding problem in number theory, or myriad other options. Providing for such needs is surely within the realm of possibility.

In the current world, firms increasingly turn to automation, as they have been doing as far back as we look—the cotton gin, for example. Currently, there is little evidence that the effects are beyond the norm. Major impacts would show up in productivity, which is in fact low by the standards of the early post–World War II era. Meanwhile, there is a great deal of work to be done—from reconstructing collapsing infrastructure, to establishing decent schools, to advancing knowledge and understanding, and far more. There are many willing hands. There are ample resources. But the socioeconomic system is so dysfunctional that it is not capable of bringing these factors together in a satisfactory way—and under the current Trump-Republican campaign to create a tiny America trembling within walls, the situation can only become worse. Insofar as robots and other forms of automation can free people from routine and dangerous work and liberate them for more creative endeavors (and, particularly in the leisure-deprived US, with time for themselves), that's all to the good. UBI could have a place, though it is too crude an instrument to achieve the preferable Marxist version.

If We Want a Future,
Green New Deal Is Key

with Robert Pollin

C. J. POLYCHRONIOU: Noam, let me start with you and ask you to share your thoughts about the uniqueness of the climate change crisis.

NOAM CHOMSKY: History is all too rich in records of horrendous wars, indescribable torture, massacres, and every imaginable abuse of fundamental rights. But the threat of destruction of organized human life in any recognizable or tolerable form—that is entirely new. The environmental crisis under way is indeed unique in human history, and is a true existential crisis. Those alive today will decide the fate of humanity—and the fate of the other species that we are now destroying at a rate not seen for 65 million years, when a huge asteroid hit the earth, ending the age of the dinosaurs and opening the way for some small mammals to evolve to pose a similar threat to life on earth as that earlier asteroid, though differing from it in that we can make a choice.

Meanwhile, the world watches as we proceed toward a catastrophe of unimaginable proportions. We are approaching perilously close to the global temperatures of 120,000 years ago, when sea levels were 6 to 9 meters higher than today. Glaciers are sliding into the sea five times faster than in the 1990s, with more than 100 meters of ice thickness lost in some areas due to ocean warming, and current losses doubling every decade. Complete loss of the ice sheets would raise sea levels by about five meters, drowning coastal cities, and with utterly devastating effects elsewhere—the low-lying plains of Bangladesh for example. This is only one of the many concerns of those who are paying attention to what is happening before our eyes.

Climate scientists are certainly paying close attention, and issuing dire warnings. Israeli climatologist Baruch Rinkevich captures the general mood succinctly:

> After us, the deluge, as the saying goes. People don't fully understand what we're talking about here. . . . They don't understand that everything is expected to change: the air we breathe, the food we eat, the water we drink, the landscapes we see, the oceans, the seasons, the daily routine, the quality of life. Our children will have to adapt or become extinct. . . . That's not for me. I'm happy I won't be here.

> Yet, just at the time when all must act together, with dedication, to confront humanity's "ultimate challenge," the leaders of the most powerful state in human history, in full awareness of what they are doing, are dedicating themselves with passion to destroying the prospects for organized human life.

C. J. POLYCHRONIOU: With rare exceptions, the mainstream political establishment in the United States continues to look the other way when it comes to climate change. Why is that?

NOAM CHOMSKY: Both political parties have drifted right during the neoliberal years, much as in Europe. The Democratic establishment is now more or less what would have been called "moderate Republicans" some years ago. The Republicans have gone off the spectrum. Comparative studies show that they rank alongside of fringe right-wing parties in Europe in their general positions. They are, furthermore, the only major conservative party to reject anthropogenic climate change, as already mentioned—a global anomaly. Two respected political analysts of the American Enterprise Institute, Thomas Mann and Norman Ornstein, describe the Republican Party since Newt Gingrich's takeover in the '90s as not a normal political party but a "radical insurgency" that has largely abandoned parliamentary politics. Under McConnell's leadership, that has only become more evident—but he has ample company in Republican Party circles.

The positions of the leadership on climate surely influence the attitudes of Republican Party loyalists. Only about 25 percent of Republicans and 36 percent of the more savvy millennials recognize that humans are responsible for global warming. Shocking figures.

And in the ranking of urgent issues among Republicans, global warming (if it is even assumed to be taking place), is almost undetectable. It is considered outrageous to assert that the Republican Party is the most dangerous organization in human history. Perhaps so, but in the light of the stakes, what else can one rationally conclude?

C. J. POLYCHRONIOU: Bob, the Green New Deal is seen as perhaps the only viable solution to avert a climate change catastrophe of the sort described by Noam above, yet many continue to regard it as unrealistic, not only from a purely economic perspective (the claim is that it is simply unaffordable), but also in the sense that modern economies and societies cannot function without fossil fuel energy. First, is the Green New Deal a detailed policy proposal to move us away from a climate change catastrophe, and, second, is it realistic?

ROBERT POLLIN: The Green New Deal has gained tremendous traction as an organizing framework over the past year. This alone is a major achievement. But it is still imperative that we transform this big idea into a viable program. In my view, putting meat on the bones of the Green New Deal starts with a single simple idea. We have to absolutely stop burning oil, coal, and natural gas to produce energy within the next thirty years at most, and we have to do this in a way that also supports rising living standards and expanding opportunities for working people and the poor throughout the world.

This version of a Green New Deal program is, in fact, entirely realistic in terms of its purely economic and technical features. Clean renewable energy sources—including solar, wind, geothermal, and to a lesser extent small-scale hydro and low emissions bioenergy—are already either at cost parity with fossil fuels and nuclear, or they are cheaper. In addition, the single easiest and cheapest way to lower emissions is to raise energy efficiency standards. A number of measures would advance this goal, including retrofitting existing buildings; making new buildings operate as net-zero energy consumers; and replacing gas-guzzler cars with expanding public transportation and electric cars.

Energy efficiency measures, by definition, will save people money—for example, your home electricity bills could realistically be cut in half without having to reduce the amount that you light, heat, or cool your house. So, the Green New Deal will not cost consumers anything over time, as long as we solve the actually quite simple problem of funding Green New Deal investments through the savings we gain by raising efficiency standards and producing cheap renewable energy. My coworkers and I have estimated that building a 100 percent clean energy system will require about 2.5 percent of global GDP per year for roughly the next thirty years. Yes, that's a lot of money in dollar terms, like about $2 trillion in 2021 and rising thereafter. But it does still mean that 97.5 percent of global economic activity can be devoted to things other than investments in clean energy.

So, absolutely, the Green New Deal can be a realistic global climate stabilization project. More specifically, the Green New Deal is capable of hitting the necessary emissions reduction targets for stabilization at a global average temperature of 1.5 degrees Celsius above preindustrial levels by 2100, as set out by the Intergovernmental Panel on Climate Change (IPCC) last October. However, the real question, of course, is not whether the Green New Deal is economically or technically feasible, but rather whether it is politically feasible. On this question, Noam is of course exactly on point in asking: Are we, the human race, going to allow ourselves to become the 21st-century asteroid clone or not?

C. J. POLYCHRONIOU: What about the claim that a transition to 100 percent renewable energy will result in the permanent loss of millions of good-paying jobs?

ROBERT POLLIN: In fact, clean energy investments will be a major source of new job creation, in all regions of the globe. The critical factor is that clean energy investments will create a lot more jobs than maintaining the existing dirty energy infrastructure—in the range of two to four times more jobs per dollar of spending in all of the countries that we have studied, including Brazil, China, India, Indonesia, South Africa, Spain, and the United States.

Of course, jobs that are tied to the fossil fuel industry will be eliminated. The affected workers and their communities must be supported through generous "just transition" measures, including guaranteeing workers' pensions, moving people into new jobs without losing incomes, and investing in impacted communities, in a range of projects. Land reclamation is just one such investment opportunity, including cleaning up abandoned coal mines and converting the residual coal ash into useful products, like paper. I can't emphasize enough that, throughout the world, "just transition" programs must be understood as absolutely central to the Green New Deal.

C. J. POLYCHRONIOU: Noam, how do we increase public awareness about the need for government action vis-à-vis climate change?

NOAM CHOMSKY: The simple answer is: work harder. There are no new special tricks. We know what the message is. We know the barriers that have to be overcome. We have to find ways to shape the message, in words and actions, so as to overcome the barriers.

The message is two-fold: first, we're facing an existential crisis that must be dealt with quickly; and second, there are ways to overcome it.

The first part is expressed simply enough in current articles in the most prestigious and reliable journals. Oxford professor of physics Raymond Pierrehumbert, a lead author of the recent IPCC report, opens his review of existing circumstances and options by writing: "Let's get this on the table right away, without mincing words. With regard to the climate crisis, yes, it's time to panic. . . . We are in deep trouble." He then lays out the details carefully and scrupulously, reviewing the possible technical fixes and their very serious problems, concluding, "There's no plan B." We must move to zero-net carbon emissions, and fast.

The second part is spelled out in convincing detail in Bob's work, briefly reviewed here.

The message must be conveyed in ways that do not induce despair and resignation among those inclined to accept it, and do not evoke resentment, anger, and even greater rejection among those who do not accept what is in fact becoming overwhelmingly clear.

In the latter case, it is necessary to understand the reasons—perhaps rejection of science altogether, or adopting economists' preference for market-based solutions which, whatever one thinks of them, are completely on the wrong timescale, or the great many who expect the Second Coming, or those who think we will be rescued by some unknown technology or great figure, perhaps the colossus perceived by scholars at Stanford University's Hoover Institution, whose "spirit seems to stride the country, watching us like a warm and friendly ghost" (Ronald Reagan).

The task will not be easy. It must be undertaken, urgently. By words and by actions, such as those being undertaken in the climate strikes of September 2019.

C. J. POLYCHRONIOU: Bob, what will it take for the labor movement as a whole to come around and embrace the Green New Deal vision?

ROBERT POLLIN: The Green New Deal has been gaining major support in the labor movement for several years now. There is still a long way to go, but progress is evident. For example, the coalition in Washington State that advanced a Green New Deal proposition in the 2018 election cycle was led by the visionary then president of the state AFL-CIO, Jeff Johnson. In the end, the initiative was defeated when oil companies flooded the airwaves with $30 million of virulent propaganda in the weeks before the November election. Similar initiatives are now being advanced in Colorado, again led by the state's mainstream labor leaders.

Of course, we need to very quickly advance beyond just these few shining examples. What is critical here is that the climate movement must be firmly committed to a just transition as one component of the Green New Deal that is of equal significance with all the others. The climate movement needs to also be clear on the point that building the clean energy economy will be supportive of increasing job opportunities and rising living standards, as I am convinced it can be.

There is no reason that the Green New Deal needs to be associated with austerity economic policies in any way. To the contrary, clean energy investments will create new opportunities for a wide range of small-scale public, cooperative, and private ownership forms. You don't need massive mining projects, pipelines, or exploration platforms to deliver clean energy. Solar panels on roofs and in parking lots and wind turbines on farms can, by themselves, get us reasonably far along in meeting the energy needs of a growing egalitarian economy. From this perspective, the Green New Deal should rightfully be seen as offering a fully viable alternative to austerity economics, along with the only realistic path for keeping us from becoming the 21st-century asteroid clone.

Trump Is Consolidating Far-Right Power Globally

C. J. POLYCHRONIOU: Noam, in 2016 Trump called U.S foreign policy "a complete and total disaster," claiming that previous administrations in the post–Cold War era were guided by unrealistic expectations that damaged America's national interests. Since taking office, he has withdrawn the country from a series of international agreements, demanding that countries pay for US protection, and seeking to advance US economic interests through tariffs and protectionism. These moves have led many analysts to speak of a new era in US relations with the world. What's your own take on Trump's foreign policy?

NOAM CHOMSKY: One of the most appropriate comments I've seen on Trump's foreign policy appeared in an article in the *New Republic* written by David Roth, the editor of a sports blog: "The spectacle of expert analysts and thought leaders parsing the actions of a man with no expertise or capacity for analysis is the purest acid satire—but less because of how badly that expert analysis has failed than because of how sincerely misplaced it is . . . there is nothing here to parse, no hidden meanings or tactical elisions or slow-rolled strategic campaign."

That seems generally accurate. This is a man, after all, who dismisses the information and analyses of his massive intelligence system in favor of what was said this morning on *Fox and Friends*, where everyone tells him how much they love him. With all due skepticism about the quality of intelligence, this is sheer madness considering the stakes.

And it continues, in ways that are almost surreal. At the recent G20 conference, Trump was asked about Putin's statement that Western liberalism is obsolete. Trump assumed he must be talking about California: *Western* liberalism. Putin "may feel that way," Trump responded: "He sees what's going on. And I guess, if you look at what's happening in Los Angeles, where it's so sad to look; and what's happening in San Francisco and a couple of other cities which are run by an extraordinary group of liberal people."

He was asked why the US alone is refusing to join the G20 in a commitment to address global warming and responded by praising the quality of US air and water, apparently not understanding the distinction.

It's hard to find a comment on foreign policy that departs from this impressive norm. Efforts to detect some coherent global strategy indeed seem to be a kind of acid satire.

Not that there is no coherent policy. There is one policy that emerges from the chaos—the kind we would expect from an egotistical con man who has one principle: ME! It follows that any treaty or agreement reached by predecessors (particularly the despised Obama) is the worst deal in history, which will be replaced by the Greatest Deal in History negotiated by the most accomplished dealmaker of all time and greatest American president. Similarly, any other action carried out in the past was misguided and harmed America, but will be corrected by the "stable genius" now in charge of defending America from those who are cheating and assaulting it on all sides.

It makes no difference what the consequences are—terrible, decent, indifferent—as long as the imagery is preserved.

It may be recalled that a president who obtains his picture of the world from *Fox and Friends* is not an entirely new phenomenon. Forty years ago, a revered predecessor (Ronald Reagan) was learning about the world from movies, and was so mesmerized that he even came to believe that he had taken part in the liberation of Nazi concentration camps (while not leaving California).

All of this tells us something about modern politics. But Trump can't be compared to Reagan, any more than farce can be compared to tragedy, to paraphrase Marx.

It's understandable that the farce elicits ridicule, and no doubt some are relishing the coming photo op of Trump and Boris Johnson upholding

Anglo-American civilization. But for the world, it's dead serious, from the destruction of the environment and the growing threats of terminal nuclear war to a long list of other crimes and horrors.

The most dangerous immediate foreign policy crisis is the conflict with Iran, which has been deemed the official source of all evil. Iran must end its "aggression" and become a "normal country"—like Saudi Arabia, which is making rapid progress in Trump's fantasy world, even "a great job in Saudi Arabia from the standpoint of women," he explained at G20.

The charges against Iran resonate through the media echo chamber with little effort to assess the validity of the accusations—which hardly withstand analysis. Whatever one thinks of Iranian international behavior, by the miserable standards of US allies in the region—not to speak of the US itself—it is not much of a competitor in the rogue state derby.

In the real world, the US unilaterally decided to destroy the well-functioning nuclear agreement (JCPOA), with ludicrous charges accepted by virtually no one with the slightest credibility, and to impose extremely harsh sanctions designed to punish the Iranian people and undermine the economy. The [US government] also uses its enormous economic power, including virtual control of the international financial system, to compel others to obey Washington's dictates. None of this has even minimal legitimacy; the same is true of Cuba and other cases. The world may protest—last November, the UN General Assembly once again condemned the US embargo on Cuba, 189-2 (only the US and Israel voted against the resolution). But in vain. The weird idea of the founders that one might have "decent respect to the opinions of mankind" has long vanished, and the pained bleatings of the world pass in silence. On Iran as well.

This is not the place to pursue the matter, but there is a good deal more to say about the US specialty of resorting to sanctions (with extraterritorial reach) to punish populations—a form of "American exceptionalism" that finds its place within what Nick Turse calls "the American system of suffering" in *Kill Anything That Moves*, his harrowing expose of the US assault on the civilian population of South Vietnam. The right to engage in this malicious practice is accepted as normal in the US doctrinal system, with little effort to analyze the actual motives in individual cases, the legitimacy of such policies, or, in fact, even their legality. Matters of no slight significance.

With regard to Iran, within the government-media doctrinal system, the only question that arises is whether the victim will respond in some way, maybe by "violating" the agreement that the US has demolished, maybe by some other act. And if it does, it obviously will be deemed to deserve brutal punishment.

In commentary made by US officials and media, Iran "violates" agreements. The US merely "withdraws" from them. The stance is reminiscent of a comment by the great anarchist writer and Wobbly activist T-Bone Slim: "Only the poor break laws—the rich evade them."

Analysts have tried hard to detect some grand strategy behind the US assault on Iran, another exercise in futility. It's easy enough to detect the goals of the thugs surrounding Trump: for Pompeo and Bolton, the goal is to smash the miscreant—from a safe distance, so that it isn't costly for us. And damn the consequences. Trump himself seems to see it quite differently. Whether he in fact called off a military strike because of his compassion for 150 possible victims, who knows? The only evidence comes from a source that is not famous for its credibility. But it seems clear that he doesn't want a war, which would spoil all the fun and games that he is so greatly enjoying, and would harm his electoral prospects. It's far better to go into the elections facing the cosmic threat of an evil enemy that only the Bold and Courageous Leader is able to confront, not any of those weak-kneed Dems, surely none of those "mere" women. Reagan grasped the principle as well when he boldly faced the threat of Nicaragua, strapping on his cowboy boots and warning that Nicaraguan troops were only two days' march from Harlingen, Texas, and declaring a national emergency because of the extraordinary threat to the security and survival of the US.

This is not the place to pursue the matter again, but in the background of the Iran conflict are some unmentionable facts. The alleged threat of Iranian nuclear weapons can readily be overcome by adopting the demand of the Arab States, Iran, and in fact virtually the entire world, to establish a nuclear weapons-free zone in the region, a policy to which the US and UK have a unique obligation, and which the US regularly blocks—for reasons that are hardly obscure: if the US were to officially acknowledge the existence of Israel's nuclear arsenal, the huge flood of aid to Israel would be illegal under US law, and of course, Israel's weapons of mass destruction cannot be subject to inspection.

What about tariffs? "Tariff man" tells us that the tariffs are designed to promote US economic interests, but whether he believes it or not, or cares, we have no idea. Political pronouncements can rarely be taken at face value, and Trump is not notorious for his truthfulness and credibility.

There is, to put it charitably, scant evidence for Trump's boast that his tariffs are forcing China to pour "billions of dollars" into the Treasury Department. "We never had 10 cents coming into our Treasury" under past administrations, he explained. "Now we have billions coming in." In the real world, the costs of the tariffs are borne by US companies (which may choose to compensate by reducing wages) and consumers, burdened with a highly regressive tax that targets mostly the less affluent. In brief, Trump's tariffs are yet another one of his policies to harm American workers and the poor.

It is, however, true that "billions" are involved. A study by the New York Fed with Princeton and Columbia Universities estimates that US companies and consumers have paid $3 billion a month in additional taxes because of tariffs on Chinese goods and on aluminum and steel from around the globe, in addition to a $1.4 billion in costs to US companies related to lost efficiency in 2018.

The tariff war against China may lead to some shifting of assembly operations from China to Vietnam and other countries with even lower labor costs, but as for the US economy, more typical is the decision of Apple a few days ago to shift Mac Pro computer assembly from Texas to China.

Trump's tariff wars seem to relate primarily to domestic policy, crafted with the coming election in view. He has to somehow convince his voting base that he is the one man in the country protecting battered Americans who are suffering from the "carnage" created by his predecessors—which is real enough for a great many Americans, as illustrated dramatically by the astonishing decline in life expectancy among white, working-age Americans, attributed to "deaths of despair," a phenomenon unknown in developed societies. Trump's trick is to wave a big club and threaten others with dire consequences unless they stop torturing poor America and agree to "play fair." When we take all this apart, a different picture emerges, much as in the case of the ominous threat of Iran. But what matters for the con game is the "alternative reality" that the conjurers are concocting.

With no little success. It's a mistake to "mis-underestimate" Trump (to borrow W. Bush's neologism). He is a canny demagogue and manipulator, who is managing to maintain the allegiance of the adoring crowds that believe he is standing up for them against the hated elites while also ensuring that the primary Republican constituency of extreme wealth and corporate power are doing just fine, despite some complaints. And they surely are, in fact, making out like bandits with help from Trump and his associates.

It is quite remarkable to see how effectively alternative reality is created. Iran is typical, but the successes are far broader. Consider the charge that "China is killing us," stealing our jobs, joined by "Mexican robbers." How is China killing us? Did China have a gun to the head of CEO Tim Cook of Apple, ordering him to end the last vestige of production of Apple computers in the US? Or Boeing, or GM, or Microsoft, or any of the others who have shifted production to China? Or were the decisions made by bankers and investors in corporate boardrooms in New York and Chicago? And if the latter, is the solution to wave a fist at China or to change the mode of decision-making in the US—by shifting it to the hands of stakeholders, workers and communities, or at least giving them a substantial role, as democratic theory would suggest? It seems a fairly obvious question. Oddly, it isn't raised, while the official mantra persists unperturbed.

It's claimed that China imposes unfair conditions on investors, demanding technology transfer (following the pattern of development of others from England and the US to the East Asian tigers). Perhaps so. If Apple and others don't like these conditions, they're free not to invest in China. Worshippers of free enterprise and the market should surely agree.

Another charge is that China is unfairly pursuing an industrial policy that subsidizes favored industries. If so, US political leaders and analysts should be cheering. According to the economic doctrines they profess, China is harming its economy by departing from the optimal free market mode of development, thus contributing to US economic hegemony. What's the problem?

Somehow, that's not what we hear. Nor do we hear much about how this is normal policy in Western state capitalist societies, notoriously in the US throughout its history, and dramatically since World War II, the basis for the creation of today's high-tech economy, and continuing today.

What appears to be a more credible charge is that China is violating the intellectual property rights regime (TRIPS) established in the World Trade Organization. Suppose so. Several questions arise. One is: Who gains, who loses? To a large extent, American consumers gain, while Big Pharma, Microsoft, and others, granted exorbitant and unprecedented patent rights, under TRIPS suffer some reduction in their enormous profits. That leads at once to another question: Is the TRIPS regime legitimate? True, it was established by interstate agreement, but who made those decisions? Did the public have any role, or even know what was happening? Hardly. The misnamed "free trade agreements" are more properly described as investor-rights agreements, often with little relation to trade in any meaningful sense, and not surprisingly, serving the interests of their designers in the investor class.

Other elements of the "China is killing us" complaints actually make sense. Concern is often openly expressed that Chinese progress might leave the US behind—for example, that Huawei's cheaper and superior technology may give them an "unfair advantage" in establishing 5G networks. Plainly that has to be stopped, US officials argue, along with Chinese economic development generally. Their concerns are reminiscent of the 1980s, when superior Japanese manufacturing techniques were undermining inefficient US enterprises, and the Reagan administration had to intervene to block Japanese imports by "voluntary export restraints"—where "voluntary" means "agree or else"—and other devices to enable backward American management to catch up.

Without proceeding, while there are some detectable strategic objectives, much of what is offered and discussed is concealing something quite different. And there is good reason to agree that the sight of experts seeking to detect some grand strategy behind Trump's antics is "the purest acid satire." But there is a strategy. And it is working quite well.

One of Trump's stated objectives behind his understanding of diplomacy is to "turn enemies into friends." Is there any evidence that he is actually pursuing such a diplomatic objective? I have in mind, in particular, the cases of North Korea and Russia.

In this case, the stated objective seems real. It elicits ridicule and bitter condemnation across the mainstream political spectrum. But whatever Trump's motives may be, the general policy makes some sense.

The Panmunjom Declaration of the two Koreas in April 2018 was a highly significant event. It called for the two Koreas to proceed toward amicable relations and eventual denuclearization "on their own accord," without the external interference that has often in the past undermined what seemed to be initiatives with some promise: repeated interference from the US, as the historical record shows, facts commonly evaded in reporting. In this declaration and related agreements, as discussed by Korea specialist Chung-in Moon in the main establishment journal *Foreign Affairs*, for the first time the two Koreas laid out specific timetables and took concrete and promising steps toward reduction of tensions and disarmament—developments that should be welcomed and supported.

To his credit, Trump has largely adhered to the request of the two Koreas. His recent meeting with Kim at the demilitarized zone, the symbolic border crossing, and possible tentative agreements are steps that with goodwill could have salutary consequences. They might facilitate efforts of the two Koreas to proceed on the difficult path toward accommodation and might offer a way to relieve the sanctions that are blocking badly needed aid to the North and contributing to a major humanitarian crisis there. All of this may infuriate commentators across the spectrum, but if there is a better way to bring peace to the peninsula and to take steps toward denuclearization and reform within the North Korean dictatorship, no one has yet informed us about it.

Putin's Russia need not be turned into a "friend," but cooperative relations with Russia are a prerequisite for survival. Trump's record on this score is mixed. Mattis's Nuclear Posture Review (February 2018) poses very severe threats, escalated since by the unbelievable decision to carry forward development of hypersonic weapons. Adversaries are doing likewise. The right approach is diplomacy and negotiations to prevent a suicidal course, but there is not a hint of that. The same is true of the INF Treaty negotiated by Reagan and Gorbachev, which significantly reduced the risks of terminal war. Each side claims that the other is violating the treaty. The right approach is to have neutral analysts investigate the claims and to negotiate an end to such violations as are discovered. The worst approach is to withdraw from the treaty, as the US is doing, with Russia following. The same considerations hold for the other major arms control treaty, New Start.

Throughout, it seems that John Bolton, consistent in his malevolence, has succeeded in blocking progress and driving policy in directions that are extremely ominous.

What's your assessment of the Trump administration's Middle East plan? And how instrumental is Jared Kushner's role in this?

I presume that Kushner is the main architect, as reported. What has been released so far is fairly straightforward and consistent with earlier policies of the administration authorizing Israel's takeover of the Golan Heights and development of Greater Jerusalem, all in violation of Security Council orders (backed at the time by the US). At the same time, the meager US aid to Palestinians has been terminated on the grounds that they do not thank the boss politely enough when he is undermining their most elementary rights.

The Kushner plan carries this forward. Israel is to be granted the fondest wishes of its expansionist leadership. The Palestinians are to be bought off by development funds provided by others (not the US). The essence of the Trump-Kushner "Deal of the Century" was captured succinctly by Israeli UN ambassador Danny Danon, in the *New York Times*: Palestinians should realize that the game is over and "surrender."

Then there can be peace, another triumph of the "great negotiator."

In this case there is an underlying strategic objective: to consolidate the alliance of reactionary states (the oil monarchies, Egypt, Israel) as a base for US power in the region. That is by no means something new, though earlier variants had somewhat different forms and were less visible than today.

These objectives fall within a broader strategy of forming a global reactionary alliance under the US aegis, including the "illiberal democracies" of Eastern Europe (Hungary's Orbán, etc.) and Brazil's grotesque Jair Bolsonaro, who, among other virtues, shares with Trump the dedication to undermine prospects for a livable environment by opening up the Amazon—"the lungs of the earth"—to exploitation by his friends in mining and agribusiness. That's a natural strategy for today's Trump-McConnell Republican party, well ensconced to the far right of the international spectrum, even beyond the European "populist" parties that were not long ago considered a contemptible fringe.

Without asking you to play the role of a Cassandra, how do you think history will assess Trump's stance on climate change, which is by far the biggest global challenge facing the world?

To borrow from Wittgenstein, with a slight tweak, "Whereof one cannot speak politely, thereof one must remain silent."

Trump's Actions on Syria Reflect the Foreign Policy of a Con Man

C. J. POLYCHRONIOU: Noam, since coming to office, Trump has shown on numerous occasions that he is not a normal foreign policy president. But can you make any sense out of his stance toward Syria?

NOAM CHOMSKY: The first of Trump's recent steps was to withdraw the small US contingent that was a deterrent to Turkey's expansion of its invasion of Syria and to authorize Erdoğan's plans to extend his atrocities and ethnic cleansing of Syrian Kurds. His second step was to move US troops to "secure" the oil-producing areas. The latter, apparently after he was told about the oil, is easy to understand. He has held all along that our only standing interest in the Middle East is to "secure" its oil for our own benefit.

As for the first step, we can only speculate, but it seems quite likely that the motive is what guides him consistently: How will the action affect me? Trump is an effective con man who has a good sense of what animates his voting base. In this case, he presumably expected (correctly it seems) that withdrawing a few hundred troops would appeal to the sector of the population that resonates to his message that America is foolishly expending its blood and treasure to help "unworthy" people who don't even thank us for our sacrifices on their behalf. Moreover, Trump is the first president to stand up for the suffering American people instead of giving everything away to foreigners out of stupidity (or treachery).

It's worth recalling that repeated polls have shown that Americans vastly overestimate the scale of foreign aid—and recommend that it be considerably higher than it actually is (putting aside what constitutes "aid").

Much has been written and said about the betrayal of the Kurds, a US ally in the war against ISIS (also known as Daesh). This isn't, however, the first time that the US has betrayed the Kurds and other former allies.

Betrayal of the Kurds has been virtually a qualification for office since Ford-Kissinger abandoned them to the mercy of Saddam Hussein when they were no longer needed. Reagan went so far as to support his friend Saddam's chemical warfare campaign against Iraqi Kurds, seeking to shift the blame to Iran and blocking congressional efforts to respond to these hideous crimes. Clinton's method was to provide the arms for the murderous government assault on Turkish Kurds, which killed tens of thousands, wiped out 3,500 towns and villages, and drove hundreds of thousands from their homes. (See Noam Chomsky, *The New Military Humanism*, chapter 3. London: Pluto Press, 1999). As Clinton's flood of military aid increased, so did the shocking crimes, and Turkey became the prime recipient of American arms (outside of Israel-Egypt, a separate category).

Trump's contribution is particularly disgusting. The Kurds lost 11,000 soldiers, men and women, leading the war against ISIS for which Trump claims credit, helped by some US special forces (five casualties are reported) and air support. Erdoğan demanded that Kurds eliminate defensive fortifications (filling in trenches, etc.) near the border, and at the request of the US command, they complied, trusting Washington's promise that it would protect them from a further Turkish assault. Trump's series of tweets on Monday, October 7, 2019, following a phone call with his counterpart Erdoğan on Sunday evening, broke that promise, leaving Kurds exposed to the invasion by Turkish-backed forces, most it seems jihadis and criminals. For years, Turkey has been helping tens of thousands of jihadis to flood into Syria for its anti-Assad war and to establish a Turkish presence. No surprises in how the extended Turkish assault has been carried out.

Former prosecutor and U.N. investigator Carla del Ponte said Erdoğan should be investigated and indicted for war crimes. What about Trump? After all, isn't he the one who gave Erdoğan the green light to launch an invasion into the Kurdish semiautonomous region in Syria?

Turkey had already invaded and occupied Kurdish-controlled regions of northern Syria, killing hundreds and displacing hundreds of thousands, with credible charges of serious war crimes. Trump's green light extended the operation with [the] alleged goal of ending a terrorist threat, but in reality it was to put an end to the highly promising social and political achievements in Kurdish-led Rojava by violence and terror, ethnic cleansing, and resettling the region with Syrians of Turkey's choosing.

On war crimes, it is well to remember the stirring words of Justice Robert Jackson, chief US prosecutor at the Nuremberg Tribunal where Nazi war criminals were judged and hanged: "We must never forget that the record on which we judge these defendants today is the record on which history will judge us tomorrow. To pass these defendants a poisoned chalice is to put it to our own lips as well. We must summon such detachment and intellectual integrity to our task that this Trial will commend itself to posterity as fulfilling humanity's aspirations to do justice."

When we ask how these words have been heeded since, we know how history should judge us, and what to expect of punishment for war crimes—especially in perfectly clear cases of aggression with no credible pretext, the "supreme international crime" of the Nuremberg judgment: the US-UK invasion of Iraq in 2003, to take a textbook example.

Continuing with the Nuremberg judgment, we might recall that "to initiate a war of aggression," such as the invasion of Iraq, "is not only an international crime; it is the supreme international crime differing only from other war crimes in that it contains within itself the accumulated evil of the whole." Included in the accumulated evil of the whole is the recruitment of such militants as Abu Bakr al-Baghdadi, who joined the resistance to the invasion. After an education in Abu Ghraib, he went on to lead the criminal enterprise ISIS, and, finally killed himself by detonating a suicide vest during a US special forces operation on October 27, 2019.

Moving to the domestic front, are the Democrats likely to benefit from impeaching Trump, or will the gamble to do so prove to be a costly one for them?

My own guess is that it will turn out to be rather like the Mueller investigation. Trump will be impeached by the House, then acquitted in the Senate, where few Republicans are likely to be principled enough to face Trump's adoring and militant voting bloc. Then Trump can declare victory for the Tribune of the People, [saying he] has once again protected "real" red-blooded Americans from the machinations of the Deep State and the treacherous liberal elites.

Economic models predict that if nothing changes with regard to the direction of the economy, Trump will win in 2020 with an even bigger margin. Is this a surprising development, given all the chaos that surrounds Trump's presidency?

These models are largely based on public perceptions of current economic trends. These take no account of the fact that the Trump economy carries onward the slow Obama recovery from the Great Recession, now with a real unemployment rate of over 7 percent with almost stagnant real wages and declining benefits—and spectacular enrichment of a tiny sector to the point where over 20 percent of the country's wealth is in the hands of 0.1 percent of the population while half the population has negative net worth.

In the past, these models have been accurate, though we should recall that the best predictor of electability, dramatically for Congress, is campaign spending, as Thomas Ferguson has shown, again in current work. But we are not in normal times. The Republican "radical insurgency," as it was called several years ago by Thomas Mann and Norman Ornstein of the American Enterprise Institute, has gone far off the traditional rails under Trump. It has undermined democracy and poses an extraordinary threat to the persistence of organized human life on earth—in the all-too-near future. How such factors will enter into the election is not easy to say, though it is unfortunately not difficult to predict the consequences of four more years of Trumpism.

To Make the US a Democracy, the Constitution Itself Must Change

C. J. POLYCHRONIOU: According to popular conception, the United States is a "nation of immigrants," although this formulation significantly excludes Native people—who were already here, and were subjected to colonization, displacement, and genocide at the hands of European immigrants—and also excludes African Americans, whose ancestors were kidnapped and enslaved. When it is described as a "nation of immigrants," the US is often portrayed as a varied nation where people have the freedom to pursue their dreams of a better life while maintaining their own cultural, ethnic, and religious distinctiveness or uniqueness. Yet, the truth of the matter is that inequality and oppression of the "Other" have been ongoing political and social realities since the origins of the republic. In fact, today we have a president in the White House who makes no bones about wishing to see nonwhite people, even elected representatives of the US Congress, leave the country because they challenge the status quo and seek a United States with a more humane and democratic polity. Meanwhile, the very rich are enjoying political privileges like never before. Noam, what are some of the tangible and intangible factors that seem to be pushing the country—socially, politically and economically—backward rather than forward?

NOAM CHOMSKY: Trump's diatribes successfully inflame his audience, many of whom apparently feel deeply threatened by diversity, cultural change, or simply the recognition that the white Christian nation of their collective imagination is changing before their eyes. White supremacy is nothing new in the US. The late George Frederickson's comparative studies of white supremacy found the US to be almost off the chart, more extreme even than Apartheid South Africa. As late as the 1960s, the US had anti-miscegenation laws so extreme that the Nazis refused to adopt them as a model for their racist Nuremberg laws. And the power of Southern Democrats was so great that until '60s activism shattered the framework of legal racism—if not its practice by other means—even New Deal federal housing programs enforced segregation, barring Black people from new housing programs.

It goes back to the country's origins. While progressive in many ways by the standards of the day, the US was founded on two brutal racist principles: the most hideous system of slavery in human history, the source of much of its wealth (and England's too), and the need to rid the national territory of Native Americans, whom the Declaration of Independence explicitly describes as "the merciless Indian savages," and whom the framers saw as barring the expansion of the "superior" race.

Immigrants . . . were supposed to be white immigrants—in fact, basically "Anglo-Saxon," in accord with weird racist myths of the Founding Fathers that persisted through the 19th century. That includes the leading Enlightenment figures. Benjamin Franklin urged that Germans and Swedes be barred because they were too "swarthy." Thomas Jefferson was greatly interested in Anglo-Saxon language and law, part of his immersion in the "Saxon myth" that English democracy and law trace back to a pre–Norman Saxon period. The first Naturalization Act, 1790, restricted the option to whites, extended to ex-slaves after the Civil war.

The country of course needed immigrants to settle the "Indian country" from which Indigenous nations were expelled or "exterminated" (as the founders put it). But they were supposed to be "white"—a somewhat flexible culturally constructed category. By the late 19th century, Asians were excluded by law. The first more general immigration law was in 1924, designed to bar Jews and Italians primarily. There is no need to review here the horrendous record of how Jews were prevented from fleeing Nazi barbarism, crimes that persisted even after the war. Truman sent Earl Harrison on a mission to inspect the concentration camps where Jews were still held, under grotesque conditions as he reported. About the only effect was to intensify efforts to ship them to Palestine.

The 1924 law remained in place until 1965. By the 1980s immigration began to be criminalized. Treatment of Haitians fleeing terror was particularly despicable. Guantánamo was first used as a detention center by the Bush I and Clinton administrations, a place to get rid of Black people fleeing in terror from the murderous coup regime that [US leaders] were supporting, despite pretenses to the contrary. They were classified as "economic migrants," a cynical pretense in gross violation of international law and minimal decency.

Another ugly story.

It's not terribly surprising, then, to read a report of a conference of conservative intellectuals where one esteemed speaker, University of Pennsylvania Law professor Amy Wax, explains learnedly that "our country will be better off with more whites and fewer nonwhites," since immigrants may not quickly come to "think, live and act just like us" because of the social and cultural climate of their places of origin.

Wax failed to elaborate on whether her parents, Jewish immigrants from Eastern Europe, came from a cultural and social climate where people were thinking and acting like "us."

It's not hard to understand why these deep currents are becoming more manifest, and ominous, today, after forty years of the "savage capitalism" unleashed by the neoliberal assault. It's enough to recall that for a large majority of the workforce, wages have either stagnated or declined since 1979, when the neoliberal assault was just taking off. From the country's origins, US workers benefited from the world's highest wages. . . . Since the 1980s, though the unusual advantages persist, working people have fallen behind the rest of the developed world by many measures. For review of their current status, see Amanda Novella and Jeff Madrick's February 2019 contribution to the journal *Challenge*.

The effects of the assault are sharp concentration of wealth and power, increasingly in largely predatory financial institutions, stagnation or decline for the majority, deterioration of benefits, astonishing collapse of infrastructure, a form of globalization designed to pit working people against one another for the benefit of international investors, weakening of institutions to protect worker rights, undermining of functioning democracy, and much else that is all too familiar.

The result, in the US and in Europe, is an upsurge of anger, resentment, and, all too often, a search for scapegoats—typically those even more disadvantaged, who are portrayed as being coddled by liberal elites. It's a dangerous mix: fertile territory for demagogues.

The threats are far more extreme than the incipient Fascist-style tendencies, which are severe enough. It cannot be overlooked that humans are facing a decision of extraordinary significance, which must be made very soon: Will organized human society survive in anything like its present form, or will it be devastated by global catastrophe? The two most ominous threats are nuclear war and environmental catastrophe, both increasing. On the latter, major energy corporations are apparently planning on a future with 5° Celsius above preindustrial levels by mid-century, and with that in mind, are racing to accelerate what climate scientists recognize to be indescribable catastrophe by maximizing the profitable production of fossil fuels, joined by the biggest banks and other major capitalist institutions.

Meanwhile the Republican administration, determined to safeguard its credentials as the most dangerous organization in human history, is anticipating a slightly less overwhelming catastrophe—a rise of 4°[C] by end of the century, also far above what scientists recognize to be a colossal danger. And it concludes from this detailed environmental assessment that we should not limit automotive emissions, because—what's the difference? We're going over the cliff anyway.

If there is anything like this in world history, I haven't found it. And this passes with scarcely a raised eyebrow.

Of course, this is only science, and as [right-wing radio host] Rush Limbaugh instructs his tens of millions of radio listeners, science is one of the "four corners of deceit," along with government, academia, and media (of the wrong sort).

All of this tells us that the tasks ahead are urgent, on many fronts.

Another common (mis)perception is that American culture and society adapt easily to change. Yet, this is a country where it is immensely difficult to change even outdated and dysfunctional political processes and

institutions, such as the Electoral College and the distribution of Senate seats. It is very hard to pass amendments to the Constitution. And so far, we have faced many barriers to moving away from the two-party system. How do we explain the inflexibility of US political processes and institutions?

In the 19th century the US Constitution was in many ways a progressive document, even though it was a "Framers' Coup" against the democratic aspirations of most of the public—the title of Michael Klarman's impressive study of the making of the Constitution, generally regarded as the "gold standard" in the scholarly literature.

The document has inherent problems, which are leading to a likely constitutional crisis. The problems are serious enough for law professor Erwin Chemerinsky, writing on "America's constitutional crisis," to entitle his article "The First Priority: Making America a Democracy" (contrary to the intentions of the Framers). He reviews some of the familiar problems. One has to do with the Electoral College, which was designed by the Framers because of their distrust of popular government. By now states with 23 percent of the population have enough electoral votes to choose the president. Even more importantly, the same radical imbalance makes the Senate a highly undemocratic institution—in accord with the intentions of the Framers. In Madison's constitutional design, the Senate was the most powerful branch of government, and the most protected from public interference. It was to represent "the wealth of the nation," the most "responsible" men, who have sympathy for property and its rights. Furthermore, though the Framers did not anticipate this, of course, social and demographic changes have placed this excessive antidemocratic power in the hands of a part of the population that is mostly rural, white, Christian, socially conservative, and traditionalist—generally sympathetic to the Wax principle.

Some of these undemocratic features were virtually unavoidable. The Constitution would never have been ratified if the smaller colonies were not granted an equal voice. But by now the effects are severe—and unchangeable by amendment because of the same radical imbalance in voting power.

These problems are exacerbated by the monopolization of politics by the two political parties and "winner take all" state laws that bar proportional representation, which can permit a variety of voices to enter the political arena, sometimes growing to major parties. Some have argued, not implausibly, that if a country with the US system tried to join the European Union, the application might be rejected by the European Court of Justice.

The impending crisis is becoming more severe because of the malevolence of the Republican leadership. They are well aware that their formula of abject service to wealth and corporate power along with mobilization of a voting base of the kind that shows up at Trump rallies is not enough to overcome their growing minority status. The solution is radical gerrymandering of the kind now authorized by the reactionary Roberts Court, and stacking the judiciary with far-right justices who will be able to hold the country by the throat for many years. Here the evil genius is Mitch McConnell, who maneuvered to block appointments under Obama, a campaign of obstruction that left 106 vacancies at the end of Obama's second term (including the scandalous case of Merrick Garland), and is now rushing through appointment of Federalist Society choices.

Another recurring theme of US history involves religious fundamentalism, which is still widespread throughout the country. Does the United States, in some ways, look more like a fundamentalist nation rather than an advanced secular republic?

Throughout its history the US has been an unusually fundamentalist society, with regular Great Awakenings and beliefs that are far off the spectrum of developed societies. Almost 80 percent of Americans believe in miracles. There is a huge evangelical community, a large part of Trump's base, which he keeps in line by throwing them crumbs. Secretary of State Mike Pompeo, a devout evangelical Christian, speculated recently that God might have sent Trump to save Israel from Iran—which is threatening Israel with destruction in the fantasy world of doctrinal verities. Fully 40 percent of Americans expect Jesus to return to earth by mid-century (23 percent certainly). It's possible that this accounts for some of the "looking away" that we were discussing earlier. All in all, it is a curious form of exceptionalism that goes back to the earliest settlers.

The United States remains a global superpower, but its domestic society is strikingly unequal and poverty is rampant. Given that, should we interpret Trumpism as a political phenomenon akin to the same dynamics that gave rise in the prewar era to Fascism and other forms of authoritarian rule in Europe and elsewhere?

Already in the 1950s, economist John Kenneth Galbraith described US society as marked by "private affluence, public squalor." It's true that in the public sphere it often resembles a "third world" country. The Infrastructure Report Card of the American Society of Civil Engineers regularly ranks the US down at the bottom, D+. And one can hardly walk through a US city or travel in poor rural areas without being shocked at the squalor. The same holds for social justice measures. Among OECD countries, the US ranks near the bottom. I don't think this relates specifically to Trumpism, except insofar as the contemporary Republican Party leadership is a virtual caricature of long-standing features of US political economy, based on business power that is unusual by historical standards, with a pervasive impact on the political system and also on the "hegemonic common sense," in Gramscian terms. The business classes are not just unusually powerful, but are also highly class conscious, constantly engaged in bitter class war, in some ways vulgar Marxists, with values inverted.

There is variation. The New Deal period brought the US somewhat closer to European-style social democracy, but from the '80s that has been sharply reversed. By now, when Bernie Sanders calls for renewing and extending the New Deal—ideas that would not have greatly surprised Eisenhower—he is considered a radical who wants to destroy "American values."

Trumpism and prewar Fascism seems to me a different matter. There surely are resemblances. Just speaking personally, Trump's Greenville, North Carolina, rally evoked my childhood memories of listening on the radio to Hitler's Nuremberg rallies, not understanding the words but the mood was apparent enough, and frightening. The not-so-subtle appeals to racism, xenophobia, misogyny, the treachery of dissent, demonization of media that do not kowtow abjectly to the Grand Leader—all this and more is reminiscent of prewar Fascism. And the social base of Trumpism has similarities to prewar Fascism as well: superrich power and petty bourgeois popular base.

But prewar Fascism was based on control of all aspects of the society—business included—by a powerful state in the hands of a totalitarian, all-powerful ruling party: *Gleichschaltung*. The situation here is quite different, almost the opposite, with the increasingly monopolized business world, particularly its financial sector, having overwhelming power in sociopolitical life and doctrinal management.

In the 1980s, Japan was regarded as the most likely power to replace US hegemony. We know what happened to that forecast. Now, many pundits see China as a future global superpower. Is this a realistic assessment of future geopolitical developments, given the huge economic and military gap that exists today between China and the United States?

The "Japan is number one" fantasy traces in large part to the incompetence of US management, which was unable to compete with superior Japanese production methods. Reagan took care of that with "voluntary export restraints"—where "voluntary" means do it or else, making clear who is number one—and a number of other devices. One was SDI ("Star Wars"), sold to the public (and maybe to Reagan himself) as defense against the evil enemy, but to the corporate world as a great business opportunity, courtesy of the taxpayer, a familiar benefactor.

As for China, it has made substantial economic and technological progress, but remains a very poor country. It is ranked 86th in the 2018 update to the UN Development Index, right below Algeria. (India is ranked 130th, barely above East Timor.) China has huge internal problems unknown in the West. It is argued that China is comparable to the US, maybe ahead, in purchasing power parity, but that means that it is far below per capita. China has been pursuing systematic plans to expand its influence through Eurasia in a somewhat uneasy partnership with an economically much weaker Russia, first through the Shanghai Cooperation Council, now with the Belt and Road Initiative. In some areas of technology—solar panels, electric cars—it may be in the lead. But it still has a long way to go to reach the level of the rich industrial societies.

The US is concerned with Chinese growth, and is seeking (pretty openly) to impede it—not a very attractive policy stance.

It's also worth bearing in mind that in the age of neoliberal globalization, national accounts are a less meaningful measure of economic power than in the past. Political economist Sean Starrs has done informative work on a different measure: proportion of world wealth held by domestically based multinational corporations. By that measure the US is far in the lead internationally, owning a spectacular 50 percent of world wealth—more than the US share of global GDP at the peak of its power in 1945—and US corporations are in the lead in just about every category.

China is sure to have a major role in world affairs. A sane policy would be accommodation and cooperation, which doesn't seem out of the range of possibility.

Worship of Markets Is
Threatening Human Civilization

C. J. POLYCHRONIOU: Noam, looking at the current state of the world, I think it is not an exaggeration at all to say that we live in ominously dangerous times—and not simply in a period of great global complexity, confusion, and uncertainty, which, after all, has been the "normal" state of the global political condition in the modem era. I believe, in fact, that we are in the midst of a whirlpool of events and developments that are eroding our capacity to manage human affairs in a way that is conducive to the attainment of a political and economic order based on stability, justice, and sustainability. Indeed, the contemporary world is fraught, in my own mind at least, with perils and challenges that will test severely humanity's ability to maintain a steady course toward anything resembling a civilized life.

How did we get to such a state of affairs, with tremendous economic inequalities and the resurgence of the irrational in political affairs on the one hand, and an uncanny capacity, on the other, to look away from the existential crises such as global warming and nuclear weapons, which will surely destroy civilized life as we know it if we continue with "business as usual"?

NOAM CHOMSKY: How indeed.

The question of how we got to this state of affairs is truly vast in scope, requiring not just inquiry into the origin and nature of social and cultural institutions but also into depths of human psychology that are barely understood. We can, however, take a much more modest stab at the questions, asking about certain highly consequential decisions that could have been made differently, and about specific cases where we can identify some of the roots of looking away.

The history of nuclear weapons provides some striking cases. One critical decision was in 1944, when Germany was out of the war and it was clear that the only target was Japan. One cannot really say that a decision was made to proceed nevertheless to create devices that could devastate Japan even more thoroughly, and in the longer term threaten to destroy us as well. It seems that the question never seriously arose, apart from such isolated figures as Joseph Rotblat—who was later barred reentry to the US.

Another critical decision that was not made was in the early 1950s. At the time, there were still no long-range delivery systems for nuclear weapons (ICBMs). It might have been possible to reach an agreement with Russia to bar their development. That was a plausible surmise at the time, and release of Russian archives makes it seem an even more likely prospect. Remarkably, there is no trace of any consideration of pursuing steps to bar the only weapons systems that would pose a lethal threat to the US, so we learn from McGeorge Bundy's standard work on the history of nuclear weapons, with access to the highest-level sources. Perhaps still more remarkably, there has, to my knowledge, been no voiced interest in this astonishing fact.

It is easy to go on. The result is seventy-five years of living under the threat of virtually total destruction, particularly since the successful development of thermonuclear weapons by 1953—in this case a decision, rather than lack of one. And as the record shows all too graphically, it is a virtual miracle that we have survived the nuclear age thus far.

That raises your question of why we look away. I do not understand it, and never have. The question has been on my mind almost constantly since that grim day in August 1945 when we heard the news that an atom bomb had wiped out Hiroshima, with hideous casualties. Apart from the terrible tragedy itself, it was at once clear that human intelligence had devised the means to destroy us all—not quite yet, but there could be little doubt that once the genie was out of the bottle, technological developments would carry the threat to the end. I was then a junior counselor in a summer camp. The news was broadcast in the morning. Everyone listened—and then went off to the planned activity—a baseball game, swimming, whatever was scheduled. I couldn't believe it. I was so shocked I just took off into the woods and sat by myself for several hours. I still can't believe it, or understand how that has persisted even as more has been learned about the threats. The same sentiments have been voiced by others, recently by William Perry [former defense secretary], who has ample experience on the inside. He reports that he is doubly terrified by the growing risk of terrible catastrophe, and the failure to be terrified by it.

It was not known in 1945, but the world was then entering into a new geological epoch, the Anthropocene, in which human activity is having a severe impact on the environment that sustains life. Warnings about the potential threat of global warming date back to a 1958 paper by Hans Suess and Roger Revelle, and by the 1970s, concerns were deeply troubling to climate scientists. ExxonMobil scientists were in the forefront of spelling out the severe dangers. That is the background for a crucial decision by ExxonMobil management in 1989, after (and perhaps because) James Hansen had brought the grave threat to public attention. In 1989, management decided to lead the denialist campaign.

That continues to the present. ExxonMobil now proudly declares that it intends to extract and sell all of the 25 billion barrels in its current reserves, while continuing to seek new sources.

Executives are surely aware that this is virtually a death knell for organized human society in any form that we know, but evidently it doesn't matter. Looking away with a vengeance.

The suicidal impulses of the fossil fuel industry have been strongly supported by Republican administrations, by now, under Trump, leaving the US in splendid isolation internationally in not only refusing to participate in international efforts to address this existential threat but in devoting major efforts to accelerate the race to disaster.

It is hard to find proper words to describe what is happening—and the limited attention it receives.

This again raises your question of how we can look away. For ExxonMobil, the explanation is simple enough: the logic of the capitalist market rules—what Joseph Stiglitz twenty-five years ago called the "religion" that markets know best. The same reasoning extends beyond, for example to the major banks that are pouring funds into fossil fuel extraction, including the most dangerous, like Canadian tar sands, surely in full awareness of the consequences.

CEOs face a choice—they can seek to maximize profit and market share, and (consciously) labor to undermine the prospects for life on earth, or they can refuse to do so, and be removed and replaced by someone who will. The problems are not just individual; they are institutional, hence much deeper and harder to overcome.

Something similar holds for media. In the best newspapers there are regular articles by the finest journalists applauding the fracking revolution and the opening of new areas for exploitation, driving the US well ahead of Saudi Arabia in the race to destroy human civilization. Sometimes there are a few words about environmental effects: fracking in Wyoming may harm the water supplies for ranchers. But scarcely if ever is there a word on the effect on the planet—which is, surely, well understood by authors and editors.

In this case, I suppose the explanation is professionalism. The ethics of the profession requires "objectivity": reporting accurately what is going on "within the beltway" and in executive suites, and keeping to the assigned story. To add a word about the lethal broader impact would be "bias," reserved for the opinion pages.

There are countless illustrations, but I think something deeper may be involved, something related to the "religion" that Stiglitz criticized. Worship of markets has many effects. One we see in the origins of the reigning neoliberal faiths. Their origin is in post–World War I Vienna, after the collapse of the trading system within the Hapsburg empire. Ludwig von Mises and his associates fashioned the basic doctrines that were quickly labeled "neoliberalism," based on the principle of "sound economics": markets know best, no interference with them is tolerable.

There are immediate consequences. One is that labor unions, which interfere with flexibility of labor markets, must be destroyed, and social democratic measures must be dismantled. Mises openly welcomed the crushing of the vibrant Austrian unions and social democracy by state violence in 1928, laying the groundwork for Austrian Fascism. Which Mises welcomed as well. He became economic consultant to the proto-Fascist Austrian Chancellor Engelbert Dollfuss, and in his major work, *Liberalism*, explained that "it cannot be denied that Fascism and similar movements aiming at the establishment of dictatorships are full of the best intentions and that their intervention has, for the moment, saved European civilization. The merit that Fascism has thereby won for itself will live on eternally in history."

These themes resonate through the modern neoliberal era. The US has an unusually violent labor history, but the attack on unions gained new force under Reagan with the onset of the neoliberal era. As the business press reported, employers were effectively informed that labor laws would not be enforced, and the US became the only industrial society apart from Apartheid South Africa to tolerate not just scabs, but even "permanent replacement workers." Neoliberal globalization, precarity of employment, and other devices carry the process of destroying organized labor further.

These developments form a core part of the efforts to realize the Thatcherite dictum that "there is no society," only atomized individuals, who face the forces of "sound economics" alone—becoming what Marx called "a sack of potatoes" in his condemnation of the policies of the authoritarian rulers of mid-nineteenth-century Europe.

A sack of potatoes cannot react in any sensible way even to existential crises. Lacking the very bases of deliberative democracy, such as functioning labor unions and other organizations, people have little choice beyond "looking away." What can they hope to do? As Mises memorably explained, echoed by Milton Friedman and others, political democracy is superfluous—indeed an impediment to sound economics: "free competition does all that is needed" in markets that function without interference.

The pathology is not new but can become more severe under supportive social and economic institutions and practices.

Yet, only a couple of decades ago, there was wild celebration among liberal and conservative elites alike about the "end of history," but, even today, there are some who claim that we have made great progress and that the world is better today than it has ever been in the past. Obviously, "the end of history" thesis was something of a Hegelian illusion by staunch defenders of the global capitalist order, but what about the optimism expressed by the likes of Steven Pinker regarding the present? And how can we square the fact that this liberal optimism is not reflected by any

stretch in the politico-ideological currents and trends that are in motion today both inside Western nations but also around the world?

The celebrations were mostly farcical, and have been quietly shelved. On the "great progress," there is serious work. The best I know is Robert Gordon's compelling study of the rise and fall of American growth, which extends beyond the US, though with some modifications. Gordon observes that there was virtually no economic growth for millennia until 1770. Then came a period of slow growth for another century, and then a "special century" from 1870 to 1970, with important inventions ranging from indoor plumbing to electrical grids and transportation, which radically changed human life, with significant progress by many measures.

Since the 1970s the picture is much more mixed. The basis for the contemporary high-tech economy was established in the last decades of the special century, mainly through public investment, adapted to the market in the years that followed. There is currently rapid innovation in frills—new apps for iPhones, etc.—but nothing like the fundamental achievements of the special century. And in the US, there has been stagnation or decline in real wages for nonsupervisory workers and in recent years, increased death rates among working-class, working-age whites, called "deaths of despair" by the economists who have documented these startling facts, Anne Case and Angus Deaton.

There is more to say about other societies. There are numerous complexities of major significance that disappear in unanalyzed statistical tables.

Realism, crystallized intellectually by Niccolò Machiavelli in *The Prince*, has been the guiding principle of nation-states behind their conduct of international relations from the beginning of the modern era, while idealism and morality have been seen as values best left to individuals. Is political realism driving us to the edge of the cliff? And, if so, what should replace the behavioral stance of governments in the 21st century?

The two major doctrines of International Relations Theory are realism and idealism. Each has their advocates, but it's true that the realists have dominated: the world's a tough place, an anarchic system, and states maneuver to establish power and security, making coalitions, offshore balancing, etc.

I think we can put aside idealism—though it has its advocates, including, curiously, one of the founders and leading figures of the modern tough-minded realist school, Hans Morgenthau. In his 1960 work, *The Purpose of American Politics*, Morgenthau argued that the US, unlike other societies, has a "transcendent purpose": establishing peace and freedom at home and indeed everywhere. A serious scholar, Morgenthau recognized that the historical record is radically inconsistent with the "transcendent purpose" of America, but he advised that we should not be misled by the apparent inconsistency. In his words, we should not "confound the abuse of reality with reality itself." Reality is the unachieved "national purpose" revealed by "the evidence of history as our minds reflect it." What actually happened is merely the "abuse of reality." To confound abuse of reality with reality is akin to "the error of atheism, which denies the validity of religion on similar grounds."

For the most part, however, realists adhere to realism, without sentimentality. We might ask, however, how realistic realism is. With a few exceptions—Kenneth Waltz for one—realists tend to ignore the roots of policy in the structure of domestic power; the corporate system is overwhelmingly dominant. This is not the place to review the matter, but I think it can be shown that much is lost by this stance. That's true even of the core notion of realism: security. True, states seek security, but for whom? For the general population? For the systems of power represented by the architects of policy? Such questions cannot be casually put aside.

The two existential crises we have discussed are a case in point. Does the government policy of maximization of the use of fossil fuels contribute to the security of the population? Or of ExxonMobil and its brethren. Does the current military posture of the US—dismantling the INF Treaty instead of negotiating disputes over violations, rushing ahead with hypersonic weapons instead of seeking to bar these insane weapons systems by treaty, and much else—contribute to the security of the population? Or to the component of the corporate manufacturing system in which the US enjoys comparative advantage: destruction. Similar questions arise constantly.

What should replace the prevailing stance is government of, by, and for the people, highlighting their concerns and needs.

The advent of globalization has been interpreted frequently enough in the recent past as leading to the erosion of the nation-state. Today, however, it is globalization that is being challenged, first and foremost by the resurgence of nationalism. Is there a case to be made in defense of globalization? And, by extension, is all nationalism bad and dangerous?

Globalization is neither good nor bad in itself. It depends how it is implemented. Enhancing opportunities for ideas, innovations, aesthetic contributions to disseminate freely is a welcome form of globalization, as well as opportunities for people to circulate freely. The WTO system, designed to set working people in competition with one another while protecting investor rights with an exorbitant patent regime and other devices, is a form of globalization that has many harmful consequences that would be avoided in authentic trade agreements designed along different lines—and it should be borne in mind that much of the substance of the "free trade agreements" is not about free trade or even trade in any meaningful sense.

Same with nationalism. In the hands of the Nazis, it was extremely dangerous. If it is a form of bonding and mutual support within some community, it can be a valuable part of human life.

The current resurgence of nationalism is in large part a reaction to the harsh consequences of neoliberal globalization, with special features such as the erosion of democracy in Europe by transfer of decision-making to the unelected Troika with the northern banks looking over their shoulders. And it can and does take quite ugly forms—the worst, perhaps, the reaction to the so-called "refugee crisis"—more accurately termed a moral crisis of the West, as Pope Francis has indicated.

But none of this is inherent in globalization or nationalism.

In your critiques of US foreign policy, you often refer to the United States as the world's biggest terrorist state. Is there something unique about the United States as an imperial state? And is US imperialism still alive and kicking?

The US is unique in many respects. That includes the opening words of the Declaration of Independence, "We the People," a revolutionary idea, however flawed in execution. It is also a rare country that has been at war almost without a break from its first moment. One of the motives for the American Revolution was to eliminate the barrier to expansion into "Indian country" imposed by the British. With that overcome, the new nation set forth on wars against the Indian nations that inhabited what became the national territory; wars of "extermination," as the most prominent figures recognized, notably John Quincy Adams, the architect of Manifest Destiny. Meanwhile, half of Mexico was conquered in what General Ulysses S. Grant, later president, called one of the most "wicked wars" in history.

There is no need to review the record of interventions, subversion, and violence, particularly since World War II, which established the US in a position of global dominance with no historical precedent. The record includes the worst crime of the postwar period, the assault on Indochina, and the worst crime of this millennium, the invasion of Iraq.

Like most terms of political discourse, "imperialism" is a contested notion. Whatever term we want to use, the US is alone in having hundreds of military bases and troops operating over much of the world. It is also unique in its willingness and ability to impose brutal sanctions designed to punish the people of states designated as enemies. And its market power and dominance of the international financial system provide these sanctions with extraterritorial reach, compelling even powerful states to join in, however unwillingly.

The most dramatic case is Cuba, where US sanctions are strongly opposed by the entire world, to no avail. The vote against these sanctions was 189-2, US and Israel, in the latest UNGA [United Nations General Assembly] condemnation. The sanctions have been in place for almost sixty years, harshly punishing Cubans for what the State Department called "successful defiance" of the US. Trump's sanctions on Venezuela and have turned a humanitarian crisis into a catastrophe, according to the leading economist of the opposition, Francisco Rodríguez. His sanctions on Iran are quite explicitly designed to destroy the economy and punish the population.

This is no innovation. Clinton's sanctions on Iraq (joined by Blair) were so destructive that each of the distinguished international diplomats who administered the "oil for food" program resigned in protest, charging that the sanctions were "genocidal." The second, Hans-Christof von Sponeck, published a detailed and incisive book about the impact of the sanctions (*A Different Kind of War*). It has been under a virtual ban. Too revealing, perhaps.

The brutal sanctions punished the population and devastated the society, but strengthened the tyrant, compelling people to rely on his rationing system for survival, possibly saving him from overthrow from within, as happened to a string of similar figures. That's quite standard. The same is reportedly true in Iran today.

It could be argued that the sanctions violate the Geneva Conventions, which condemn "collective punishment" as a war crime, but legalistic shenanigans can get around that.

The US no longer has the capacity it once did to overthrow governments at will or to invade other countries, but it has ample means of coercion and domination, call it "imperialism" or not.

Why is the United States the only major country in the world displaying consistently an aversion to international human rights treaties, which include, among many others, the Convention on the Elimination of all Forms of Discrimination Against Women (CEDAW)?

The US almost never ratifies international conventions, and in the few cases where it does, it is with reservations that exclude the US. That's even true of the Genocide Convention, which the US finally did ratify after many years, exempting itself. The issue arose in 1999, when Yugoslavia brought a charge of war crimes to the ICJ [International Court of Justice] against NATO. One of the charges was "genocide." The US therefore rejected World Court jurisdiction on the grounds that it was not subject to the Genocide Convention, and the Court agreed—agreeing, in effect, that the US is entitled to carry out genocide with impunity.

It might be noted that the US is currently alone (along with China and Taiwan) in rejecting a World Court decision, namely, the 1986 Court judgment ordering the US to terminate its "unlawful use of force" against Nicaragua and to pay substantial reparations. Washington's rejection of the court decision was applauded by the liberal media on the grounds that the court was a "hostile forum" (*New York Times*), so its decisions don't matter. A few years earlier the court had been a stern arbiter of justice when it ruled in favor of the US in a case against Iran.

The US also has laws authorizing the executive to use force to "rescue" any American brought to the Hague—sometimes called in Europe "the Hague Invasion Act." Recently it revoked the visa of the chief prosecutor of the ICC [International Criminal Court] for daring to consider inquiring into US actions in Afghanistan. It goes on.

Why? It's called "power," and a population that tolerates it—and for the most part probably doesn't even know about it.

Since the Nuremberg trials between 1945 and 1949, the world has witnessed many war crimes and crimes against humanity that have gone unpunished, and interestingly enough, some of the big powers (US, China, and Russia) have refused to support the International Criminal Court, which, among other things, can prosecute individuals for war crimes. In that context, does the power to hold leaders responsible for unjust wars, crimes against humanity, and crimes of aggression hold promise in the international order of today?

That depends on whether states will accept jurisdiction. Sometimes they do. The NATO powers (except for the US) accepted ICJ jurisdiction in the Yugoslavia case, for example—presumably because they took for granted that the court would never accept the Yugoslavian pleas, even when they were valid, as in the case of the targeted destruction of a TV station, killing sixteen journalists. In the more free and democratic states, populations could, in principle, decide that their governments should obey international law, but that is a matter of raising the level of civilization.

John Bolton and other ultranationalists, and many others, argue that the US must not abandon its sovereignty to international institutions and international law. They are therefore arguing that US leaders should violate the Constitution, which declares that valid treaties are the supreme law of the land. That includes in particular the UN Charter, the foundation of modern international law, established under US auspices.

Trump's "Economic Boom" Is a Sham

C. J. POLYCHRONIOU: Noam, I want to start by asking you to reflect on Trump's political posturing and leadership style and explain to us how this apparently "irrational" president continues to enjoy unquestionable support among nearly half of all voters and has managed to turn the GOP into his own fiefdom.

Noam Chomsky: Whatever one thinks of Trump, he is a highly skilled politician, with a good sense of how to gain popular approval, even virtual worship in some circles. His job approval just passed 50 percent for the first time, according to the latest Zogby poll.

He certainly has taken control of the GOP, to quite a remarkable extent. He's been very successful with his two constituencies: the primary one, wealth and corporate power; and the voting base, relatively affluent fairly generally, including a large bloc of Christian evangelicals, rural whites, farmers, workers who have faith in his promises to bring back jobs, and a collection of others, some not too admirable.

It's clear why the primary constituency is mostly delighted. Corporate profits are booming. Wealth continues to be concentrated in very few hands. Trump's administration is lavishing them with gifts, including the tax bill, the main legislative achievement; across-the-board deregulation; and rapidly increasing fossil fuel production. He and McConnell—in many ways the evil genius of the administration—are packing the judiciary with reactionaries, guaranteeing the interests of the corporate sector and private wealth even after these "glory days" are past. They don't like his trade wars, which are causing disruption of global supply chains, but so far at least that's outweighed by his dedicated service to their welfare.

To keep the rest in line is sometimes easy, among them the Christian right, white supremacists, ultranationalists, and xenophobes, and those in terror of "hordes" of immigrants. It is easy to throw them occasional chunks of red meat. But sometimes maintaining their allegiance takes the kind of demagoguery at which he is expert. Thus, many who are understandably aggrieved by the economic policies of the neoliberal years still seem to feel that he's the one person standing up for them by shaking his fist at those they blame for taking away their jobs: immigrants and "the scheming Chinese," primarily.

Numerous press reports reveal how the scam works. Thus, in the *New York Times*, Patricia Cohen investigates the attitude of owners of large farms to Trump's trade wars, which sharply cut their exports to China and cause severe financial hardships. In general, she finds, they continue to support the president. "I get why he's doing it," her major informant says: "America has been bullied" by China. And if the trade war persists through the 2020 election, "I would be OK with that." He's sure that Trump will do everything possible to help. Furthermore, "It makes me feel really good to hear Trump say farmers are important to this country. That's what makes me want to stick with the president."

Shaking a fist at the "Yellow Peril" and a little sweet talk carry the day, helped by $16 billion to compensate for export losses.

The gift is largely paid by a new hidden tax on the general public. Tariffs are in effect a tax on consumers (contrary to Trump's pretenses about China paying for them). The New York Fed estimates the cost to consumers at $1.6 billion annually, a tax of $831 for the average American household. Hence, Trump's tariffs tax the general public to maintain the loyalty of a prime constituency.

With regard to immigrants, while there may be some cases where they take jobs from US citizens, in general that is not the case (and decent wages for all wouldn't exactly hurt). On the contrary, many studies indicate that immigrants improve the economy, and they commonly take jobs that US citizens don't want.

The case of China is more interesting. It's quite true that huge numbers of jobs have fled to China, but who is responsible for that? China? Is China holding a gun to the heads of Apple, GM, IBM, GE…and forcing them to ship jobs to China? One can't even say that it's the fault of the managers of the corporations. Their responsibility, in fact legal obligation, is to make profits for shareholders, and that purpose is served by shifting jobs to China, Mexico, Vietnam, Bangladesh….

Those who object to these practices should be demanding that such decisions should not be in the hands of management and the board of directors, but rather in the hands of those who actually do the work of the enterprise, as democratic principle might suggest. Perhaps along the lines of a 19th century writer whose initials are K.M. But somehow one doesn't see this interesting idea explored in mainstream commentary. Passing strange.

Trump is taking all credit for the current state of the economy, which includes a historically low rate of unemployment. First, exactly what sort of economic policies has Trump implemented since coming to office that can explain the present economic boom, and, second, how really sound is the current state of the economy?

To begin with, there is reason for caution about the low rate of unemployment. In the (very good) economics journal *Challenge*, relying on Bureau of Labor Statistics figures, economist John Komlos estimates that "the real unemployment rate in the fall of 2018 was closer to 7.4 percent of the labor force. Among those without a high school diploma, it was twice as high," reaching 28 percent unemployed among African Americans. The prime reason for the discrepancy in figures—all from the same government sources—is the significant decline in labor force participation. Many have dropped out of the labor force in their prime years. The high actual unemployment rate, Komlos plausibly suggests, is part of the reason why "there is so much despair in the society."

Gallup polls regularly measure stress, worry, and anger. The US ranks high by these measures, reaching new highs in 2018, by now even higher than during the Great Recession. In reported stress levels, the US has "one of the highest rates out of the 143 countries studied and it beat the global average (35 percent) by a full 20 percentage points." The US is even above Venezuela in its current distress.

The dire emotional state of Americans is illustrated dramatically by the "deaths of despair" (death by suicide, drugs, and alcohol) documented by Anne Case and Angus Deaton among working-class whites; tellingly, those "who would have entered the market starting in the early 1980s," when the neoliberal assault took off. The deaths of despair are estimated at 150,000 a year, contributing to the decline in life expectancy in the US for the past two years, the first time since World War I and the 1918 flu pandemic—a phenomenon unprecedented in developed societies.

All of this is happening in the most powerful state in world history, with extraordinary advantages not approached anywhere. Worth contemplating.

"The alleged full employment," Komlos writes, "is a statistical mirage designed to hide the real pain in the labor market," exacerbated by wage stagnation for forty years and actual decline: "Real median household incomes have been declining for every educational group since the turn of the twenty-first century," for those without a college degree by 17 percent, continuing the stagnation or decline in real hourly wages since the '80s. Add to this Alan Greenspan's "greater worker insecurity," the foundation of his success in economic management as he boasted to Congress, and we get a more realistic picture than what is in the headlines, and an explanation for the general despair. Much the same is true throughout the regions afflicted by the neoliberal/austerity plague, though deaths of despair seem to be an American phenomenon.

The "economic boom" is a continuation of the slow recovery that began under Obama. The McConnell-Ryan Congress restricted a needed government stimulus during the Obama years, wailing about deficits, but as usual, when they took office it turned out that "Reagan taught us that deficits don't matter" (says Dick Cheney) when Republicans create them. Trump's one legislative achievement, the tax giveaway to the rich and corporate sector, provided a stimulus to the economy (without the promised investment). A Brookings Institution study by Robert Barro and Jason Furman (conservative, liberal) estimated that the boost of Trump's tax cut law to short-term GDP growth was 1.1 percent for the first quarter of 2019, accounting for the increase from the consensus expectation of 2 percent. The tax cut, of course, exploded the deficit, which can now provide a pretext for cutting social spending.

The continuing increase in employment has led to a slight increase in wages, with opportunities for those at the lower end of the income scale, but it doesn't come close to making up what has been lost during the period of stagnation from the early '80s.

Recent data indicates that the counties that voted for Donald Trump have experienced more job growth than the counties that voted for Hillary Clinton. What can explain this discrepancy?

There's a good analysis in Bloomberg news. Jobs are growing slightly faster in Trump-supporting rural and exurban counties than in the urban, mostly Clinton counties. At the same time, real wages declined slightly in Trump counties and increased slightly in Clinton counties, in both cases a decline from the Obama years. Their analysis, which doesn't include the effect of his recent trade wars, attributes the growth mainly to expansion of energy production, manufacturing (in part energy-related), and truck driving.

Trump's tariff wars against China are escalating, even though US economic interests may suffer more than those of China. What is really behind Trump's trade wars with China and even with the EU, which the "tariff man" has called "a brutal trading partner"? Is it the vision of MAGA, or pure politics?

Both national economies will suffer, very likely the weaker party (China) more so. But as always, the framework of national conflict obscures a good deal. The estimated $6 trillion cost of the "war on terror" re-declared by President Bush in 2001 (renewing Reagan's war on terror of twenty years earlier) is borne in varying ways among the population, and the same is true of the trade wars. One illustration has already been mentioned: higher taxes to keep Trump's constituency in line.

It's of considerable interest to explore the justification for the trade war, to inquire into just how "naïve America has been bullied by China." I've already discussed China's responsibility for job loss. Other complaints have to do with their unfair economic practices, such as targeting funds to specific industries—something we'd never dream of doing, and would not have stooped to in earlier years. That aside, why is this a complaint, rather than a cry of joy? Ultranationalist True Believers should be celebrating China's stupidity, which, according to received free market doctrine should be harming their economy, hence contributing to US economic power.

As an aside, it should be noted that US economic power is in fact astonishing. In recent articles and an important forthcoming book titled *American Power Globalized: Rethinking National Power in the Age of Globalization*, international economist Sean Kenji Starrs argues persuasively that in the recent years of globalization, national accounts mean much less than they used to. A more realistic estimate of economic power is the share of global wealth owned by nationally based multinational corporations. For the US, that comes to the staggering figure of about half of world wealth, more than US national economic power at its height after World War II. How this will be affected by Trump's wrecking ball, with its possibly complex effects on global supply chains, remains to be seen. Again, this colossal wealth, of course, does not devolve to the population.

Another charge is that China steals US technology by forcing firms to hand over secrets as a condition on investment (already dealt with) and by violating World Trade Organization rules on intellectual property (TRIPS). Again, other questions arise, discussed particularly by economist Dean Baker for many years. Putting aside the legitimacy of these highly protectionist devices, which raise patent protection far beyond the historical norm, we can ask who gains and who loses if, say, China uses discoveries in US research labs to produce cheaper drugs than the corporations that have gained the patents, or to develop a better alternative to the Windows operating system? American consumers gain, while Big Pharma's huge profits are somewhat reduced and Bill Gates might decline slightly in the ranks of richest men in the world.

More generally, one might ask, what right does the US have to try to impede Chinese development, as generally assumed without argument? Or even to impose sanctions? That the Chinese state is harsh, brutal, and oppressive is not in doubt. China's "reeducation camps" for perhaps a million Uyghurs, which may well be the largest mass incarceration of a racial or religious group since the Holocaust, is surely a major crime, meriting harsh condemnation. Is it a worse crime than the imprisonment of 2 million Palestinians in "the world's largest open-air prison" in Gaza, Israel's favorite punching bag, which is soon to become unlivable, international monitors estimate? Why then does the former merit US sanctions, while the latter is lavishly funded by Washington?

A rhetorical question of course, but one worth raising nevertheless.

It seems that more and more Democrats may be warming up to the idea of an impeachment. Is this a good idea? My personal view is that such a course of action will only serve to increase Trump's popularity among his base, and maybe even beyond.

I agree. Charges of impeachment go to the Senate for trial. Trump's lock on the Republican majority should be enough to clear him of any charges. The effect will then be much like that of the Mueller investigation. He will claim to have been proven innocent of the charges, which he will depict as a malicious and underhanded effort by the Democrats and the Deep State to silence the Tribune of the People, behavior that may even be treasonous, as he is now intimating with regard to the Mueller investigation. His base will be energized, if not infuriated, by what these "traitors" are trying to do to their defender. It's a losing effort for the Democrats, I think, just as their laser-like focus on Mueller and "Russiagate" has proven to be—not a great surprise.

Ocasio-Cortez and Other Newcomers Are Rousing the Multitudes

C. J. POLYCHRONIOU: After thirty-five days of a partial government shutdown, Trump signed a three-week funding bill but without securing money for the border wall. Leaving aside for the moment the surrealist nature of contemporary US political life, do you detect some hidden political strategy behind Trump's funding conflict over the border wall with the Democrats?

NOAM CHOMSKY: There's a political strategy, but I'm not convinced that it's hidden. With Trump, everything is pretty much on the surface. There have been constant efforts by political analysts to discern some deep geostrategic or sociopolitical thinking behind his performances, but they seem to me unconvincing. What he does seems readily explained simply on the well-grounded assumption that his doctrine is simple: ME!

Trump understands that he has a primary constituency—extreme wealth and corporate power—and that he has to serve its interests or he's finished. That task has largely been assigned to the Ryans and McConnells, who have performed it admirably. Profits are skyrocketing, real wages are barely increasing despite low unemployment, regulations that might limit greed (and help mere people) are being dismantled, and the one legislative achievement—the tax scam—put lots of dollars in the right pockets and created a deficit that can be used as a pretext to undermine benefits. All is working smoothly—with analogues worldwide.

But Trump must maintain enough of a voting base to stay in power. That requires posturing as the defender of the ordinary guy against hated "elites" (always suppressing the true "masters of mankind," to borrow Adam Smith's phrase for the merchants and manufacturers who were "the principal architects" of policy). This act is helped along by such figures as Rush Limbaugh, who instructs his tens of millions of followers that they should beware of "the four corners of deceit: government, academia, science and media," institutions that "are now corrupt and exist by virtue of deceit." So, he argues, just listen to ME.

Meanwhile, Trump must rise to the defense of the masses from awesome threats, chief among them now the hordes of "rapists," "murderers," and "Islamic terrorists" he says are being mobilized down south to storm across the border and slaughter decent, law-abiding, white Christian Americans. We must therefore have a "beautiful wall"—which *they* will pay for. Trump promised that, and to back down would not only betray the trembling masses but also be a defeat, which his ego cannot tolerate.

The game is not really new. After all, the revered Ronald Reagan bravely donned his cowboy uniform and declared a National Emergency to protect the country from the Nicaraguan army, supposedly poised to destroy us all only two days' drive from Harlingen, Texas. Trump is only carrying it further, helped by the fading of such infantile notions as "truth"—or "false realities," to borrow Jared Kushner's innovation. Former secretary of state Dean Acheson's admonition that policy makers must be "clearer than truth" has long passed into obsolescence. They can do far better in the atmosphere of "alternative facts" for those liberated from the four pillars of deceit.

I doubt that there is any deeper political strategy.

Furthermore, such performances are rather natural, perhaps even necessary. As both parties have drifted to the right during the neoliberal assault on the population, the Democrats abandoned the working class and became pretty much what used to be called "moderate Republicans" (something that is beginning to change now in promising ways) while Republicans climbed so deeply into the pockets of the super-rich and corporate power that it became impossible for them to gain anywhere near enough votes on their actual policies. Antics of the Trump style fit the requirements, along with a variety of measures to suppress voting and increased reliance on the many regressive aspects of the constitutional system, which by now make it possible for a small minority of white Christian traditional rural older citizens to have effective control of the government. The tendency is increasing and may soon lead to a major political crisis since it is virtually ineradicable given the structure of the Senate, designed by the Framers so that the small states would ratify the mostly unpopular federal Constitution. A topic for another day.

Responding to Alexandria Ocasio-Cortez's call for measures to tackle climate change, press secretary Sarah Huckabee Sanders made the incredible statement that climate change should be left to God. Don't you find it utterly mysterious and indeed dangerous that such thinking still prevails among US public officials in the 21st century? And, really, how well do you think that such messages resonate with the American public today?

Sanders's insight is not new. She is in good company. After all, the former chair of the Senate Committee on Environment and Public Works, James Inhofe, condemned efforts to address global warming as sacrilege: "God's still up there," he proclaimed, and "the arrogance of people to think that we, human beings, would be able to change what He is doing in the climate is to me outrageous." It seems to work, at least in Oklahoma, where the senior senator has been in office since 1994. Doubtless well beyond Oklahoma, in a society with fundamentalist religious commitments that are far beyond the norm.

Yes, mysterious and dangerous—as is the fact that half of Republicans deny that global warming is even taking place, and of the rest, barely more than half think that humans have some responsibility for it. But there's good news too. Trump's new acting administrator of the EPA, former coal industry lobbyist Andrew Wheeler, agrees that global warming is probably happening—a problem he considers to be an "eight or nine" on a one-to-ten scale of concern, he informed Congress at his confirmation hearings.

Venezuela seems to be in the throes of a civil war. The US backs Juan Guaidó as interim president, in turn forcing Nicolás Maduro to consider

expelling US diplomats, a decision he eventually backed away from, all while the leaders of China, Russia, and Turkey slam Trump's stance in Venezuela. First, what's your assessment of what's happening in Venezuela, and, second, why is it that much of the left worldwide continues to support Maduro when it is obvious that he has been a complete disaster?

Maduro has been a disaster, and the best the opposition has to offer is the self-declared president Juan Guaidó. About him little is known, apart from his great admiration for the neofascist Brazilian president Jair Bolsonaro, whom Guaidó praised for his commitment to "democracy [and] human rights," as illustrated, for example, by his criticism of Brazil's military dictatorship—because it . . . didn't murder 30,000 people as in neighboring Argentina, the worst of the vicious military dictatorships that swept across South America from the '60s.

The roots of the Venezuelan disaster go back to failures of the Chávez administration, including its failure to diversify the economy, which is still almost entirely reliant on oil export. Venezuelan opposition economist Francisco Rodríguez, former chief Andean economist for the Bank of America, notes the failure of the government to set aside reserves during the period of high oil prices so it would not be at the mercy of international financial markets when prices dropped sharply in 2014. Venezuela has been blocked from access to credit by harsh US sanctions, which have exacerbated the effects of what Rodríguez describes as the "atrocious" mismanagement of the economy under Maduro. Writing in *Foreign Policy*, Rodríguez observes that the policy of "starving the Venezuelan economy of its foreign currency earnings risks turning the country's current humanitarian crisis into a full-blown humanitarian catastrophe." Arguably, that is the purpose, following the Nixon-Kissinger script of "making the economy scream" to undermine the Allende regime. (That was the soft track; the hard track, soon implemented, was brutal military dictatorship.)

The drift toward civil war, with outside interference, is all too apparent. There is still room for negotiations among the contending parties, but it diminishes daily as the crisis deepens. Maduro is digging in and Washington is intensifying its intervention, imposing new sanctions and selecting the egregious Elliott Abrams to join Bolton and Pompeo in what has been called "Trump's axis of evil." If skeletons can shudder, many must be doing so in the Central American countries that Abrams helped to ravage during Reagan's terrorist wars.

Israel and Iran seem to be moving ever further closer toward a full-blown war. Why are they clashing in Syria?

Iran joined Russia in ensuring Assad's victory in Syria, along with Iran's Lebanese ally Hezbollah. Israel has been bombing Syria regularly. Four months ago the IDF reported over two hundred strikes against Iranian targets since 2017, and they have been increasing since.

Israel, of course, has overwhelming military dominance in the Middle East, even apart from its close alliance with the US, which lavishly funds its military with the most advanced weapons in the US arsenal and even uses Israel to pre-position US weapons. And, of course, Israel is the region's sole nuclear power, the reason why Washington has regularly blocked international efforts, led by the Arab states and Iran, to establish a nuclear weapons-free zone (furthermore, WMD-free) in the Middle East. That would end any imagined Iran nuclear threat, but it is unacceptable because the primary US client state in the region would have to open its nuclear arsenal to inspection, and those who regard US law as having some force would have to stanch the flood of military support for Israel.

Iran is not under US control and is therefore an enemy. Furthermore, the US and Israel recognize that Iran is a deterrent to their free resort to force in the region. The same is true of Hezbollah, whose Iranian-supplied missiles target large parts of Israel. The US and Israel have been threatening to attack Iran for years ("all options are open") in radical violation of the UN Charter (hence the US Constitution), but that is a matter of no concern for lawless states with overwhelming power. And Trump has, of course, escalated the confrontation by withdrawing from the Iran nuclear agreement. An actual invasion of Iran would be too costly and dangerous, but the US-Israel might consider attacking from a distance after somehow neutralizing Hezbollah (which would mean destroying much of Lebanon). The consequences could be devastating.

In Davos, the multibillionaires expressed annoyance at and even fear of the presence of radical Democrats in the US Congress and their talk of "soaking the rich" on taxes. Has a global financial oligarchy replaced democracy in today's advanced capitalist world?

It's impossible to replace something that has never really existed, but it's true that the partial democracies of the West have been undermined further by the financialization of the international economy during the neoliberal years. That's a large part of the reason for the bitterness, anger, and resentment, mislabeled "populism," that is shaking the foundations of the Western democracies, where the centrist political parties that have run the political system are crumbling in election after election.

Many analysts have to account for the rise of such "populism" throughout the neoliberal capitalist world on the basis of psychic disorders—in one respected version, impulses "deep in our psyches and bodies beyond matters of fact: physical pain, fear of the future, a sense of our own mortality." It is, however, not really necessary to appeal to an epidemic of irrationality and "emotional appeals" somehow spreading over the domains subjected to the neoliberal assault of the past generation, including the enormous growth of largely predatory financial institutions with its deleterious impact on democratic systems of governance.

Fear that the "rascal multitude" will threaten the property of the self-designated "men of best quality" traces back to the first modern democratic revolution in 17th century England, and was a major concern of the Framers of the US Constitution in its successor a century later. It reappears constantly when there is even a minor threat to overwhelming power, as in the famous "Powell Memorandum" of 1971, which warned that the world is practically coming to an end because of the slight infringement on overwhelming business domination of the society. The influential manifesto, sent to the US Chamber of Commerce, helped set off the harsh counterattack in the years since.

It's not surprising that these fears are surfacing in Davos as a few young Democratic representatives are arousing the rascal multitude again.

For many years, a considerable majority of the US population has favored higher taxes on the rich, while they regularly decline. And now, a few recently elected members of Congress are advocating what the public wants, most vocally Alexandria Ocasio-Cortez, who even went so far as to suggest tax rates at a level regarded as optimal for the economy by the most prominent specialists (Nobel laureate Peter Diamond, Emmanuel Saez, among others). Scandalous indeed.

What else can one expect when twenty-six people now have as much wealth as half the world's population, according to the latest of the regular Oxfam reports on inequality?

No wonder the "masters of mankind" are trembling.

Moral Depravity Defines US Politics

C. J. POLYCHRONIOU: Noam, with people still arguing about winners and losers from the 2018 midterm elections (and there is clearly a lot to say about what those elections mean), what do you consider to be the most striking features of the latest manifestation of American democracy in action?

NOAM CHOMSKY: The most striking features are brutally clear.

Humanity faces two imminent existential threats—environmental catastrophe and nuclear war. These were virtually ignored in the campaign rhetoric and general coverage. There was plenty of criticism of the Trump administration, but scarcely a word about by far the most ominous positions the administration has taken: increasing the already dire threat of nuclear war, and racing to destroy the physical environment that organized human society needs in order to survive.

These are the most critical and urgent questions that have arisen in all of human history. The fact that they scarcely arose in the campaign is truly stunning, and carries some important, if unpleasant, lessons about our moral and intellectual culture.

To be sure, not everyone was ignoring these matters. They were front and center for those who are constantly vigilant in their bitter class war to preserve their immense power and privilege. Several states had important ballot initiatives addressing the impending environmental catastrophe. The fossil fuel industry spent huge, sometimes record-breaking, sums to defeat the initiatives—including a carbon tax in the mostly Democratic state of Washington—and mostly succeeded.

We should recognize that these are extraordinary crimes against humanity. They proceed with little notice.

The Democrats helped defeat these critically important initiatives by ignoring them. They scarcely mentioned them "in digital or TV ads, in their campaign literature or on social media," a *New York Times* survey found. Nor, of course, were they mentioned by the Republicans, whose leadership is dedicated to driving humanity off the cliff as soon as possible—in full knowledge of what they are doing, as easily demonstrated.

The *Times* article goes on to explain that, "environmental activists and political scientists say it is a reflection of the issue's perpetual low ranking among voters, even Democratic voters, and of the intense polarization along party lines that has developed around global warming." The article failed to add that this assessment is an incredible indictment of the country and its political, social, economic, and media institutions, all of which, so the assessment claims, have sunk to such a level of depravity that the question of whether organized human society can survive in any minimally tolerable form, in the near future, is of little consequence.

Whether that unspoken indictment is correct, we cannot be sure. It is perhaps of some significance that one Democratic candidate, Sean Casten, flipped a Republican district while making impending climate disaster the centerpiece of his campaign.

There is plenty of competition for moral depravity in the current remarkable moment of human history. Perhaps the prize goes to a bureaucracy, maybe in honor of Kafka: Trump's National Highway Traffic Safety Administration. Right in the midst of the campaign, it produced a detailed study calling for an end to regulations on emissions, with a rational argument—extrapolating current trends, it turns out that by the end of the century the game will be over. Automotive emissions don't contribute very much to the catastrophe, so there isn't any point trying to limit them.

In brief, let's rob while the planet burns, putting poor Nero in the shadows.

This surely qualifies as a contender for the most evil document in history. Again, not an issue in the campaign.

There have been many monsters in the past, but it would be hard to find one who was dedicated to undermining the prospects for survival of organized human society, in the immediate future to put a few more dollars in overstuffed pockets.

It's hard to find words to describe what is happening before our eyes.

The same is true of the second truly existential threat, nuclear war. A few weeks before the election, Trump announced that the US is withdrawing from the Intermediate-Range Nuclear Forces Treaty (INF), which eliminated short-range missiles deployed in Western Europe and Russia—extremely hazardous weapons, which have only a few minutes flight-time to Moscow, posing a decapitation threat, a sudden attack that would destroy any possibility of response. That, of course, sharply increases the danger of a nuclear response to warnings generated by automated systems that have often failed in the past.

Anyone familiar with the record knows that it's a virtual miracle that we have so far avoided terminal nuclear war. The threat, which was already grave, was heightened by the Trump nuclear posture review authorizing new destabilizing weapons and lowering the threshold for nuclear attack. This latest move increases the threat further. Scarcely a mention on the campaign trail or in coverage.

The US is withdrawing from the treaty on the grounds that China is not a partner and that the Russians have violated it. China, in turn, claims that the US has violated the treaty. It's plain how to address these problems—through inspections and diplomacy, neither of which has been attempted. Rather, let's just blithely increase the threat of total destruction. And let's ignore all of this in the vast outpourings during the political campaign.

Again, we have to ask some serious questions about the prevailing moral and intellectual culture—and about the urgency of providing remedies, very soon.

Let's put aside what are merely the most significant questions in human history, and turn to what is within the realm of discussion.

A striking fact about the election is that it once again demonstrated the failure of the Democratic Party as a whole to deal with issues that matter to working people. While working-class people of color largely supported the Democratic Party in 2018, even more than before, the party lost the non-college-educated white population. What's more, it seems to be of little concern, at least to Democratic Party leaders, or the "Wall Street Democrats" as they are sometimes called. They were exultant about their successes in the affluent suburbs, where normally Republican voters were disgusted by Trump's vulgarity. Whether they come naturally or are feigned, Trump's antics help keep his white working-class constituency in line while his party stabs them in the back at every turn and serves its real constituency, great wealth and corporate power, with impressive dedication.

The betrayal of working-class America could hardly be clearer, though fortunately, some are breaking free of the treachery. One positive feature of the midterms was the success of a diverse group of young progressive candidates, mostly women—a tribute to the popular activism of recent years, and a hopeful sign for the future, if this trend can expand and flourish.

On the surface, it seems that Trump's success with much of the voting constituency can be attributed to racist and xenophobic appeals, particularly concerning the imminent threat of "invasion" by hordes of terrorists and criminals approaching our borders. Recall that he focused his tantrums on this up to the election, then dropped the topic when it was no longer needed to rally the faithful.

Few seem to have recalled that Trump was pulling a leaf from Reagan's playbook. As noted, In 1985, our intrepid leader strapped on his cowboy boots and declared a national emergency because Nicaraguan troops were a two days' drive from Harlingen, Texas—and people didn't collapse in laughter. Trump made a similar move in warning that if people fleeing from misery and oppression (misery and oppression for which we are largely responsible) reach our borders they'll try to kill us all. Heavily armed militias traveled to the border to back up the thousands of troops deployed to defend us. This seems to have worked; surveys report that people voted for Trump because he was the candidate that could save us from destruction by these criminal hordes. That also carries some lessons.

But when we ask why Trump's strategy works, we find something deeper, which extends pretty much worldwide, with particularities from place to place. In conditions of economic distress, a sense of hopelessness, justified contempt for institutions, and understandable anger and resentment about what is being done to them, people can become easy prey to demagogues who direct their anger toward scapegoats, typically those even more vulnerable, and who foster the symptoms that tend to rise to the surface under such circumstances. That's been happening, worldwide. We see it in election after election in many countries, and in other ways.

In the US, working-class people have suffered forty years of stagnation while wealth concentrates in very few hands, leading to staggering inequality. The Democrats have ignored all this, and worse, the party has carried forward the neoliberal policies that took off with Reagan and Thatcher and have imposed these consequences, by design. And for the designers, the neoliberal programs have been brilliantly successful, in ways that we need not review here.

Despite low unemployment, wage growth, after a rise in 2014–15, is now barely keeping up with inflation while corporate profits are skyrocketing, particularly for the predatory financial institutions; they emerged from the crisis for which they were responsible even richer and more powerful than before. A side effect is that the country's wealth is being shifted from R&D, innovation, and product development, to financial transactions in the interests of the very rich. Fine for them, but disastrous for the health and future of the society.

The concentration of wealth and enhancement of corporate power translate automatically to decline of democracy. Research in academic political science has revealed that a large majority of voters are literally disenfranchised, in that their own representatives pay no attention to their wishes but pay heed to the demands of the donor class. It is furthermore well established that elections are pretty much bought; electability, hence policy, is predictable with remarkable precision from the single variable of campaign spending, both for the executive and Congress. Thomas Ferguson's work is particularly revealing, going far back and including the 2016 election. And that is a bare beginning. Legislation is commonly shaped, even written, by corporate lobbyists, while representatives who sign it have their eyes on funding for the next election.

The midterms highlighted other ominous developments. The Republicans increased their Senate majority—with barely 40 percent of the votes cast. Right now, sixty senators are elected by states with 25 percent of the population, which means some 15 percent of the vote (mostly rural, white, religious, skeptical of science, heavily armed). And the tendency is increasing. It's hard to see how some form of civil conflict can be avoided unless the Democrats reverse course sharply and become a political party that doesn't simply abandon the working class to its bitter class enemy, as they have done for forty years.

How do we explain the fact that while US politics seems nastier, more polarized, and more divided than any other time in recent history, both parties stay away from addressing the most critical issues facing the country and the world at large?

In 1895, the highly successful campaign manager Mark Hanna famously said: "There are two things that are important in politics. The first is *money,* and I can't remember what the second one is."

Those who control the wealth of the country have their own priorities, primarily self-enrichment and enhancement of decision-making power. And these are the priorities that prevail in a neoliberal democracy with the annoying public dismissed to the back rooms where they belong.

The CEOs of major banks surely understand the extraordinary threat of environmental catastrophe but are increasing investment in fossil fuels because that's where the money is. Like the energy corporations, they are hardly eager to support candidates warning of the serious crimes they are committing. Lockheed-Martin and its cohorts are quite happy to see vast increases in the military budget and are surely delighted with such declarations as the Trump administration's new National Defense Strategy, just released by the US Institute of Peace (lacking a sense of irony, the bureaucracy is quite happy to caricature Orwell).

This somber document warns that our dangerously depleted military, which almost overwhelms the rest of the world combined, might not be able to prevail in a two-front war against Russia and China. Of course, neither military industry nor the distinguished authors of the report believe that such a war could even be fought without terminal destruction, but it's a great way to siphon taxpayer dollars away from absurdities like health and education and into the deserving pockets of the captains of industry and finance.

Not many political figures will dare to dismiss such awesome threats to our security.

As for the nastiness, it's largely a result of the drift to the right of both parties during the neoliberal years, the Democrats becoming what used to be called "moderate Republicans" (or often worse) and the Republicans drifting off the spectrum, and their devotion to wealth and corporate power is so extreme that they cannot possibly win elections on their actual policies. They have therefore been compelled to mobilize voting constituencies on "cultural issues," diverting attention away from actual policies. To keep them in line, it's natural for the leadership to demonize the political opposition as not merely wrong but intent on demolishing their most deeply held values—and for the latter to resort to contempt for the "deplorables." Soon antagonisms degenerate to warfare.

There are many illustrations of how the Republican leadership has sought to organize a voting constituency, some of which we've discussed before. One revealing case is abortion rights. In the '60s, the Republican Party was strongly pro-choice, including the leadership (Reagan, Ford, George H. W. Bush, and others). Same with voters. In 1972, two-thirds of Republicans believed abortion to be a private matter, and that the government should have no role in it.

Nixon and his cohorts realized that they could attract the Catholic vote, traditionally Democratic, by adopting an anti-abortion plank. Later in the '70s, evangelicals began to organize for political action. Among their demands was maintaining segregated schools. Republican operative Paul Weyrich recognized an opportunity. An open call for segregated schools wouldn't work, but if the Republican Party pretended to oppose abortion, it could pick up the huge evangelical vote, now a core part of Trump's voting base. The leadership accordingly shifted to passionate "pro-life" advocates, including those who it is sometimes believed had some character and honesty, like Bush I, who shifted along with the rest.

Meanwhile, the actual constituency of the Republican Party remains great wealth and corporate power, even more dramatically so under Trump. It is quite an achievement to serve this actual constituency with dedication while maintaining a hold on the voting base.

As their voting base shrinks, Republican leaders understand that the GOP is becoming a minority party, which is why they are so dedicated to finding modes of voter suppression and packing the courts with reactionaries who will support their efforts.

It should also be noted that popular opinion differs from the party leadership on many central issues. But as already mentioned, since the majority of the population is disenfranchised, it doesn't matter much. To take just one example, for forty years of polling the population has strongly favored higher taxes on the rich—as taxes on the rich decline.

Bernie Sanders was reelected to the Senate while his protégé Alexandria Ocasio-Cortez won a smashing victory over her Republican opponent for New York's 14th District and became, in fact, the youngest woman elected to Congress. In fact, there are now probably as many Democratic Social-ists in the House as there are conservative Democrats, so the question is whether progressives should go on to form a third party or try to change the Democratic Party from within. What's your take on this matter?

In the 18th century, with all of its extreme flaws, the US constitutional sys-tem was a major step forward in democratic participation as compared with Europe. Even the concept "We the People," though grossly misleading, was a conceptual breakthrough. Over the years, however, by comparative stan-dards the system increasingly ranks as quite regressive. It is doubtful, for example, that Europe would admit a country with the US system as a new member. In particular, the system is radically rigged against any challenge to the governing duopoly. To develop a basis for a third party would require a serious and sustained effort in popular mobilization—not impossible, but not now on the horizon. There do seem to be possibilities to shift the char-acter of the Democratic Party, at least back to its modern New Deal origins, and beyond (it already is considerably beyond in some respects as a result of the civilizing effect of the activism of the '60s and its aftermath).

There are possibilities for development of independent parties, begin-ning at the local level, adopting fusion policies for more general elections, perhaps gaining enough traction to take part more actively in the political system.

But we should never forget that electoral politics, while not to be dis-missed, should not be the prime focus of serious radical political action, which aims to change the basic institutions that undergird the political sys-tem, to dismantle hegemonic ideologies, and to help develop the kind of mass consciousness that must be the basis for badly—even desperately—needed social and political change.

Trump Is Willing to Dismantle Democracy to Hold on to Power

C. J. POLYCHRONIOU: **Noam, with slightly more than two weeks away from the most important national elections in recent US history, Trump's campaign continues to harp on the message of "law and order"—a political tactic that authoritarian leaders have always relied on in order to control people and to strengthen their grip on a country—but refuses to accept a "peaceful transition to power" if he loses to Biden. Your thoughts on these matters?**

NOAM CHOMSKY: The "law and order" appeal is normal, virtually reflexive. Trump's threat to refuse to accept the result of the election is not. It is something new in stable parliamentary democracies.

The fact that this contingency is even being discussed reveals how effective the Trump wrecking ball has been in undermining formal democracy. We may recall that Richard Nixon, not exactly revered for his integrity, had some reason to suppose that victory in the 1960 election had been stolen from him by Democratic Party machinations. He did not challenge the results, placing the welfare of the country above personal ambition. Al Gore did the same in 2000. The idea of Trump placing anything above his personal ambition—even caring about the welfare of the country—is too ludicrous to discuss.

James Madison once said that liberty is not protected by "parchment barriers"—words on paper. Rather, constitutional orders presuppose good faith and some commitment, however limited, to the common good. When that is gone, we've moved to a different sociopolitical world.

Trump's threats are taken quite seriously, not only in extensive commentary in mainstream media and journals, but even within the military—which might be compelled to intervene, as in the tinpot dictatorships that are Trump's model. A striking example is an open letter to the country's highest-ranking military officer, Chairman of the Joint Chiefs General Mark Milley, from two highly regarded retired military commanders, Lt. Colonels John Nagl and Paul Yingling. They warn Milley: "The president of the United States is actively subverting our electoral system, threatening to remain in office in defiance of our Constitution. In a few months' time, you may have to choose between defying a lawless president or betraying your Constitutional oath" to defend the Constitution against all enemies, "foreign and domestic."

The enemy today is domestic: a "lawless president," Nagl and Yingling continue, who "is assembling a private army capable of thwarting not only the will of the electorate but also the capacities of ordinary law enforcement. When these forces collide on January 20, 2021, the US military will be the only institution capable of upholding our Constitutional order."

With Senate Republicans "reduced to supplicant status," having abandoned any lingering shreds of integrity, General Milley should be prepared to send a brigade of the 82nd Airborne to disperse Trump's "little green men," Nagl and Yingling advise. "Should you remain silent, you will be complicit in a coup d'état."

Hard to believe, but the very fact that such thoughts are voiced by sober and respected voices, and echoed throughout the mainstream, is reason enough to be deeply concerned about the prospects for US society. I rarely quote *New York Times* senior correspondent Thomas Friedman, but when he asks whether this might be our last democratic election, he is not joining us "wild men in the wings"—to quote McGeorge Bundy's term for those who don't automatically conform to approved doctrine.

Meanwhile, we should not overlook how leading elements of Trump's "private army" [the US Border Patrol] are showing their mettle in their usual terrain of deployment: the cruel Arizona desert to which the US, since Clinton, has driven miserable people fleeing from our destruction of their countries so that we may evade our responsibility—both legal and moral—to offer them an opportunity for asylum.

When Trump decided to terrorize Portland, Oregon, he didn't send the military, probably expecting that it would refuse to follow his orders, as had just happened in Washington, DC. He sent paramilitaries, the most fierce of them the tactical unit BORTAC of the Border Patrol, which is given virtually free rein with the "damned of the earth" as its targets.

Immediately on returning from carrying out Trump's orders in Portland, BORTAC returned to its regular pastimes, smashing up a flimsy medical aid center in the desert where volunteers seek to provide some medical aid, even water, to desperate people who managed somehow to survive.

Not content with this achievement, BORTAC soon returned to the task. Perhaps those who may be facing Trump's private army might want to learn more about them. Here's an excerpt from an authoritative report from the scene offered by the humanitarian organization No More Deaths:

> After sunset yesterday, October 5th, US Border Patrol entered No More Deaths' humanitarian aid station, Byrd Camp, with a federal warrant, for a second nighttime raid in two months. Volunteers were held for 3 hours while 12 people who were receiving medical care, food, water, and shelter from the 100+ degree heat were apprehended.
>
> In a massive show of armed force, Border Patrol, along with the Border Patrol Tactical Unit (BORTAC), descended on the camp with an armored tank, ATVs, a helicopter, and many marked and unmarked vehicles. Agents, armed with assault rifles, chased and terrorized those who were receiving care, all while the helicopter hovered low above them kicking up dust and debris, making it nearly impossible to see. Border Patrol smashed windows, broke doors, and destroyed essential camp infrastructure as well as supplies. This was after heavily surveilling the camp and patrolling its perimeter, creating an antagonistic and distressing environment for those receiving care, since late Saturday night on the 3rd.
>
> Since the previous raid on July 31st, Border Patrol has refused on multiple occasions to meet with volunteers to discuss previous shared agreements that upheld the right to provide humanitarian aid. The Tucson sector chief sent No More Deaths representatives a formal letter asserting this refusal.

Those are the professional elements of Trump's private army, buttressed by the armed militias that are upholding the doctrines of white supremacy that the FBI and Department of Homeland Security regard as the major domestic threat in the US, sharply increasing during the Trump years from 20 percent of terrorism-related crimes in 2016 to close to 100 percent by 2019.

Those are the forces that may be upholding "law and order" if in fact the top military command decides to be "complicit in a coup d'état." It seems unimaginable, but, regrettably, not inconceivable.

Meanwhile, Trump and his Republican cohorts are working overtime to implement their strategy of undermining the election or discrediting it if it comes out the wrong way, setting the stage for a possible coup.

In preparation, an "Army for Trump" is being mobilized to descend on polls to intimidate the "wrong voters." What was once the Justice Department is easing election fraud inquiry constraints in case that path becomes necessary.

In general, no stone is left unturned in Trump's campaign to dismantle democratic forms and hold on to power.

Perhaps there is some slight comfort in the fact that we are not alone. Other major democracies are also decaying, also falling into the hands of leaders with traits of Fascism, if not the ideologies (many, including leading scholars of Fascism, regard this characterization of Trump as much too charitable).

The world's largest democracy, India, is now run by a Trump-style wrecker, Narendra Modi, who is destroying Indian secular democracy and turning India into a cruel ethnocracy while also crushing Kashmir.

The world's oldest democracy, Britain, has not approached Trump's demolition job, but Prime Minister Boris Johnson is trying to join the club. His dismissal of Parliament so that he could ram through his version of Brexit, quickly overturned by the Supreme Court, caused outrage in British legal circles, with charges that he was undermining the presumption of good faith on which the British constitutional order has rested for centuries. He has since moved on to violating international law—admittedly, but only "a little bit"—by reversing a crucial provision of the agreement he had just reached with the EU, which is now suing Britain for this breach.

We may add, the second largest democracy in the western hemisphere, run by a Trump clone who tries in every way to imitate his model, for example, by trying to fire investigators for daring to look at the corruption and alleged criminality that surrounds him and his family. The US has gone farther down the road toward autocracy. When inspectors general tasked with overseeing executive malfeasance followed the same course, the would-be dictator in the White House simply fired them. He did so without a peep from the Republican Senate that had instituted this effort to protect the public, by now "reduced to supplicant status."

Perhaps it is mere coincidence, but there is a remarkable correlation between the dedication of leaders to demolish the democratic order and their expediting the slaughter of their own populations by COVID-19. The current ranking of cases and deaths, reported by the authoritative South China *Morning Post* (Hong Kong), are, from the top:

United States: 7,551,428 cases, 211,844 deaths

India: 6,835,655 cases, 105,526 deaths

Brazil: 5,000,694 cases, 148,228 deaths

They are followed far behind by a stellar democracy, Russia: 1,253,603 cases, 21,939 deaths. Others are left in their wake.

This is, of course, not the full picture. It's important to factor in death rates and other variables. But the general picture, and the correlation, are hard to overlook.

What is happening in the US, India and Brazil also cannot fail to evoke memories of the early 1930s—for me, bitter personal memories. One common feature is the fanatic adoration of the Maximal Leader by his loyal followers. There is one curious difference. Mussolini and Hitler were providing their worshippers with something: social reforms, a place in the sun. Trump is stabbing them in the back with virtually every legislative and executive action, and seriously harming the US in the international arena. The same is true of his companions in arms in India and Brazil.

Trump's commitment to cause maximal suffering to the American population is stunning to behold. It goes well beyond his truly colossal crimes: racing toward the abyss of environmental catastrophe and sharply increasing the threat of nuclear war. In far lesser ways, once again no stone is left unturned in ways to cause severe harm to the public.

Let's just keep to the pandemic, the least of the grave crises humanity faces. There is an international consortium, COVAX, working to facilitate the search for vaccines by cooperative efforts and to give at least some consideration to the distributional problems, ensuring that potential vaccines and other treatments will be available to those who need them rather than monopolized by the rich.

Trump's contribution? The usual one: to withdraw from the effort that over 170 countries have committed to.

The wrecker-in-chief always has a pretext: In this case, the World Health Organization (WHO) is involved, and the WHO serves Trump as a scapegoat as he flails around to deflect attention from his slaughter of tens of thousands of Americans.

Aside from the characteristic cruelty in pursuit of self-interest, withdrawal means that Americans will be deprived if vaccines are developed elsewhere—perhaps in China, which according to some reports may be in the lead.

As in 2003, after the SARS epidemic, scientists are now warning that another coronavirus pandemic is likely, probably more severe than this one. We've discussed before how Trump dismantled the protections that were in place against the current pandemic, leaving the US singularly unprepared. He is now resolutely pursuing the same course, not just by withdrawing from COVAX.

The countries of the world are now participating in a UN Biodiversity Summit "to try and slow humanity's rapid destruction of nature." The UN official leading the convention, Elizabeth Maruma Mrema, emphasizes that averting another pandemic is one crucial target. If we want to avoid another COVID, she warns, "we have to take action. . . . We either conserve and protect that nature, biodiversity, or it will make us suffer as we do now."

Trump is again helping out in the usual way: by refusing to take part.

The media are also helping in this case. The cited two minutes on NPR may have exhausted the coverage, a cursory search suggests.

Meanwhile, "humanity's destruction of nature" proceeds apace. A major study of the destruction of biodiversity by the Royal Botanical Gardens, Kew, found that "two-fifths of the world's plants are at risk of extinction. . . . We are 'ignoring the potential treasure chest of wild species' that offers potential fuels, foods and medicines to humanity, says conservation scientist Colin Clubbe."

This study received three minutes on BBC. We have to keep to priorities, after all.

Trump's approach to international conventions and initiatives is simple: If I didn't create it, demolish it, claiming it's the worst deal in history. If I created it, it's "the deal of the century," the greatest achievement in memory. And with his media echo chamber, and congressional supplicants, he can get away with it. Pity the country, and the world.

True, Trump's methods are achieving something. Waving the big stick does sometimes bring results. When the US approached the UN Security Council to demand that it renew harsh sanctions against Iran, it refused with almost total unanimity, including even Britain. No matter. Secretary of State Mike Pompeo, in good Mussolini-Hitler fashion, returned to the Security Council to inform them that the UN sanctions are renewed.

"The United States took this decisive action," Pompeo instructed his Security Council servants, "because, in addition to Iran's failure to perform its JCPOA commitments, the Security Council failed to extend the UN arms embargo on Iran." Such disobedience of course cannot be tolerated by the Dear Leader of the world.

More broadly, the Trump administration is steadily firming up the reactionary international headed by Washington, the one geostrategic initiative that can be detected in the administrative chaos. Prime members are Trump's companions Modi and Bolsonaro. In the Middle East, they are joined by Egypt's General Abdul Fattah al-Sisi, Trump's "favorite dictator," who has driven Egypt to new depths of despair. And of course the Gulf dictatorships, headed by the estimable Mohammed bin Salman, responsible for Khashoggi's brutal murder as one of his lesser crimes. Another welcome member is Israel, now scarcely concealing its drift to the far right. The recent formalization of tacit relations between Israel and the Gulf dictatorships finds its natural place in this system. There are also members beyond, like Viktor Orbán's Hungarian illiberal democracy, and waiting in the wings, such attractive figures as Italy's Mario Salvini, celebrating the drowning of thousands of the damned in the Mediterranean, adding to Italy's contribution to Europe's genocidal record.

On the bright side, Trump's reactionary international is now countered by the new Progressive International, which grew from the Sanders movement in the US and a European counterpart, DiEM25, a transnational movement seeking to preserve and strengthen what is of value in the European

Union while overcoming its severe flaws. It has also drawn in a wide range of representatives from the Global South. Its first international conference just took place in Iceland, where the prime minister is a member. Though it of course lacks the resources of violence and wealth of the reactionary international, it has promise to become a people's representative in the global class war that is underway to determine the contours of the post-pandemic world.

Typical of authoritarian leaders, Trump relies heavily on the use and promotion of conspiracy theories, apparently fully aware of the fact that conspiracy theories intensify political polarization. Why do conspiracy theories thrive in politics, and what do they mean for political reality at the end of the second decade of the 21st century in the United States?

One reason why conspiracy theories flourish is that people want explanations, sometimes out of intellectual curiosity, sometimes for more personal and often wrenching reasons. That's particularly true when things fall apart. That's happened in many ways.

Consider the neoliberal disaster of the past forty years. Its essence was announced with much clarity by Thatcher and Reagan, and their economic guru Milton Friedman, right at the start: There is no society; individuals have to face the ravages of the market alone, with no defense, surely not labor unions, which have to be destroyed. Governments are the problem, flawed by the fact that they are partially responsive to the public. Decisions therefore have to be transferred to private hands, in effect, the corporate sector. Corporations must be dedicated solely to self-enrichment—not a principle of economics, but an ethical judgment.

There are further nuances, but this is the essence. Putting these principles together, it is not hard to draw some conclusions about likely consequences.

The Rand Corporation has just released a study on the scale of the (hardly unexpected) effects. They estimate the sum "transferred" from the middle and working classes to the very rich since Reagan-Thatcher-Friedman to be $47 trillion. "Robbery" might be a more accurate term.

Rand takes the very rich to be the top 10 percent. That's misleading. It is overwhelmingly a tiny fraction of these. The top 0.1 percent have seen their share of the nation's wealth double since Reagan, to 20 percent.

This is only part of the grim story, amplified by Clinton's radically anti-labor globalization program, post-Thatcher austerity, Obama's bailout of the perpetrators of the housing crash and rejection of legislation to help the victims as well, and much else.

It should not come as a great surprise that the epidemic of "deaths of despair" that has plagued the US, primarily among white men of working age, is now beginning to haunt Britain. Nor that much of the world is consumed by rage, resentment, contempt for institutions. This offers fertile territory to demagogues and con men—sometimes, like Trump, highly skilled—who can parade as the saviors of the public while slavishly serving their oppressors. With ample help from the information system, they can divert attention away from the sources of popular discontent to the standard scapegoats, exploiting deep-seated prejudices and fears. No need to review how it is done.

In such a climate, conspiracy theories can flourish.

There are other factors to consider. The real world is complex. Pick any event you like and even the most solid accounts will have plenty of loose ends, odd coincidences, unexplained features. That's why scientists do experiments, abstracting radically from the observed phenomena. Again, that encourages conspiracy theories.

Furthermore, some of the theories might have some validity. Adam Smith was consciously exaggerating when he declared that "People of the same trade seldom meet together, even for merriment and diversion, but the conversation ends in a conspiracy against the public, or in some contrivance to raise prices." But he wasn't concocting a fantasy. It happens all the time. Some of these escapades are well documented. In many other cases there are grounds for suspicion.

To take just one current example, the staid and respectable German national broadcaster *Deutsche Welle* recently interviewed the prominent US political scientist Norman Ornstein of the American Enterprise Institute on some curious doings involving Trump, Deutsche Bank, and the US Supreme Court.

To quote the opening words:

> The explosive *New York Times* report on the tax situation of US President Trump is raising some uncomfortable questions for Germany's largest

lender, Deutsche Bank, namely: why did Deutsche Bank loan Mr. Trump 2 Billion dollars at the same time other banks, including all US banks, were not willing to do so? And while Deutsche Bank may be handling the loans, we cannot say tonight who or what is behind that money. In other words, we don't know who owns the debt of US President Donald Trump. And adding to the puzzle is the role played by the son of a former Supreme Court Justice. Justin Kennedy, son of former Justice Anthony Kennedy, was a division head and contact for Trump at Deutsche Bank. Kennedy was close to the then future president while continuing to lend him money.

Another part of the puzzle, as Ornstein elaborates, is the premature retirement of Justice Kennedy, the swing vote on the Court, permitting Trump to nominate the young, far-right Brett Kavanaugh, Justin Kennedy's protégé, to replace him.

"The optics look terrible," Ornstein concludes, calling for investigation by the State of New York, not the federal prosecutors, who are now in the pockets of Trump's legal representatives, formerly known as the Justice Department.

It's not a conspiracy theory, but can easily be recrafted as one.

In brief, in a fetid swamp, conspiracy theories flourish, and some might turn out to have considerable bearing on the world that has been created by systems of state and private power.

Trump Is Quite Capable of an "October Surprise"

C. J. POLYCHRONIOU: Since coming to power, Trump has taken various steps to rule like an autocrat. One of his latest tactics is to send federal agents into cities to crush protests. Can you talk about the political aims behind Trump's abuse of his law enforcement powers, and whether his actions have precedent in modern US history?

NOAM CHOMSKY: The renowned economist James Buchanan—one of the leading figures of US-style "libertarianism"—observed in his major work *The Limits of Liberty* that the ideal society should accord with fundamental human nature, which makes good sense. Then comes the next question: What is fundamental human nature? He had a very simple answer: "In a strictly personalized sense, any person's ideal situation is one that allows him full freedom of action and inhibits the behavior of others so as to force adherence to his own desires. That is to say, each person seeks mastery over a world of slaves."

It is not easy to find real human beings who suffer from this pathology, but Trump seems to be a good candidate. When inspectors general began to fulfill their duty of inquiring into the swamp of corruption he'd created, he fired them. The US attorney for the Southern District of New York was summarily dismissed when he made the same error, replaced by a flack for private equity.

Next in turn was the military: "The White House is intensifying an effort to hire Pentagon personnel with an undisputed allegiance to President

Trump . . . current and former officials said." When the Senate did not quickly confirm his choice, retired Gen. Anthony Tata, to fill "the Pentagon's top policy job," Trump simply appointed him without the required Senate approval. This has been standard procedure under Trump. Why bother with the legal formality of Senate confirmation?

Practices are much the same when the population dares to raise its head. They are then threatened with "ominous weapons" and "vicious dogs" —the latter invokes/recalls attacks on civil rights protesters that aroused horror and contempt when used in the deep South sixty years ago. Overruling state and local officials, [Trump] sent paramilitaries to assault protesters in Portland, Oregon, including the elite Border Patrol Tactical Unit (BORTAC), trained to use violence with little oversight against miserable refugees dying in the harsh Arizona desert not far from where I live.

Confronting Portland's "Wall of Moms" with brute force does not go over too well with the general public, even arousing protests that it can't happen here: We're not Italy under Mussolini!

BORTAC was ultimately withdrawn from Portland, but shortly thereafter returned to its mission of demonstrating that it *can* and *does* happen here, even if we choose not to look. A few days after leaving Portland, heavily armed BORTAC units raided a humanitarian aid station for fleeing refugees in the Arizona desert, "detaining over thirty people who were receiving medical care, food, water, and shelter from the 100+ degree heat. In a massive show of force, Border Patrol, along with BORTAC, descended on the camp with an armored vehicle, three ATVs, two helicopters, and dozens of marked and unmarked vehicles," a No More Deaths news update reports.

There's plenty more.

One reaction is that "the Western-led world order is in crisis. If the US reelects Donald Trump, this will be terminal." A few years ago, you might have encountered these sentiments on a street corner, with someone holding a sign reading "The end is nigh." Today, you read them in the world's leading business journal, the London *Financial Times*, expressed by the sober and highly respected economic-political analyst Martin Wolf. Much of the world has had more than enough of the Western-led world order in the past centuries, but would hardly favor what is likely to come if Trump were to administer a terminal blow.

Are there precedents in American history? One has to search fairly hard to find any, though a possible candidate is Trump's hero Andrew Jackson. When Jackson defied the Supreme Court's orders to stop his campaign of brutal Indian removal, he is alleged to have directly challenged the sitting Supreme Court Chief Justice: "John Marshall has made his decision now let him enforce it."

We should also not overlook the fact that popular support for autocracy runs disturbingly high. Few signs are clearer than attitudes toward the media. Almost one-fourth of Republicans agree that "President Trump should close down mainstream news outlets, like *CNN, The Washington Post* and *The New York Times*." Twice that number of Republicans, almost half, agree that "the president should have the authority to close news outlets engaged in bad behavior" and that "the news media is the enemy of the American people," engaged in bad behavior. Democrats are not that extreme, but the numbers are not overly reassuring.

What about his suggestion that the November general election be delayed, from which he refuses to back down? Given that he is not constitutionally empowered to enforce such an extraordinary proposal, how can he be stopped from doing so?

He could be stopped by mass popular protests, perhaps a general strike, inducing the real masters to intervene to preserve the society they largely own. If it comes to a true show of force, Trump can be stopped by the military—if they decide to uphold the US Constitution. These strange days it must have occurred to many that Trump's attempted purge of the military command might be tactical, anticipating this contingency—something else that would have been unthinkable a few years ago.

It might be worthwhile to pay attention to some analogies in today's decaying global social order. Recently, Trump's mimic in Brazil, President Jair Bolsonaro, sought to fire investigators looking into his family's sordid activities. He was blocked by the Supreme Court.

The world's oldest parliamentary democracy is also tottering, under the regime of Prime Minister Boris Johnson, who stands out in Europe for his Trump-like failure to responsibly handle the pandemic. When Johnson wanted to ram through his version of Brexit, he simply suspended

Parliament—an unprecedented act that was bitterly condemned by British legal authorities, and quashed by the Supreme Court. The US trails behind.

Trump's attacks on the US Postal Service are increasing in the year of the mail-in ballot. In fact, his new postmaster general, Louis DeJoy, has already taken steps to slow down the delivery of mail, and there is even talk of post offices shutting down across the country in an apparent effort to disenfranchise voters. What does Donald Trump's success in undermining democratic governance reveal about the state of the US political system and US democracy in the 21st century?

Several factors converge in the actions of Trump's choice to undermine the postal service. One is the narrow concern with the elections. Republicans know that they have a problem. They're a party of a shrinking minority. They cannot approach voters with their actual policies of unstinting service to extreme wealth and corporate power, and therefore have to mobilize voters on so-called "cultural issues," not a very secure stand. To hold onto office, they have to resort to such devices as massive purging of voters to ensure that the "wrong people" don't contaminate the elections, a remarkable story exposed by investigative journalist Greg Palast. Slowing mail service might open the door to challenges to the election if they can't steal it by other means.

But there are deeper reasons that we've discussed before. The modern Republican Party has a visceral hatred of the [US] Postal Service, for good reasons. It is a highly efficient government institution, a fact that can give voters the subversive idea that government might be of, by and for the people. It offers no opportunities for private profit, and performs major services to the population, and could do a great deal more if it were freed of congressional malevolence. These are lessons that have to be kept from the eyes of the dangerous masses. Even worse, the worshipers of the so-called Founding Fathers might not be able to continue to suppress the fact that they conceived of the postal service as a subsidy to a free, independent press; anathema.

The implications for what remains of democratic governance after forty years of the neoliberal assault, enhanced by Trump's wrecking ball, need hardly be elaborated.

Trump has tried to use the coronavirus pandemic in a way that serves his reelection purposes, rather than serving the interests and needs of the American public. With coronavirus cases and deaths hitting new records almost daily, isn't it possible that he may use COVID as a means to bolster his suggestion for postponing the November election?

He is desperate enough to try almost anything. And he'll have plenty of support. Business leaders may cringe at Trump's antics. That's especially true for those who like to present themselves as humane and cultivated managers of "soulful corporations" in '50s rhetoric, regularly recycled when needed to overcome "reputational risks." But as long as Trump recognizes where real power lies and follows the rules, they prefer him to uncertain alternatives that might be subject to pressures from people who care about the common good.

As Joe Biden bends to activist pressures and rises in the polls, the true masters of the universe are becoming increasingly alarmed. Front-page headlines tell us that "Investors Start to Ask: What If Biden Becomes President?" The stories report that investors are concerned that the gravy train may be slowed down if their champion is kicked out.

Fossil fuel industries are particularly worried. A headline in the Texas press reads, "Oil donors flock to Trump as Biden hardens climate stance." It reports that they "are writing checks to President Donald Trump with greater zeal than they did four years ago, as Biden campaigns on a climate plan that seeks to eliminate carbon emissions by mid-century," possibly earlier, along with his $2 trillion program to address some of the many problems that have to be dealt with—not enough, but a substantial step forward.

Many polls indicate that Trump is trailing Biden by double digits. What could possibly happen between now and November that could turn the race around?

Biden's victory is anything but a sure thing. Election tampering is now a huge industry, and massive campaign funding in the last days can have a major effect. This seems to have happened in 2016. The leading specialist on campaign funding, Tom Ferguson, found that a "dual wave of money" donated to presidential and Senate races had a substantial and probably decisive impact in the final days of the '16 campaign. And we've already discussed the possibility that Republican interference with mail balloting might muddy the waters. Apart from all of these devices to undermine the limited integrity of elections, Trump is quite capable of an "October surprise." It's not hard to conjure up a variety of options. This is no time for letting one's guard down, beguiled by dubious hopes.

We Must Not Let
Masters of Capital Define
the Post-COVID World

C. J. POLYCHRONIOU: It's been argued by many, from various quarters, that COVID-19 has been a game changer. Do you concur with this view, or are we talking of a temporary situation, with a return to the "business as usual" approach being the most likely scenario once this health crisis is over?

NOAM CHOMSKY: There is no way to predict. Those who have primary responsibility for the multiple crises imperiling us today are hard at work, relentlessly, to ensure that the systems they created, and from which they have greatly benefited, will endure—and in an even harsher forms, with more intense surveillance and other means of coercion and control. Popular forces are mobilizing to counter these malign developments. They seek to dismantle the destructive policies that have led us to this uniquely perilous moment of human history, and to move toward a world system that gives priority to human rights and needs, not the prerogatives of concentrated capital.

We should take a few moments to clarify the stakes for ourselves in the bitter class war taking shape as the post-pandemic world is being forged. The stakes are immense. All are rooted in the suicidal logic of unregulated capitalism, and at a deeper level in its very nature. All are becoming more apparent during the neoliberal plagues of the past forty years. The crises have been exacerbated by malignancies that have surfaced as these destructive tendencies took their course. The most ominous are appearing in the most powerful state in human history—not a good omen for a world in crisis.

The stakes were spelled out in the setting of the Doomsday Clock last January. Each year of Trump's presidency, the minute hand has been moved closer to midnight. Two years ago, it reached the closest it has been since the clock was first set after the atomic bombings. This past January, the *Bulletin of Atomic Scientists* abandoned minutes altogether and moved to seconds: 100 seconds to midnight. The analysts reiterated the prime concerns: nuclear war, environmental destruction, and deterioration of democracy, the last of these because the only hope of dealing with the two existential crises is vibrant democracy in which an informed population is directly engaged in determining the fate of the world.

Since January, Trump has escalated each of these threats to survival. He has continued his project of dismantling the arms control regime that has provided some protection against nuclear disaster. So far this year, he has terminated the Open Skies Treaty, proposed by Eisenhower, and imposed frivolous conditions to block the renegotiation of New Start, the last pillar of the system. He is now considering ending the moratorium on nuclear tests, "an invitation for other nuclear-armed countries to follow suit," said Daryl Kimball, executive director of the Arms Control Association.

The military industry can scarcely control its euphoria over the flood of gifts from the public to develop new weapons to destroy us all, encouraging adversaries to do likewise so that down the road, new grants will flow to try to counter the new threats to survival. A hopeless task, as virtually every specialist knows, but that is not pertinent; what matters is that public largesse should flow into the right pockets.

Trump also has continued his dedicated campaign to destroy the environment. that sustains human life. His FY 2020 budget proposal, issued while the pandemic was raging, called for further defunding of the Centers for Disease Control and Prevention and other health-related components for government, compensated by increased support for the fossil fuel industries that are destroying the prospects for survival. And, as usual, he called for more funding for the military and for the [border] wall that is a central part of his electoral strategy. The corporate leaders Trump has installed to supervise environmental destruction are quietly eliminating regulations that somewhat constrain the damage and that protect the population from poisoned water supplies and poisoned air. The latter reveals sharply the malevolence of the Trump phenomenon. In the midst of an unprecedented respiratory pandemic, Trump's minions are seeking to increase air pollution, which makes COVID-19 more deadly, endangering tens of thousands of Americans. But it doesn't much matter. Most have no choice but to live near the polluting plants—[those] who are poor and Black, and who vote the "wrong" way.

Again, there are beneficiaries: his prime constituency of private wealth and corporate power.

Turning to the third concern of the Doomsday Clock analysts, Trump has accelerated his program to dismantle American democracy. The executive branch has been virtually dismantled, converted to a collection of cowardly sycophants who do not dare to offend the master. His latest step was to fire the State of New York prosecutor who was investigating the swamp that Trump has created in Washington. He was carrying forward the investigation of the inspectors general whom Trump purged when they were getting too close. The next projected step, we have just learned, is to be a purge of the military command, to ensure faithful obedience to the aspiring tin-pot dictator in the event of an international or domestic crisis of his making.

Trump is mimicked closely by Jair Bolsonaro; farce imitating tragedy. But in Brazil, there is still a slim barrier to executive criminality: the Supreme Court, which blocked Bolsonaro's moves to purge the authorities investigating his own swamp. The US trails well behind.

It is quite an achievement to have significantly escalated all three of the threats to survival that have moved the Doomsday Clock toward midnight in a mere six months, while at the same time, administering a spectacular failure to deal with the pandemic. Under Trump's leadership, the US, with 4 percent of the world's population, has by now registered 20 percent of [COVID-19] cases. According to a study in a leading medical journal, almost all cases are attributable to the refusal by Trump and associates to respect the advice of scientists.

In late March, the US and EU had about the same number of coronavirus cases. Europe adopted the results of US scientific studies, and cases have very sharply declined. Under Trump, cases have increased to over five times the EU level. European researchers are wondering whether the US has just given up. Europe is now considering a ban on travelers from the pariah state that Trump and associates are constructing.

The idea that the US government has given up is mistaken; a more accurate conclusion is that the rulers simply don't care. Their concern is to maintain power and to shape the future society in their image. The fate of the general population is someone else's business.

The task of forging the future world is not left to executive orders. It is by now virtually the sole concern of the Senate, with a Republican majority that is perhaps even more subservient to the master than the executive. Mitch McConnell's Senate has virtually abandoned any pretense of being a deliberative or legislative body. Its task is to serve wealth and corporate power while packing the judiciary, top to bottom, with young ultraright Federalist Society products who will be able to protect the reactionary Trump-McConnell agenda for many years, whatever the public might want.

The latest Republican effort to punish the population is to call upon the Supreme Court to terminate the Affordable Care Act ("Obamacare")—as always, offering nothing in its place but empty promises.

Trumpian malevolence is merely bringing to light far deeper malignancies of the socioeconomic order that cannot be ignored if we are to avoid the next and probably worse pandemic, or to deal with the truly existential threats to survival that Trump is working hard to make much more severe.

These are the questions we face as we ask ourselves what we can do to shape the emergence from the current health crisis.

Since the eruption of nationwide demonstrations in defense of Black lives and in support of defunding the police, we have witnessed massive shifts in public attitudes on racism and growing defiance of Trump by leading establishment figures and even leaders within his own party. Can you analyze racism in the Trump era, and speculate as to whether the country is ready for a new era in race relations?

Some insight into "racism in the Trump era" is provided by the record of racially motivated violence. According to the Anti-Defamation League, in 2016, before Trump took office, this curse accounted for 20 percent of terrorism-related deaths in the US. By 2018, the figure rose to 98 percent. And it has continued since. FBI Director Christopher Wray reported that racially and ethnically motivated extremists had been the primary source of ideologically motivated lethal incidents and violence since 2018, and that 2019 marked the deadliest year of white supremacist violence since the Oklahoma City bombing in 1995, *Foreign Affairs* reports.

That is one face of racism in the Trump era, regularly fanned from the White House. The current demonstrations reflect critical tendencies in the opposite direction. The demonstrations are unprecedented, in scale, in commitment, in solidarity, and in popular support —reaching well beyond what Martin Luther King Jr. achieved when he was still a popular figure.

These remarkable demonstrations testify to significant changes in popular consciousness. Trump, of course, has been trying hard to stir up his white supremacist voting bloc while tweeting wild charges about how the country is under siege by the violent radicals who run the Democratic Party. But his familiar techniques do not seem to be working as before.

So far, the [short-term] goals of the demonstrators seem to be mostly focused on policing. This focus on police practices leads directly to inquiry into much more fundamental features of American society. There is ample evidence that police violence in the US is well beyond comparable societies, but it doesn't take place in a social vacuum. The US is a far more violent society.

Violence, of course, isn't in the genes. It arises from social maladies that are reflected in many aspects of the society, not least its very low ranking among OECD [Organization for Economic Cooperation and Development] countries in social justice measures. It's clear why these maladies have a radically disproportionate impact on the Black community. Police violence is a symptom, which cannot be cured while ignoring its roots.

The spread of protests, especially to small-town America, has also brought to light the utterly weird phenomenon of the militia movement in the United States. To what extent is the political ideology of the Republican Party under Trump linked to the extreme anti-government ideology of the militia movement?

Apart from the assault on the Michigan State Legislature by the armed Michigan Liberty Militia ("very good people," Donald Trump assured us), the most dramatic recent case was at the village of Bethel, Ohio. A peaceful demonstration of a few dozen people in support of Black Lives Matter was attacked by seven hundred counterprotesters from motorcycle gangs, "back the blue" groups, and proponents of the Second Amendment, many armed or with baseball bats and clubs. The Second Amendment has nothing to do with demonstrations like these, but it has become a rallying cry among right-wing groups. It has constantly been evoked by Trump, always irrelevantly, to inflame the "tough guys" he is counting on.

As for political ideology, modern Republicans like to intone Reagan's slogan that government is the problem, not the solution. But always tongue-in-cheek. Their idol expanded the federal government (while almost tripling the national debt). It's true that the ideology of the modern Republican Party is in part anti-government. For them, government has a serious flaw; it is somewhat responsive to the general public. The flaw can be remedied by transferring policy making to private tyrannies that are completely unaccountable to the public.

But government is sometimes the solution for Republicans. One instance is when state power is needed to crush popular interference with the doctrines of the faith, that is, the neoliberal doctrines. Government is also the solution for the huge public subsidies for the corporate sector, and more visibly, when the corporate crime wave that has been unleashed by neoliberal principles crashes the economy, as has been happening regularly since Reagan. The masters then run hat in hand to the nanny state to be bailed out. That is happening again today, though this time the corporate greed mandated by neoliberal doctrine is only partially responsible. When the pandemic struck, corporations that had enriched wealthy shareholders and management with stock buybacks have been demanding, and receiving, public largesse as usual via several Congressional Covid aid packages.

On top of that, it always makes sense not to let an opportunity go to waste. Thanks to friends in high places, "nearly 82 percent of the benefits from the tax law change [in the coronavirus stimulus] will go to people making $1m or more annually in 2020."

The guiding neoliberal principle is simply a sharper version of the traditional understanding that government's proper function is to "protect the minority of the opulent against the majority," as James Madison instructed at the Constitutional Convention. Government's prime concern is the welfare of "the men of best quality," as they called themselves a century earlier during the first modern democratic revolution in 17th-century England. The "rabble" will somehow fend for themselves.

How? In the neoliberal world, the solution for them is to join the precariat, deprived of support systems ("there is no society"), health programs, child care, vacations, secure pensions, in fact any way to escape the ravages of the market, whatever it brings.

Pensions illustrate neoliberal logic well. The first step has been to dissolve them into private 401(k)s. That might lead to higher returns for those who are lucky, and to disaster for those who are not, but either way, withdrawal of security turns people's minds way from "dangerous illusions" like solidarity and mutual support to isolation in an uncertain market. The next step has just been taken by Eugene Scalia, who was chosen to be labor secretary on the basis of his credentials as a corporate lawyer strongly opposed to labor rights. Under the cover of the pandemic, he quietly opened the 401(k) market to the destructive private equity firms, offering them a huge source of profit and inflated management fees.

Proceeding further, after firing the US attorney for the Southern District of New York, who stepped out of line by exploring his swamp in Washington, Trump nominated Jay Clayton as his replacement. Clayton, a private equity lawyer, is a long-time advocate of changing federal law "to let asset managers funnel more money from retirees to those high-risk, high-fee firms," David Sirota reports in another of his invaluable exposés of state-corporate crimes. The Securities and Exchange Commission (SEC), which monitors these shady organizations, issued another scathing report on their malpractice, which Sirota interprets, plausibly, as a "desperate cry for help" to prevent the stagecoach robbery underway. But to head off that threat, Sirota notes further, the Supreme Court quietly "restricted the SEC's power to punish private equity firms."

The circle tightens. Hold on to your hats as the new age is forged by the masters, step by step—if we let them have their way.

Since the outbreak of coronavirus, Joe Biden seems to have recognized that many of the problems facing the contemporary United States are

structural, not cyclical. Indeed, Biden seems to have moved further to the left since Bernie Sanders suspended his presidential campaign in April. This raises the interesting question of whether Biden himself has changed or whether it is the politics and culture of the Democratic Party itself that have changed. Can you comment on the policy agenda of Biden and on the possibly changing face of the Democratic Party?

What Biden recognizes I don't know. We can however read his program, which has been pressed well to the left. Not by the Democratic National Committee or the donor class. Rather by direct engagement of Sanders and his associates, and most important, by the constant activism of the groups that the Sanders campaign brought together and inspired. Whether the face continues to change depends on whether these forces will continue to mobilize and to act.

It's well to remember the traditional left perspective on the quadrennial extravaganzas, including the current one. There is an official doctrine that politics reduces to voting in an election, and then going home to leave matters to others. That's a wonderful way to suppress the population and maintain authoritarian control. The terminology that is used to implement this technique of control is "vote for X," and you've fulfilled your responsibility as a citizen.The establishment doctrine is available both for those who favor government policy and those who oppose it. In the latter form, it has recently been called "lesser evil voting," given the acronym LEV.

The traditional left doctrine is very different. It holds that politics consists of constant activism to resist oppression, not only from government, but from even harsher private power, and to develop people's movements to promote justice and popular control of institutions. Every few years an event comes around called an "election." One takes a few minutes to see if there is a significant difference between the candidates, and if there is, to take another few minutes to vote against the worst one and then get back to work. To illustrate the choice, consider global warming, plainly a critical matter (for some, like me, the most critical in human history, along with nuclear war). Democrats and Republicans differ sharply on the issue. The latest study by the Pew Research Center finds that Americans continue to be deeply politically divided over how much human activity contributes to climate change. About seven-in-ten Democrats (72%) say human activity contributes a great deal to climate change, compared with roughly two-in-ten Republicans (22%), a difference of 50 percentage points. The difference is even wider among those at the ends of the ideological spectrum. A large majority of liberal Democrats (85%) say human activity contributes a great deal to climate change. Only 14 percent of conservative Republicans say the same.

This coming November, the difference between the candidates is a chasm.

Amid Protests and Pandemic, Trump's Priority Is Protecting Profits

C. J. POLYCHRONIOU: Noam, for the past forty or so years, we have been witnessing in the US the supremacy of the ideology of market fundamentalism and the demolition of the welfare state. We're now at the point that the country is unable to deal with a major health crisis, let alone resolve long-standing issues like large-scale poverty, immense economic inequalities, racism, and police brutality. Yet, in the midst of the George Floyd protests, Donald Trump did not hesitate to declare that, "America is the greatest country in the world," while seeking to start a new civil war in this country through tactics of extreme polarization. Can you comment on the above observations?

NOAM CHOMSKY: I don't think Trump wants a civil war. Rather, as he says, he wants to "dominate" by violence and terrify any potential opposition. That is his standard reflex. Just look at his outburst when one Republican Senator, Lisa Murkowski, broke strict party discipline and raised some mild doubts about the magnificence of His Royal Majesty. Or his firing of the scientist in charge of vaccine development when he raised a question about one of Trump's quack medicines. Or his purge of the inspector generals who might investigate the fetid swamp he's constructed in Washington.

It's routine. He's a radically new phenomenon in American political history.

Another Trump reflex is his call for "the most vicious dogs, and most ominous weapons, I have ever seen" when peaceful protesters appear near his abode. The phrase "vicious dogs" evokes the country's horror when images of vicious dogs attacking Black demonstrators appeared on the front pages during the civil rights movement. Trump's use of the phrase was either by intent, to stir up racist violence, or reflexive, arising from his innermost sentiments. I leave it to others to judge which is worse, and what either tells us about the malignancy at the center of global power.

With that qualification, there is no inconsistency. Both the claim that America is the greatest country in the world, in his special sense, and his call for domination, follow from his guiding doctrine: ME!

A direct corollary to this doctrine is that Trump must satisfy the demands of extreme wealth and corporate power, which tolerate his antics only insofar as he serves their interests abjectly. He does with admirable consistency in his legislative programs and executive decisions, such as the recent Environmental Protection Agency decision to increase air pollution "in the midst of an unprecedented respiratory pandemic." This choice risks tens of thousands of deaths, disproportionately Black, the business press reports, but increases wealth for those who matter.

The success of his tactics was revealed clearly at the January extravaganza at the Davos ski resort, where the masters of the universe, as they are called, meet annually to cavort and congratulate one another. This year's meeting departed from the norm. There was visible concern about "reputational risk"—recognition that the peasants are coming with their pitchforks. Therefore, there were solemn declarations that *we realize we've made mistakes, but we are changing, you can put your faith in us, we will become "soulful corporations,"* to borrow the phrase used in accolades to corporate America in the '50s.

The keynote address was, of course, handed to Trump, the Godfather. The elegant figures assembled don't like him. His vulgarity and general brutishness disrupt their preferred image of enlightened humanism. But they gave him rousing applause. Antics aside, he made clear that he understands the bottom line: which pockets have to be stuffed lavishly with more dollars.

Another direct corollary of the guiding doctrine is that the con man in charge must control his voting base while he is stabbing most of them in the back with his actual programs—a difficult feat, which he has so far carried off with much skill. The voting base includes not only avid white supremacists, but others in the grip of the fear of "them" that is a core part of the culture—and is of course not without foundation. One consequence of bitter repression is that "they" often resort to crime—that is, the retail crime of the weak, not the wholesale crime of the powerful.

For Trump's prime constituency of great wealth and corporate power, America is indeed the greatest country in the world. How can one fault a country where CEO compensation has reached 287 times that of workers, 0.1 percent of the population hold 20 percent of the wealth, and the majority try to survive from paycheck to paycheck? And calls for domination by vicious dogs placates much of the voting base.

So, all falls into place.

The actor George Clooney responded with an essay for the *Daily Beast* to the killing of George Floyd by saying that racism is America's pandemic, "and in 400 years we've yet to find a vaccine." Why is racism so entrenched and intractable in the United States?

The answer is given by what happened in those 400 years. It's been reviewed before, but for me at least it's useful to take a few minutes to think it through again until it becomes deeply ingrained in consciousness. In summary:

The first 250 years created the most vicious system of slavery in human history once the colonies had gained their liberty, the foundation of much of the nation's wealth. It was unique not only in hideous cruelty but also in that it was based on skin color. That is ineradicable, a curse reaching to future generations. Other minorities were brutally treated, even barred from the country by racist laws. This includes Jews and Italians, the prime target of the 1924 immigration law, which endured for forty years —long enough to condemn European Jews to crematoria, and post-war, to ensure that survivors went to Palestine, whatever they might have preferred. But this stigma was not permanent, as they could be assimilated into whiteness.

Also unique is the fervor of American racism. The "one drop of blood" criterion for US anti-miscegenation laws that were enforced until the 1960s civil rights movement was so severe and rigid that the Nazis rejected it when searching for models for the racist Nuremberg laws—though they did appeal to the American precedent as the only one they could find.

Formal slavery ended in 1865, and a decade of Reconstruction offered Black people a taste of freedom, which they used with remarkable effectiveness, given the horrifying legacy. That soon ended. A North-South compact offered southern racists free rein to murder and repress, and to provide a fine workforce for agribusiness and the southern industrial revolution by criminalizing Black life and offering employers a disciplined workforce with zero rights. One of the best general books on the post-Reconstruction period is called *Slavery by Another Name*, by *Wall Street Journal* Atlanta Bureau Chief Douglas Blackmon.

That stain on American history lasted pretty much until WWII, when free labor was needed for the war industry. I remember well when Black domestic servants disappeared from middle-class homes. During the great growth period after the war, some opportunities opened for Black Americans, though serious impediments remained. The educational opportunities offered by the GI Bill, a major contribution to the health of the society, were denied to Black people. Homeownership, the basis for wealth for most people, was restricted by federal laws barring Black people from federally funded housing—laws that were hated by the liberals who voted for them, but there was no recourse if there was to be any housing at all, thanks to the iron grip of influential southern Democrats, whose racist passions shifted to the Republicans under Nixon's southern strategy.

By the time these racist laws were withdrawn under pressure of the activism of the '60s, the opportunities for many Black Americans were lost. The economy suffered stagflation in the '70s and then the hammer blow of neoliberalism, designed to keep the poor and working people in their place, with Black communities as usual the most brutally affected. That assault was compounded by a new wave of criminalization of Black life initiated by the deeply racist Reagan administration. That was amplified by Clinton under the cloak of "I am one of you," and on to George Floyd.

It's not hard then to answer the question, at least on one level. At a deeper level, we can ask why the disease is so hard to cure.

It is worth bearing in mind that racism is not unique to the US. It has always existed in one form or another, but it was not until the Age of Enlightenment and the imperial conquests that it assumed its contemporary virulence. To see it on display in Europe, it is enough to view the intensive efforts of "civilized" Europeans to prevent the victims of centuries of hideous European slaughter and terror from "soiling" their shores. Better that tens of thousands should die in the Mediterranean, fleeing from Libya, the scene of the first post–World War I genocide at the hands of the Italian Fascist regime—which, we might recall, was highly praised in the liberal democracies of the West. Ludwig von Mises, the guru of "libertarianism," wrote in 1927 that "it cannot be denied that Fascism and similar movements aimed at the establishment of dictatorships are full of the best intentions and that their intervention has for the moment saved European civilization. The merit that Fascism has thereby won for itself will live on eternally in history." (His apologists plead that he only intended for these "best intentions" to be a temporary means to "save civilization"; the Blackshirts could then retire.)

Aside from Trump's criminal negligence of the spread of COVID-19, and his complete insensitivity to the frustration and anger of the people seeking justice through their street protests against the killing of George Floyd and police brutality generally, the United States does not seem to be well served by its version of federalism.

Federalism in its modern form dates back to the Civil War, which changed the phrase "United States" from plural to singular (in English at least). But the problems with US federalism trace back to the country's founding, and are becoming very severe. In the late 18th century, the US Constitution was a progressive doctrine in comparative terms. However, it was also a "framers' coup" against popular pressures for democracy, to borrow the title of the fine study by Michael Klarman that is the gold standard for scholarship on the establishment of the Constitution.

Yet even the words "We the People" were a serious challenge to the regimes of the day, meaningful enough to evoke the venerable domino theory among leaders of the time. King George III feared that the example of the American Revolution might lead to erosion of the empire. The Tsar and Klemens von Metternich had similar concerns about "the pernicious doctrines of republicanism and popular self-rule" spread by "the apostles of sedition" in the colonies that had cast off the British yoke.

That was then. By today's standards, the US political system is so regressive that if the US were to apply for membership in the European Union, it would probably be turned down by the European Court of Justice. The Senate is a travesty of democracy. Wyoming, with 500,000 people, has the same number of senators as California, with 40 million. This extreme perversion of democracy affects the Electoral College as well. The House was carefully designed by Madison with measures to reduce the threat of democracy, but all of that has been effaced by radical gerrymandering and an array of devices, mainly devised by contemporary Republicans, to suppress voting by the "wrong people." The powers of the presidency have been constrained by good faith and trust, the way the British Constitution functioned for centuries (now eroding). With a wrecker like Trump in office, backed by a party of trembling cowards, these powers verge on dictatorship, as we are now seeing.

By now a small minority—rural, white, devoutly Christian or evangelical—can run Congress. Furthermore, this is ineradicable. The small states can block a constitutional amendment.

These remarks keep to the formalities of the democratic system, putting aside those whom Adam Smith called "the masters of mankind," FDR's "economic royalists." Smith recognized them to be the "principal architects of policy" in 18th century England, the model of democracy in his day. As he wrote, they made sure that policy served their interests, however "grievous" their impact on the general population. Today, they virtually own the political system, from campaign funding to the overwhelming force of lobbyists and innumerable other devices to keep the government securely in their pocket.

Though their power is immense, it is fragile. Hence the concern at Davos about "reputational risks," and the statements of top executives that they are mending their ways. They don't have to read David Hume to learn that the "governors have nothing to support them but opinion—which can be withdrawn —since FORCE is always on the side of the governed."

The power of the masters is indeed fragile. It can be restricted, even overturned, by a public dedicated to different goals. But that requires organization. Thatcher and Reagan knew what they were doing when they launched the neoliberal era with sharp attacks on labor unions, traditionally the spearhead of social justice struggles.

Just keeping to the formal democratic system, a serious constitutional crisis is inevitable for structural reasons—and Trump is edging toward it. It is a matter of concern in high places committed to the constitutional order. For example, there is no precedent for the denunciation of his call for violent suppression of protest by some of the highest military officers—the two previous chairmen of the Joint Chiefs of Staff, his former defense secretary and former chief of staff, the former commander of NATO and US forces in Afghanistan, all top-ranking generals—some of whom went on to eloquently support the protesters.

More important, also without precedent is the remarkable mobilization of whites all over the country to participate in the mass nonviolent protests, braving the serious threat of succumbing to the virus along with some police violence. A poll in the first days of June found 64 percent of American adults were "sympathetic to people who are out protesting right now," while 27 percent said they were not and 9 percent were unsure.

Where this will lead is anyone's guess, and more may be coming as a fateful election approaches. It's hard to determine what is more ominous: another four years for the malignancy to spread its poison, or an electoral loss that Trump will declare illegitimate, refusing to leave the White House, calling on the heavily armed "tough guys" he regularly urges on to defend their "Second Amendment rights" by protecting the self-declared "chosen one," eyes lifted to heaven.

Is this a wild fantasy? Maybe, maybe not. It's being discussed in respectable circles. Specialists on the topic have warned that Trump is bringing Fascism to the US. Personally, I think that gives him too much credit. Fascism is too sophisticated a doctrine for him to grasp. It is, furthermore, a doctrine that is antithetical to his own simplistic conception of how the world should be run: by the masters of the universe, with Trump wielding the wrecking ball at whim. Fascist ideology calls for strict control of the society by the Fascist Party led by the maximal leader; crucially, control of the compliant business classes. That is almost the opposite of what prevails and what Trump's limited vision seeks to entrench further. He may advocate Fascist tactics, but that's far from Fascism. It resembles more closely a tinpot dictatorship.

Nevertheless, well-regarded analysts in the mainstream are concerned. One is former CIA analyst Robert Baer, who has had lots of experience in tin-pot dictatorships. "If I were a foreign intelligence officer assigned to Washington, I'd ask how close he is to imposing martial law because it looks pretty close to me," Baer said. "I mean, he said he will. He's preparing for it. He's got a secretary of defense right now who's balking. It's very easy to remove him and put somebody in his place. This president is very insecure. And we've watched him go after the FBI and the Department of Justice, and he will go after the Pentagon until he gets the officers in that don't countermand his orders. . . . I have never seen this in the United States, never heard since the Civil War. . . . If I were a foreigner, I would really wonder . . . what's happening to American democracy."

We can remind ourselves of how fateful the coming election is by keeping our eyes on current science. For example, the recent report from the Scripps Institute of Oceanography, the main monitor of atmospheric CO_2, shows that levels have not only long surpassed all of human history, but are approaching the highest they have been for 3 million years, when sea levels were 50 to 80 feet higher than they are today.

The coronavirus dip is a statistically insignificant deviation, though it does serve to instruct us that there is still time to avert a cataclysm, though not much.

The countries of the world are seeking to do something to respond, not enough, but at least something. The country that is doing the least is the United States, in the hands of the wrecker-in-chief.

Trump does not waste a minute in his relentless drive to race toward the cliff. His February 2020 budget proposal, while naturally calling for continued defunding of the Centers for Disease Control and Prevention in the midst of a raging pandemic, also called for further subsidies to the fossil fuel industries that are laboring to destroy organized human life. And to accelerate the disaster, Trump is using the cover of the pandemic to dismantle "federal regulations designed to protect workers, consumers, investors and the environment," rescind requirements for factories and power plants to monitor or report emissions, waive environmental laws for pipelines and other projects, and instruct "agencies across the government to rescind, modify or simply stop enforcing regulations if they burden the economy."

The last phrase is a euphemism for interfering with profits. Helping the economy would actually mean building infrastructure and productive capacity, not pouring funds into keeping stock prices high for the benefit of rich investors and predatory financial capital.

"The White House will seek to make many of those roughly 600 deregulatory actions permanent," according to a former White House official speaking on the condition of anonymity. Trump's May 19 proclamation, on which this press account is based, drops enough hints to render the prediction plausible. The heads of all agencies are instructed to "review any regulatory standards they have temporarily rescinded, suspended, modified, or waived" and other actions they have taken, and "determine which, if any, would promote economic recovery *if made permanent*," subject to conditions that are meaningless; and to consider an array of actions that "temporarily *or permanently*" relate to "regulatory standards that may inhibit economic recovery" (emphasis added).

The phrase "economic recovery" has always had a definite meaning in the Trumpian lexicon that there is no need to review.

Trump's dedication to destroying human life for the sake of short-term profit for his constituency is by far the worst of his crimes, in fact it is the most extreme crime in human history. It is approached in malignancy only by his systematic dismantling of the arms control regime that has reduced the severe threat of terminal nuclear war; and, concomitantly, his promotion of more advanced weapons that enemies can use to destroy us.

Amazingly, none of this enters into current discussion, except at the margins.

In the age of COVID-19, we have seen the sudden return of economic thinking guided however loosely by Keynesian ideas (such as increasing government spending and lowering taxes in order to boost economic activity, and maintaining a solid welfare state) especially in Western Europe. Is this an indication that neoliberalism is finally on its way out? Or will we see a return to the "normal state of affairs" once the health crisis is over, especially in the United States, where there is significant resistance to the ideas of social democracy?

Like a lot of good questions, this one is virtually impossible to answer. The forces that created the current socioeconomic regime, including the pandemic and the race to self-destruction, are not wasting a moment to ensure that the neoliberal disaster persists, indeed in harsher form, with more sophisticated means of surveillance and control. They will succeed unless the general population withdraws consent, makes use of the power that is in the hands of the governed, and becomes organized to create a world that is more humane and just—in fact, survivable.

That requires at the very least constructing a minimal social state. We can see what a difficult step that will be by looking at the liberal commentary on the Sanders campaign: good ideas, but the American people aren't ready for it. That is an incredible indictment of American society, which, according to this judgment, is not able to rise to what is normal elsewhere: universal health care and free higher education, Sanders's major planks.

But for a progressive popular movement, "joining the world" should be the least of our objectives. Why should decisions about our lives be transferred from elected representatives, over which people have at least some control, to unaccountable private hands, as neoliberal doctrine dictates? Going further, why should people spend almost all of their waking lives under controls so extreme that Stalin couldn't have dreamed of them—what is called "having a job"? Work under external command is an attack on fundamental human rights and dignity that had been regarded with contempt from classical Greece and Rome until the 19th century, and was bitterly condemned by working people in the early Industrial Revolution.

That's only a bare beginning. A different world is possible, a very different one.

COVID-19 Has Exposed the US under Trump as a "Failed State"

C. J. POLYCHRONIOU: Noam, it is widely accepted by now that the US coronavirus response not only was delayed, but it remains mired in contradictions as Trump battles with scientists over policy. Moreover, the country as a whole was shown to be completely unprepared for a major health crisis. Are we talking here not simply of an incompetent administration but also of a failed state?

NOAM CHOMSKY: Fifteen years ago, I wrote a book called *Failed States*, a common locution in the day, referring to states that are incapable of meeting the needs of citizens, in the most important case because of deep policy choices, and are a danger not only to their own citizens but the world. The prime example was the United States. Extensive evidence was reviewed. That's not of course the intended use of the phrase in the doctrinal system, just as "rogue state" means some enemy, not ourselves, the prime example.

I still stand by that judgment, which was not mine alone. A few years later, a Gallup/WIN international poll found that the US is regarded as the greatest threat to world peace—no other state even came close. And the severe threats of government policy to the domestic population, already quite apparent when the book appeared, became much clearer a year later when the housing bubble burst and the financial crisis ensued. Obama's response —to bail out the perpetrators, who became richer and more powerful than before, and forget about the congressional legislation that called for some aid to those who lost their homes in corporate scams facilitated by the

Clinton-Rubin-Summers deregulation extravaganza —extended the neo-liberal assault that took off under Reagan.

That's a large part of the background for what finally brought us the Trump malignancy—which may, quite literally, doom human society on Earth. We've discussed elsewhere why this is not an exaggeration. I hope that the basic facts and their dread import are well understood, and won't review them here.

Trump has indeed hit America, but also much of the world with a hammer blow—a matter we should not overlook. Just keeping to the current COVID-19 crisis, it is remarkable to see how little attention has been given to his sadistic assaults against poor and suffering people around the world in pursuit of his goal of enhancing his electoral prospects.

There has been some attention to the extension of his vicious attacks against refugees fleeing from misery and oppression, his way of appealing to a deluded voter base that has been led to believe that refugees are the source of their suffering.

But there is hardly a word about his attacks against poor people in Africa, where countless numbers will die thanks to his defunding of the World Health Organization (WHO); the efforts of the WHO had been protecting them from a wide range of diseases, and now this new plague. There is silence about the fate of Palestinians in the occupied territories, victims of Israel's racist contempt for their health and other basic needs, amplified by Trump's defunding of their meager health, educational and support systems because—as he explained—they don't treat him with enough respect while he's smashing them in the face.

Withholding funds from the WHO was just Trump's first step in his campaign to destroy the organization. The campaign provides real insight into the deeply rooted malevolence not only of Trump, but of the gang he has collected around him—most of whom cower in silence (though some speak out), sometimes even outdoing the boss. Secretary of State Mike Pompeo has been at the forefront of demonizing the WHO, in support of Trump's increasingly desperate efforts to find a scapegoat for his terrible crimes against Americans. It doesn't matter how many people perish in Africa and elsewhere in the Global South as crucial WHO services are undermined. Just "shithole countries" anyway, as the Dear Leader has explained.

It is by now common understanding that the US under Trump is a failed state, and a serious danger to the world. Diplomats speak in muted tones, not wanting to offend the raging beast in Washington with unlimited power to destroy. But the meaning is clear when a "senior European official" says that "the US administration is very fixated on the reelection campaign and on who can get blamed for this catastrophic covid-19 situation in the US. They are blaming WHO and China for it. Therefore it is very difficult to agree on a common language about the WHO."

The "common language" in question has to do with a UN Security Council resolution the Trump administration is blocking. The resolution calls for "a global ceasefire pertaining to armed conflict in response to the pandemic [and urges] member states to 'share timely and transparent information regarding the outbreak of COVID-19.'" But the resolution is unacceptable to the White House, because it calls on countries to "support the full implementation of the WHO International Health Regulations." As the senior European official said, asking countries to implement procedures to contain the crisis is harmful to Trump's reelection campaign.

In brief, the dedication to slaughtering poor and suffering people in pursuit of personal gain is so complete that even references to WHO health regulations cannot be made. The WHO is reaching the status of *climate change*, a phrase that has to be excised from official documents dealing with the environment. Across the board, Trump and his acolytes are echoing the words of Francisco Franco's Fascist Gen. Millán Astray: "Down with intelligence! Long live death!"

Turning directly to your question, I think "incompetent" is not the right word for Trump's malevolence, which turned serious problems in the US into devastating crises. But we should not overlook the serious problems inherited by the cruel gang in today's White House. It's crucial to understand this background if we hope to contain the next pandemic, likely to be worse than this one, because of the impact of the global warming that is a far more severe threat.

At the root, there are three factors: general capitalist logic; the more brutal neoliberal variant; and reactions by individual governments.

In 2003, after the SARS epidemic, scientists were well aware that a pandemic was likely, probably a related coronavirus. They also understood how to prepare for it—just as scientists today have a good idea as to how to prepare for a future pandemic.

But it's not enough to know. Someone has to pick up the ball and run with it. The obvious candidate is Big Pharma, with huge resources, thanks to the profits from exorbitant patent rights granted under the highly protectionist "free trade" agreements. They're ruled out, however, by normal capitalist logic. There's no profit in preparing for a catastrophe down the road. And in fact it can be in their interest to impede a constructive response.

Next, the government could step in, but that's blocked by the neoliberal intensification of capitalism's inherent inhumanity. As Reagan declaimed in his inauguration speech, government is the problem, not the solution. Translation: Take decision-making away from government, which is at least partially responsive to public influence, and hand it over to private tyrannies that are unaccountable to the public. An essential component of neoliberalism, overt since its origins in interwar Vienna, is that democracy is a threat that must be contained, even destroyed by state violence if necessary. These principles were advocated in word and action by the gurus of the movement—Ludwig von Mises, Friedrich Hayek, and others. Furthermore, as Milton Friedman counseled in the Reagan years, the unaccountable tyrants who control decision-making must be guided by sheer greed. Any concern for others would shake the foundations of civilization.

The creed was not strictly observed. Obama tried to evade it slightly, but the efforts were quickly smashed by capitalist logic (the ventilator-Covidien affair, soon to be discussed, is an example). But government intervention was largely blocked.

The third factor is the reactions of individual governments. They varied. China very quickly provided the WHO and the world with all relevant information. By early January, Chinese scientists had identified the virus and sequenced the genome. Some countries at once reacted, including Taiwan, South Korea, Singapore, New Zealand, a few others. Each now seems to have the crisis largely under control. Europe dithered but finally acted, with varying degrees of success.

At the bottom of the barrel is Trump, reflecting his dedication to his primary constituency—private wealth and corporate power, lightly hidden under a farcical display of "populism." Throughout his term in office,

Trump has systematically pursued policies that enrich his primary constituency while harming others, including his adoring crowds. One part of this program was steadily defunding the Centers for Disease Control and Prevention (CDC) and dismantling programs and organizations that could have provided advance warning of what was likely to happen. As a result, the US was singularly unprepared.

Though the US and a few other failed states had all the information that led functioning societies to react appropriately, of course not all was entirely clear. That could hardly have been possible in such tumultuous circumstances. Like others, leading US health officials had some uncertainty about what exactly was happening and how best to handle it. Nevertheless, it was possible to take effective action, as shown by the record of governments that have some concern for their citizens. US intelligence and health officials understood more than enough. Through January and February, they were trying to get through to the White House, but Trump was too busy watching his TV ratings. In the style of petty dictators, he has surrounded himself with sycophants or comical figures. So, nothing from them. Or from the Republican Party, now trembling in fear of the crowds that can be mobilized by Trump and his corporate sponsors.

When some dare to inject a little rationality into administration discussions, they quickly learn their lessons, like the physician in charge of developing vaccines who was dismissed in April for warning against one of the quack medicines that Trump was advertising.

"Down with intelligence! Long live death!"

Trump should be given credit for his considerable achievements. It's not easy to get away with holding up a banner with one hand saying, "I love you, I'm our savior, I'm chosen by heaven to protect you," while the other hand is stabbing you in the back. But Trump is doing it, brilliantly. He's the supreme con man, who makes P. T. Barnum look like an amateur. He's in a long tradition, from the trickster trading tales for fun in the Old West, to the self-declared King of France in Huckleberry Finn, to the guy who'll sell you the Brooklyn Bridge. Moving to a different sphere, we might also include the president who won the "marketer of the year" award from the Association of National Advertisers for his political campaign—easily defeating Apple and other amateurs—and who went on to win a Nobel Peace Prize for some pleasant rhetoric.

But Trump is in a class by himself. Not just as a con man, but much more significantly as a dedicated enemy of the human race. That much is demonstrated by policies that have accelerated environmental catastrophe and dismantled an arms control regime that has provided some protection from terminal nuclear war, aside from a stream of peccadilloes of the kind already mentioned.

While praising Trump for his considerable achievements, we must also bear in mind that the health system that he has been wrecking was already in terrible shape. The privatized, profit-driven health system in the US was an international scandal long before Trump, with costs about twice as high as comparable countries and some of the worst outcomes. On the eve of the pandemic, the costs of this dysfunctional system were estimated at $450 billion in wasted expense and 68,000 deaths annually by *The Lancet*, one of the world's leading medical journals.

Beyond that, the neoliberal business model dictates that hospital care must be "efficient": the minimum number of nurses and hospital beds to just get by in normal times—not much fun for patients even in normal times even at the world's best hospitals, as many can attest (myself included). And if anything goes wrong, tough luck.

It should be added that contrary to common belief, the US does have universal health care. It's called "emergency rooms." If you can drag yourself to one, they'll take care of you, often with superb care—and often a hefty bill. It's the most cruel and expensive form of universal care known, but at least it's there.

Bad as the situation was that Trump inherited, he has been committed to making it worse. One illustration of the commitments (and moral level) of the White House is the budget it submitted for the coming year on February 10, while the pandemic was raging. It called for still further cuts to the CDC, along with increased subsidies to the fossil fuel industries that are driving us to final catastrophe. And, of course, more funding for the bloated military and for the famous wall that will protect us from the rapists and murderers surging across the border.

That barely skims the surface. Failed state? Four more years?

Are the anti-lockdown protests, which Trump is openly encouraging, merely about the shutting down of the economy and quarantines?

We have enough experience to see that virtually everything Trump does is about himself—the country and the world be damned. In this case, one can detect a strategy behind the ongoing circus. Trump has been casting about to find someone to blame for his crimes. After evoking the Yellow Peril and laboring to destroy the WHO, with grim effects, he's pretty much run out of targets. A rational next step is to tell governors that it's your business: the federal government, which has all the resources, can't do anything for you. If anything goes wrong, it's your fault, not mine. And if something happens to go right somewhere, it demonstrates what a stable genius I am, and it will be trumpeted by Sean Hannity as the most brilliant decision in human history.

This is similar to the strategy of saying one thing today and the opposite tomorrow, each echoed rapturously by Fox News while the liberal press dutifully tots up the lies (20,000?). If you shoot arrows at random, some may hit the target. And if one does? I'm vindicated and the scam goes on. You can't lose.

The governors ploy is about the same: enforce lockdown, open up the economy, and protect our "Second Amendment rights," which has nothing to do with anything but pushes the right buttons. If it makes life harder for the governors and leads to many deaths, that's OK too. It's all the fault of the urban centers where diseases and other maladies fester among those who are poisoning our lily-white society.

Malevolent, but not stupid.

It's tempting to add the injunction to the states by Mitch McConnell, the real evil genius of the Republican organization—"Go bankrupt." The Republican Senate is not going to compensate you for your foolish decision to give pensions to firefighters, teachers, policemen, and other undeserving takers. We have to save the money for the makers, like the airline industries that need $50 billion because in the glory days of high profits, instead of improving services and building the enterprises, they spent close to $50 billion in buybacks to inflate stock prices and compensation for management. After all, first things first. There's no need to elaborate. His vileness has been so egregious that there's been plenty of commentary in the mainstream press.

In defense of Trump, McConnell, and the rest of the merry gang, they are carrying to an extreme the only way of dealing with the dilemma that the Republicans have faced since they turned to pure service to the business world. It's hard to go to voters and say, "Look, we're the more extreme of the two business parties. We're designing policies to benefit our primary constituency of great wealth and corporate power, and to throw you into the waste bin. So vote for us."

Somehow, that doesn't work well. Consequently, it's important to divert attention to "cultural issues," to pretend to be adamantly opposed to abortion rights and love assault rifles, to be terrified of *them*, to dismiss global warming as a Commie plot, and all the rest. The word "pretend" is quite appropriate, but I won't go into that here.

The Democratic establishment has its own sins to answer for, but it is nothing like this; more like the moderate Republicans of the days before the Gingrich-Hastert-McConnell era. And it is subject to popular pressures, which have moved the party considerably to the left in recent years. That's not insignificant.

Approval ratings for most world leaders' have soared as a result of how they have handled the coronavirus crisis, with the exception of Donald Trump. Could it be the determinant element that will put an end to four years of a nightmarish scenario written, directed, produced, and carried out by the most dangerous buffoon this country has had for president? Trump's Waterloo, so to speak?

Trump benefited from the usual leadership bump when he finally acknowledged that the crisis was real, two months late, and assumed the proper presidential pose. His approval ratings have since receded to the norm from the beginning of his presidency. That's a pretty impressive performance considering what he's done to the country. I can't guess where it will go from here. It's really hard to say. He's damned resilient, and his voting base and media echo chamber stay loyal. Current statistics show that he seems to be back to his norm of approval, which hasn't varied a great deal through his term. And if it looks bad, they might pull something before November. Like concocting an incident and bombing Iran.

Why is Trump bent on destroying the US Postal Service (USPS)?

What does the postal service contribute to private wealth and corporate power (Trump's primary constituency)? Essentially nothing. Just means that they have to pay taxes for rural mail service and other services for ordinary people—insofar as they pay taxes, another interesting topic that I'll put aside. If the USPS is privatized, it can contribute to private wealth and corporate power, and they can run it "efficiently," like the health care system.

A good deal more is involved. It's important to them to drive the idea that democracy might work out of people's heads, that a public system can serve the needs of the general public. In much of the country, the local post office not only serves people's needs efficiently but is even a place where you can stop by and chat with a human being and meet your friends.

And—horror of horrors—activists might be able to help people realize why the postal service was set up by the ounders. Its prime function in early years was to deliver journals and magazines cheaply, a subsidy to an independent press, what the founders seem to have had in mind in framing the First Amendment. These matters are explored in depth in scholarly work by Robert McChesney and Victor Pickard, who carry the discussion right to the twentieth-century struggles to join the world in having vibrant public media, a critical matter for media activists today.

That's dangerous turf. Better to destroy the virus of democracy before it infects too many people.

Joe Biden expressed the fear last week that Trump might attempt to delay the November 2020 election. Is this a likely scenario? Does the sitting president have the authority to do so on account of a national crisis?

No constitutional authority, but Trump is quite capable of imitating his ludicrous friend Jair Bolsonaro and declaring, "I am the Constitution." Unlike the Brazilian judiciary, the Roberts Supreme Court might back such a statement up. And if granted another four years of court-packing up and down the line with young ultraright figures, virtually anything will be possible. Anything, that is, but mildly progressive measures. Their fate will be dim for a generation or more.

It's also not beyond imagination that if Trump loses the Electoral College (not just the popular vote), he'll declare the election illegitimate, claiming that the Democrats brought in undocumented immigrants, and insist on staying in office, surrounded by armed militias.

I can't verify it, but it's been credibly reported that if he has to leave the White House, Trump may be facing serious charges brought by states' attorneys. That aside, given his mental state, Trump might not be able to handle defeat and walk away like a normal human being.

Many on the left feel, naturally, and with much justification, extremely uncomfortable about Joe Biden. In fact, we hear now from some quarters the same arguments we heard in 2016 about Hillary Clinton, which is to say that it would be unconscionable for progressives to accept the "lesser of two evils" principle. How can we understand the political and conceptual context of electoral choices made by progressives and the left in November 2020?

These questions are plainly important. They are a matter of intense discussion and often impassioned debate on the left, and plenty of invective. That makes them worth discussing. To be quite frank, I don't see much other reason for discussing them. I've tried to explain in recent interviews, and judging by the reactions, have failed. So, I will repeat in more detail.

I've been around for a long time and can't think of a candidate about whom I was not "extremely uncomfortable," at least since FDR (and I was too young to have considered opinions then).

In Biden's case it's easy to think of reasons to be extremely uncomfortable. We can begin with his participation in the destruction of Libya and Honduras, in Obama's global assassination campaign, in breaking all records in deportation—and on from there. But while continuing with constant efforts to change that world, we have to take off a few minutes to each make our own choices on Election Day.

Let's think through the two concepts that lie behind the question: "unconscionable" and "lesser of two evils principle."

Let's start with "unconscionable." There are those—including close personal friends and long-time activists whom I greatly respect—who take the position that some actions are simply "unconscionable," whatever the consequences. I will ignore this position. To me, frankly, it seems not worth discussing. In the moral domain, what matters is the predictable consequences of your actions, those you are well aware of but choose to ignore. No one cares if you feel your conscience is clear.

Let's turn to the lesser of two evils principle.

Throughout my lifetime of activism (almost eighty years), I've been familiar with two doctrines about voting. One is the official doctrine.

Official doctrine holds that politics consists of showing up every few years, pushing a lever, then going back to one's private pursuits. Citizens are "spectators," not "participants in action," according to official doctrine. They can choose one or another member of the leadership class ("the responsible men") but that's the limit of popular participation. I happen to be quoting Walter Lippmann, a respected public intellectual of the 20th century (a Wilson-FDR-JFK liberal), from his "progressive essays in democracy," but the ideas are representative of prevailing liberal opinion. They trace back to the framers of the Constitution. That's why the "gold standard" in constitutional scholarship, a fine and illuminating study by Michael Klarman, is called "The Framers' Coup"—a coup against the popular demand for democracy.

On the right, views are much harsher.

A second doctrine is the one that has always prevailed on the left, call it "left doctrine." Politics consists in constant direct popular engagement in public affairs, including a wide variety of activism on many fronts. Occasionally an event comes up in the formal political arena called an "election." For left activists, it requires spending a brief period assessing the options (a very brief period for legitimate activists, who've been following everything relevant closely). Then comes a decision as to whether it's worthwhile to take a few minutes away from ongoing political work to push a lever in the quadrennial extravaganza. It's at most a brief departure from political engagement.

That's the doctrine that I've followed all my life, sometimes abstaining because the show didn't seem to matter and there's no point legitimizing the charade by participating, sometimes voting for a third party, sometimes voting for Jones if it's important to block Smith. I've sometimes voted for a Republican, in years when the Republicans were still a bona fide political party and had a better candidate.

There are, of course, myriad other cases, but the general point of left doctrine seems clear.

In recent years, a third doctrine has made an appearance and is now consuming much debate on the left: the lesser of two evils principle. I'd never heard of it before, in a lifetime of intensive political engagement (in the left doctrine sense). And it seems quite strange to me. It obviously is quite different from left doctrine, the prevailing doctrine on the left. The intensive debate about it falls within official doctrine, with its laser-like focus on the elections.

My own feeling about the lesser of two evils principle, of course, is that we should reject it in favor of left doctrine. It has no merits that I can see, so I think we can put it aside, along with the often-fevered debate about it.

Let's now consider the immediate case in hand. If the traditional left doctrine were applied to the current situation, it would require comparing Trump and his entourage with Biden and his, and asking whether there is a difference between them.

I personally think the difference is colossal. First and decisive, another four years of Trump, and we'll have approached or possibly passed tipping points on the path toward environmental catastrophe toward which Trump is racing. His "party" will be in tow, virtually isolated in the world, certainly in the political system here.

Just as important, the arms control regime will be dismantled, sharply increasing the threat of terminal war. The severe threats that Trump has incited in the Middle East will have increased, if not exploded. The Doomsday Clock, already reduced to seconds under Trump, will probably be close to abandoned. The reactionary international led by the White House that Trump is establishing will be well solidified.

At home, the judiciary will be so packed by ultraright young judges that no progressive initiatives will be able to be implemented for a generation. By the wayside we'll be observing other horrors, like children sent to concentration camps on the border and Black people murdered on a whim.

An advocate of left doctrine will spend a few minutes reviewing the familiar facts, then take off another few minutes to push a lever, then go back to work.

I know of only one proposed counterargument. We have to put pressure on the Democratic establishment. To begin with, it's not a counterargument. It simply reiterates the main thesis of left doctrine: constant pressure. The only remaining question is how to impose pressure. There are, basically, two proposals on the table. The first is left doctrine. The second is refusing to vote for Biden.

Let's take a look at these.

First, left doctrine. We continue with what has been done, and has been very effective. One illustration is the Sanders campaign, which has been a remarkable success in shifting debate and policy choices to the left. The activism of the Sunrise Movement—aided by young congresswomen brought to office in the Sanders wave, notably Alexandria Ocasio-Cortez—has brought to the legislative agenda a Green New Deal, with the cooperation of liberal Democrat Ed Markey, senator from Massachusetts. Some version of a Green New Deal is essential for survival.

There have also been significant shifts in other areas (health care, minimum wage, harsh repression in vulnerable communities, women's rights, on and on). We can, in fact, see this in Biden's program, which is well to the left of previous Democratic front-runners. That's why Biden is supported against Trump by Sanders (who had a large role in bringing the shift about) and also by longtime labor activists like Lawrence Mishel and Jared Bernstein. It's not my program, or yours, but we can hardly doubt that it is an improvement over what preceded.

Left doctrine efforts can work, as they often have before. We all know that that has been the main source of progress over the years, particularly when there were administrations susceptible to activist pressure.

It could be argued that political programs are just words. True, but irrelevant. Left doctrine efforts can keep Biden's feet to the fire, as has often happened in the past. And there will be opportunities to go far beyond, an urgent necessity.

In contrast, we can be sure that a Trump administration will be rock solid in opposition.

The second approach is to refuse to vote for Biden in the hope that withholding the vote will convince the Democratic establishment to take us seriously down the road. I can't honestly construct a plausible version of this view, and it would be unfair to try.

Turning finally to your question, "How can we understand the political and conceptual context of electoral choices made by progressives and the left in November 2020?"

To me the answer seems clear. We should assess whether there is meaningful difference between the candidates, and also recognize that, for most of us, voting takes a few minutes. Then we go back to our real activist work.

To Heal from COVID-19, We Must Imagine a Different World

with Robert Pollin

C. J. POLYCHRONIOU: Noam, what are some of the deeper lessons we can draw from the global health crisis caused by coronavirus?

NOAM CHOMSKY: Pandemics have been predicted by scientists for a long time, particularly since the 2003 SARS pandemic, which was caused by a coronavirus similar to COVID-19. They also predict that there will be additional, and probably worse, pandemics. If we hope to prevent these future crises, we should therefore ask how this happened, and change what went wrong. The lessons arise at many levels, from the roots of the catastrophe to issues specific to particular countries. I'll focus on the US, though that's misleading since it is at the bottom of the barrel in competence of response to the crisis.

The basic factors are clear enough. The damage was rooted in a colossal market failure, exacerbated by the capitalism of the neoliberal era. There are particularities in the US, ranging from its disastrous health system and weak social justice ranking—near the bottom of the OECD—to the wrecking ball that has taken over the federal government.

The virus responsible for SARS was quickly identified. Vaccines were developed, but were not carried through the testing phase. Drug companies showed little interest—they respond to market signals, and there's little profit in devoting resources to staving off some anticipated catastrophe. The general failure is illustrated dramatically by the most severe immediate problem: lack of ventilators, a lethal failure, forcing doctors and nurses to make the agonizing decision of who to kill.

The Obama administration had recognized the potential problem. It ordered high-quality, low-cost ventilators from a small company that was then bought by a large corporation. But Covidien shelved the project, apparently because the products might compete with its own high-cost ventilators. It then informed the government that it wanted to cancel the contract because it was not profitable enough.

So far, normal capitalist logic. But at that point the neoliberal pathology delivered another hammer blow. The government could have stepped in, but that's barred by the reigning doctrine pronounced by Ronald Reagan —government is the problem, not the solution. So nothing could be done.

We should pause for a moment to consider the meaning of the formula. In practice, it means that government is not the solution when the welfare of the population is at stake, but it very definitely can address the concerns of private wealth and corporate power. The record is ample under Reagan and since, and there should be no need to review it. The mantra "Government bad" is similar to the vaunted "free market"—easily skewed to accommodate exorbitant claims of capital.

Neoliberal doctrines entered for the private sector too. The business model requires "efficiency," meaning maximal profit, consequences be damned. For the privatized health system, it means no spare capacity: just enough to get by in normal circumstances, and even then, bare bones, with severe cost to patients but a good balance sheet (and rich rewards for management). When something unexpected happens, tough luck.

These standard business principles have plenty of effects throughout the economy. The most severe concern the climate crisis, which overshadows the current virus crisis in its import. Fossil fuel corporations are in business to maximize profits, not to allow human society to survive, a matter of indifference. They are constantly seeking new oil fields to exploit. They do not waste resources on sustainable energy and dismantle profitable sustainable energy projects because they can make more money by accelerating mass destruction.

The White House, in the hands of an extraordinary collection of gangsters, pours fuel on the fire through its dedication to maximizing fossil fuel use and by dismantling regulations that hinder the race to the abyss, in which they proudly take the lead.

The reaction of the Davos crowd—the "masters of the universe," as they are called—is instructive. They dislike Trump's vulgarity, which contaminates the image of civilized humanism they seek to project. But they applaud him vigorously when he rants away as keynote speaker, recognizing that he has a clear understanding of how to fill the right pockets.

These are the times we live in, and unless there is a radical change of direction, what we are seeing now is a bare foretaste of what is to come.

Returning to the pandemic, there was ample evidence that it was coming. Trump responded in his characteristic manner. Throughout his term, budgets for health-related components of government were slashed. With exquisite timing, "two months before the novel coronavirus is thought to have begun its deadly advance in Wuhan, China, the Trump administration ended a $200 million pandemic early-warning program aimed at training scientists in China and other countries to detect and respond to such a threat"—a precursor to Trump's fanning "Yellow Peril" flames to deflect attention from his catastrophic performance.

The defunding process continued, astonishingly, after the pandemic had struck with full force. On February 10, the White House released its new budget, with further reductions for the beleaguered health care system (indeed anything that might benefit the population) but "the budget promotes a fossil fuel 'energy boom' in the United States, including an increase in the production of natural gas and crude oil."

Perhaps there are words that can capture the systematic malevolence. I can't find them.

The American people are also a target of Trumpian values. Despite repeated pleas from Congress and the medical profession, Trump did not invoke the Defense Production Act to order companies to produce badly needed equipment, claiming that it is a "break the glass" last resort and that to invoke the Defense Production Act for the pandemic would be to turn the country into Venezuela. But in fact, the *New York Times* points out that the Defense

Production Act "has been invoked hundreds of thousands of times in the Trump years" for the military. Somehow the country survived this assault on the "free enterprise system."

It was not enough to refuse to take measures to procure the required medical equipment. The White House also made sure that stocks would be depleted. A study of government trade data by Congresswoman Katie Porter found that the value of US ventilator exports rose 22.7 percent from January to February and that in February 2020, "the value of US mask exports to China was 1,094 [percent] higher than the 2019 monthly average."

The study continues:

> As recently as March 2, the Trump Administration was encouraging American businesses to increase exports of medical supplies, especially to China. Yet, during this period, the US government was well aware of the harms of COVID-19, including a likely need for additional respirators and masks.

Writing in the *American Prospect*, David Dayen comments: "So manufacturers and middlemen made money in the first two months of the year shipping medical supplies out of the country, and now they're making more money in the next two months shipping them back in. The trade imbalance took precedence over self-sufficiency and resiliency."

There was no doubt about the coming dangers. In October, a high-level study revealed the nature of the pandemic threats. On December 31, China informed the World Health Organization of an outbreak of pneumonia-like symptoms. A week later, it reported that scientists had identified the source as a coronavirus and sequenced the genome, again providing the information to the general public. For several weeks, China did not reveal the scale of the crisis, claiming later that the delay had been caused by failure of local bureaucrats to inform the central authorities, a claim confirmed by US analysts.

Neverthless, what was happening in China was well known. In particular, to US intelligence, which through January and February was beating on the doors of the White House trying to reach the president. To no avail. He was either playing golf or praising himself on TV for having done more than anyone in the world to stem the threat.

Intelligence was not alone in trying to get the White House to wake up. As the *New York Times* reports, "A top White House adviser [Peter Navarro] starkly warned Trump administration officials in late January that the coronavirus crisis could cost the United States trillions of dollars and put millions of Americans at risk of illness or death . . . imperiling the lives of millions of Americans [as shown by] the information coming from China."

To no avail. Months were lost while the Dear Leader flipped up and back from one tale to another—ominously, with the adoring Republican voting base lustily cheering every step.

When the facts finally became undeniable, Trump assured the world that he was the first person to have discovered the pandemic and his firm hand had everything under control. Throughout, the performance was loyally parroted by the sycophants with whom he has surrounded himself, and by his echo chamber at Fox News—which also seems to serve as his source for information and ideas, in an interesting dialogue.

None of this was inevitable. It was not only US intelligence that understood the early information that China provided. Countries on China's periphery reacted at once, very effectively in Taiwan, also in South Korea, Hong Kong, and Singapore. New Zealand instituted a lockdown at once, and seems to have virtually eliminated the epidemic.

Most of Europe dithered, but better organized societies reacted. Germany has the world's lowest reported death rate, benefiting from spare capacity they had in reserve. The same seems to be true of Norway and some others. The European Union revealed its level of civilization by the refusal of the better-off countries to help others. But fortunately, they could count on Cuba to come to their rescue, providing doctors, while China provided medical equipment.

Throughout, there are many lessons to learn, crucially, about the suicidal features of unconstrained capitalism and the additional damage caused by the neoliberal plague. The crisis shines a bright light on the perils of transferring decision-making to unaccountable private institutions dedicated solely to greed, their solemn duty, as Milton Friedman and other luminaries have explained, invoking the laws of sound economics.

For the US there are special lessons. As already noted, the US ranks near the bottom of the Organisation for Economic Co-operation and

Development in social justice measures. Its privatized, for-profit health care system, pursuing business models of efficiency, is a disaster, with twice the per-capita costs of comparable countries and some of the worst outcomes. There is no reason to live with that. Surely the time has come to rise to the level of other countries and institute a humane and efficient universal health care system.

There are other simple steps that can be taken at once. Corporations are again rushing to the nanny state for bailouts. If granted, strict conditions should be imposed: no bonuses and pay for executives for the duration of the crisis; permanent ban on stock buybacks and resort to tax havens, modes of robbery of the public that run to tens of trillions of dollars, not small change. Is that feasible? Clearly so. That was the law, and was enforced, until Reagan opened the spigot. They should also be required to have worker representation in management and to adhere to a living wage, among conditions that quickly come to mind.

There are many further short-range steps that are quite feasible and could expand. But beyond that, the crisis offers an opportunity to rethink and reshape our world. The masters are dedicating themselves to the task, and if they are not countered and overwhelmed by engaged popular forces, we will be entering a much uglier world—one that may not long survive.

The masters are uneasy. As the peasants are picking up their pitchforks, tuned in corporate leaders are changing. High-level executives have joined to show that they are such nice guys that the well-being and security of all is assured, if left in their caring hands. It's time for corporate culture and practice to become more caring, they proclaim, concerned not just with returns to shareholders (mostly very wealthy), but with stakeholders—workers and community. It was a leading theme of the last Davos conference in January.

They aren't reminding us that we've heard this song before. In the 1950s the phrase was "the soulful corporation." How soulful, it did not take long to discover.

C. J. POLYCHRONIOU: Bob, can you help us understand the economic shock of coronavirus? How severe will the socioeconomic impact be, and who is likely to be most affected?

ROBERT POLLIN: The breakneck speed of the economic collapse resulting from COVID-19 is without historic precedent.

Over the week of April 4, 6.6 million people filed initial claims to receive unemployment insurance. This is after 6.9 million people filed the previous week, and 3.3 million filed the week before that. Prior to these three weeks, the highest number of people filing claims was in October 1982, during the severe Ronald Reagan double-dip recession. At that time, the record number of claims added up to 650,000. This disparity between 1982 and today is eye-popping, even after one takes account of the relative size of the US labor force today versus in 1982. Thus, in 1982, the 650,000 unemployment insurance claims amounted to 0.6 percent of the US labor force. The 6.6 million people who filed claims in the first week of April and 6.9 million the week before both equaled fully 4 percent of the US labor force. As a percentage of the labor force, these weekly filings for unemployment claims were 7 times higher than the previous record from 1982. Adding up the past three weeks of unemployment insurance claims gets us to 16.8 million newly unemployed people, amounting to over 10 percent of the US labor force. The expectation is that this figure is going to keep rising for many more weeks to come, potentially pushing unemployment in the range of 20 percent, a figure not seen since the depths of the 1930s Great Depression.

The situation for unemployed people in the US is worse still because a large share of them had health insurance coverage through their employers. That insurance is now gone. The stimulus bill that Trump signed into law on March 27 provides no funds for treating people who are infected. The Peterson-Kaiser Family Foundation estimated that treatment could cost up to $20,000, and that even people with health insurance coverage through their employer could end up with $1,300 in out-of-pocket bills. Thus, fully in the spirit of our corporate-dominated and egregiously unfair US health care system, COVID-19 will hit millions of people with major medical bills at exactly when they are most vulnerable. If Medicare for All were operating in the US today, everyone would be covered in full as a matter of course.

In addition to the situation for people losing their jobs, we also need to recognize conditions for people working in frontline essential occupations. These people are putting themselves at high risk by showing up at work. A report by Hye Jin Rho, Hayley Brown, and Shawn Fremstad of the

Center for Economic and Policy Research shows that more than 30 million US workers (nearly 20 percent of the entire US workforce) are employed in six broad industries that are now on the front lines of the response. These workers include grocery store clerks, nurses, cleaners, warehouse workers and bus drivers, among others, and fully 65 percent of them are women. A disproportionate share of them are also low-paid and lack health insurance. These essential workers are putting themselves at high risks of infection, and if they do become sick, they will face the prospect of a severe financial crisis on top of their illness.

The coronavirus is also hitting low-income African American communities in the US most brutally. For example, in Illinois, African Americans account for more than half of all deaths from COVID-19, even while they account for only 14 percent of the state's population. In Louisiana, 70 percent of those who have died thus far are African American, while the African American share of the population is 32 percent. Comparable patterns are emerging in other states. These figures reflect the simple fact that lower-income African Americans do not have the same ability to protect themselves through social distancing and staying home from their jobs.

As severe as conditions are now for people in the US and other advanced economies, they are going to seem mild once the virus begins to spread, as it almost certainly will, with catastrophic impacts, in the low-income countries of Africa, Asia, Latin America, and the Caribbean. To begin with, the strategies of social distancing and self-isolation that have been relatively effective in high-income countries in slowing down the infection rate will be mostly impossible to implement in the poor neighborhoods of, say, Delhi, Nairobi, or Lima, since people in these communities are mostly living in very tight quarters. They also largely have to rely on crowded public transportation to get anyplace, including to their jobs, since they cannot afford to stay home from work.

This problem is compounded by the conditions of work in these jobs. In most low-income countries, about 70 percent of all employment is informal, meaning workers do not receive benefits, including paid sick leave, provided by their employers. As the Indian economists C. P. Chandrasekhar and Jayati Ghosh write, these workers and their families "are clearly the most vulnerable to any economic downturn. When such a downturn comes in the wake of an unprecedented public health calamity, the concerns are obviously multiplied."

In addition, most low-income countries have extremely limited public health budgets to begin with. They have also been hard-hit by the collapse of tourism, as well as sharp declines in their export revenues and remittances. Thus, in recent weeks, eighty-five countries have already approached the International Monetary Fund (IMF) for short-term emergency assistance, roughly double the number that made such requests in the aftermath of the 2008 financial crisis. The situation is likely to get worse very quickly.

C. J. POLYCHRONIOU: Noam, will coronavirus kill globalization?

NOAM CHOMSKY: Globalization in some form goes back to the earliest recorded history—in fact, beyond. And it will continue. The question is: In what form? Suppose, for example, that a question arises as to whether to transfer some enterprise from Indiana to northern Mexico. Who decides? Bankers in New York or Chicago? Or perhaps the workforce and the community, perhaps even in coordination with Mexican counterparts. There are all sorts of associations among people—and conflicts of interest among them—that do not coincide with colors on maps. The sordid spectacle of states competing when cooperation is needed to combat a global crisis highlights the need to dismantle profit-based globalization and to construct true internationalism, if we hope to avoid extinction. The crisis is offering many opportunities to liberate ourselves from ideological chains, to envision a very different world, and to move on to create it.

The coronavirus is likely to change the highly fragile international economy that has been constructed in recent years, profit-driven and dismissive of externalized costs such as the huge destruction of the environment caused by transactions within complex supply chains, not to speak of the destruction of lives and communities. It's likely that all of this will be reshaped, but again we should ask, and answer, the question of whose will be the guiding hands.

There are some steps toward internationalism in the service of people, not concentrated power. Unions are still called "internationals," for example, reminiscent of dreams that do not have to be idle, and sometimes are not. Longshoremen have refused to unload cargo in acts of international solidarity. Yanis Varoufakis and Bernie Sanders issued a call for a progressive international to counter the international of reactionary states being forged by the Trump White House. There have been many impressive examples of international solidarity at state and popular levels. At the state level, nothing compares with Cuban internationalism—from Cuba's extraordinary role in the liberation of southern Africa, described in depth by Piero Gleijeses, to the work of its doctors in Pakistan after the devastating 2005 earthquake, to overcoming the failures of the European Union today.

Similar efforts can take many forms. I know of nothing to compare with the flow of Americans to Central America in the 1980s to help victims of Reagan's terrorist wars and the state terrorism that he supported, from all walks of life, some of the most dedicated and effective from church groups in rural America. There has been nothing like that in the prior history of imperialism, to my knowledge.

Without proceeding, there are many kinds of global interaction and integration. Some of them are highly meritorious and should be actively pursued.

C. J. POLYCHRONIOU: Governments around the world are responding to the coronavirus economic fallout with massive stimulus measures. In the US, the Trump administration is prepared to spend $2 trillion of stimulus money approved by Congress. Bob, is this enough? And will it test the limits of how much more debt the US can bear?

ROBERT POLLIN: The stimulus program that Trump signed into law in March is the largest such measure in US history. At $2 trillion, it amounts to roughly 10 percent of US gross domestic product (GDP), which the government aims to distribute quickly in the coming months. By contrast, the 2009 Obama fiscal stimulus was budgeted at $800 billion over two years, or about 3 percent of GDP per year over the two years.

Despite its unprecedented magnitude, it is easy to see that the current stimulus program is too small and will deliver too little, in most of the ways that matter. This is while recognizing that, adding everything up, the stimulus provides massive giveaways to big US corporations and Wall Street—i.e., the same people who benefited the most only eleven years ago from the Obama stimulus and corresponding Wall Street bailout. I noted above the fact that the stimulus provides no health care support for people infected by COVID-19. It also offers minimal additional support for both hospitals fighting the virus on the front lines as well as for state and local governments. State and local governments are going to experience sharp falls in their tax revenues—from income taxes, sales taxes, and property taxes—as the recession takes hold. During the 2007–09 Great Recession, state and local tax revenues fell by 13 percent. We can expect a drop now of at least equal severity. Absent a large-scale injection of funds from the federal government—i.e., an injection of roughly three times what has been allocated thus far through the stimulus—state and local governments will be forced to undertake large-scale budget cuts and layoffs, impacting school teachers, health care workers and police officers who, in combination, represent the bulk of their payroll spending.

Even the Trump administration appears to recognize that the stimulus bill is far too small. That is why both Trump and the congressional Democrats are already talking about another stimulus bill that could amount to another $2 trillion. The US does have the capacity to maintain borrowing these enormous sums. Among other considerations, as was true during the 2007–09 Great Recession, US government bonds will be recognized as the safest assets available on the global financial market. This will place a premium on US bonds relative to every other credit instrument on the global market. The Federal Reserve also has the capacity, as needed, to buy up and effectively retire US government bonds if the debt burden becomes excessive. No other country, or entity of any sort, enjoys anything like this privileged financial status.

Working from this position of extreme privilege, the Fed has now committed to providing basically unlimited and unconditional support for US corporations and Wall Street firms. Indeed, between March 18 and 31 alone, the Fed purchased $1.14 trillion in Treasury and corporate bonds, at a rate of over $1 million per second. The *Financial Times* reports projections that the Fed's asset holdings could reach $12 trillion by June—i.e., 60 percent of US GDP—with further increases to follow. By comparison, just prior to the 2007–2009 financial crisis, the Fed's bond holdings were at $1 trillion. They then spiked to $2 trillion during the crisis—a figure equal to only about 1/5 where the Fed's interventions are heading over the next couple of months.

The US and global economy do need a gigantic bailout now to prevent suffering by innocent people resulting from both the pandemic and economic collapse. But the bailout needs to be focused, in the immediate, on delivering health care provisions needed by everyone and keeping people financially whole.

Taking a broader structural perspective, we also need to stop squandering the enormous financial privileges enjoyed by the US on propping up the neoliberal edifice that has denominated economic life in the US and the world for the last forty years. The fact that the US government has the financial wherewithal to bail out giant corporations and Wall Street twice within the past eleven years means that it also has the capacity to take control over some of the most dysfunctional and antisocial private enterprises. We could start by replacing the private health insurance industry with Medicare for All. The federal government could also take a controlling interest in the fossil fuel industry that must be put out of business, in any case, over the next thirty years. Other targets for at least partial nationalizations should include the airlines that face desperate straits now, but that squandered 96 percent of their cash on buybacks over the past decade. The Wall Street operators who helped to engineer such financial practices need to face both strong regulations and competition from large-scale public development banks capable of financing, for example, the Green New Deal.

In short, the US economy that will emerge out of the present crisis cannot be permitted to return to the neoliberal status quo. It was clear during the Great Recession that some of the biggest US corporations and Wall Street firms could not survive without government life supports. Now, only eleven years later, we are about to rerun the same movie, only this time on a jumbotron screen. Forty years' worth of neoliberal indoctrination has pampered big business and Wall Street into believing that corporate socialism will always be theirs for the asking—that they can hoard profits for themselves at will while foisting their risks, as needed, onto everybody else. At this moment especially, if businesses want to insist that they exist only to maximize profits for their owners, then the federal government needs to sever their lifelines. Progressives should keep fighting hard for these principles.

C. J. POLYCHRONIOU: Noam, coronavirus seems to be producing an uplift in solidarity among common people in many parts of the world, and perhaps even the realization that we are all global citizens. Obviously, coronavirus itself won't defeat neoliberalism and the resulting atomization of social life that we have been witnessing since its advent, but do you expect a shift in economic and political thinking? Perhaps the return of the social state?

NOAM CHOMSKY: Those possibilities should remind us of the powerful wave of radical democracy that swept over much of the world under the impact of the Great Depression and the anti-Fascist war—and of the steps taken by the masters to contain or crush such hopes. This history yields many lessons for today.

The pandemic should shock and prompt an appreciation of genuine internationalism, to a recognition of the need to cure ailing societies of the neoliberal plague, then on to more radical reconstruction directed to the roots of contemporary disorder.

Americans in particular should awaken to the cruelty of the weak social justice system. Not a simple matter. It is, for example, quite odd to see that even at the left end of mainstream opinion, programs such as those advocated by Bernie Sanders are considered "too radical" for Americans. His two major programs call for universal health care and free higher education, normal in developed societies and poorer ones as well.

The pandemic should awaken us to the realization that in a just world, social fetters should be replaced by social bonds, ideals that trace back to the Enlightenment and classical liberalism. Ideals that we see realized in many ways. The remarkable courage and selflessness of health workers is an inspiring tribute to the resources of the human spirit. In many places, communities of mutual aid are being formed to provide food for the needy and help and support for the elderly and disabled.

There is indeed "an uplift in solidarity among common people in many parts of the world, and perhaps even the realization that we are all global citizens." The challenges are clear. They can be met. At this grim moment of human history, they must be met, or history will come to an inglorious end.

Ventilator Shortage Exposes the Cruelty of Neoliberal Capitalism

C. J. POLYCHRONIOU: Noam, the outbreak of the new coronavirus disease has spread to most parts of the world, with the United States now having more infected cases than any other country, including China, where the virus originated. Are these surprising developments?

NOAM CHOMSKY: The scale of the plague is surprising, indeed shocking, but not its appearance. Nor the fact that the US has the worst record in responding to the crisis.

Scientists have been warning of a pandemic for years, insistently so since the SARS epidemic of 2003, also caused by a coronavirus, for which vaccines were developed but did not proceed beyond the pre-clinical level. That was the time to begin to put in place rapid-response systems in preparation for an outbreak and to set aside spare capacity that would be needed. Initiatives could also have been undertaken to develop defenses and modes of treatment for a likely recurrence with a related virus.

But scientific understanding is not enough. There has to be someone to pick up the ball and run with it. That option was barred by the pathology of the contemporary socioeconomic order. Market signals were clear: there's no profit in preventing a future catastrophe. The government could have stepped in, but that's barred by reigning doctrine. "Government is the problem," Reagan told us with his sunny smile, meaning that decision-making must be handed over even more fully to the business world, which is devoted to private profit and is free from concern about the common good. The years that followed injected a dose of neoliberal brutality to the unconstrained capitalist order and the twisted markets it constructs.

The depth of the pathology is revealed clearly by one of the most dramatic—and murderous—failures: the lack of ventilators that is one the major bottlenecks in confronting the pandemic. The Department of Health and Human Services foresaw the problem, and contracted with a small firm to produce inexpensive, easy-to-use ventilators. But then capitalist logic intervened. The firm was bought by a major corporation, Covidien, which sidelined the project, and, "in 2014, with no ventilators having been delivered to the government, Covidien executives told officials at the [federal] biomedical research agency that they wanted to get out of the contract, according to three former federal officials. The executives complained that it was not sufficiently profitable for the company."

Doubtless true.

Neoliberal logic then intervened, dictating that the government could not act to overcome the gross market failure, which is now causing havoc. As the *New York Times* gently put the matter, "The stalled efforts to create a new class of cheap, easy-to-use ventilators highlight the perils of outsourcing projects with critical public-health implications to private companies; their focus on maximizing profits is not always consistent with the government's goal of preparing for a future crisis."

Putting aside the ritual obeisance to the benign government and its laudatory goals, the comment is true enough. We may add that focus on maximizing profits is also "not always consistent" with the hope for "the survival of humanity," to borrow the phrase of a leaked memo from JPMorgan Chase, [the US's] largest bank, warning that "the survival of humanity" is at risk on our current course, including the bank's own investments in fossil fuels. Thus, Chevron canceled a profitable sustainable energy project because there's more profit to be made in destroying life on Earth. ExxonMobil refrained from doing so, because [it] had never opened such a project in the first place, having made more rational calculations of profitability.

And rightly so, according to neoliberal doctrine. As Milton Friedman and other neoliberal luminaries have instructed us, the task of corporate managers is to maximize profits. Any deviation from this moral obligation would shatter the foundations of "civilized life."

There will be recovery from the COVID-19 crisis, at severe and possibly horrendous costs, particularly for the poor and more vulnerable. But there will be no recovery from the melting polar ice sheets and the other devastating consequences of global warming. Here, too, the catastrophe results from a market failure—in this case, of truly earth-shaking proportions.

The current administration had ample warning about a likely pandemic. In fact, a high-level simulation was run as recently as last October. Trump has reacted during his years in office in the manner to which we have become accustomed—by defunding and dismantling every relevant part of government, and assiduously implementing instructions from his corporate masters to eliminate the regulations that impede profits and save lives. He is also leading the race to the abyss of environmental catastrophe, by far his greatest crime—in fact, the greatest crime in history when we consider the consequences.

By early January, there was little doubt of what was happening. On December 31, China informed the World Health Organization (WHO) of the spread of pneumonia-like symptoms with unknown etiology. On January 7, China informed the WHO that scientists had identified the source as a coronavirus and had sequenced the genome, which they made available to the scientific world. Through January and February, US intelligence was trying hard to reach Trump's ear, but failed. Officials informed the press that "they just couldn't get him to do anything about it. The system was blinking red."

Trump was not silent, however. He issued a stream of confident pronouncements informing the public that it was just a cough; he has everything under control; he gets a 10 out of 10 for his handling of the crisis; it's very serious but he knew it was a pandemic before anyone else; and the rest of the sorry performance. The technique is well-designed, much like the practice of reeling out lies so fast that the very concept of truth vanishes. Whatever happens, Trump is sure to be vindicated among his loyal followers. When you shoot arrows at random, some are likely to hit the target.

To crown this impressive record, on February 10, when the virus was sweeping the country, the White House released its annual budget proposal, which made even sharper cuts in all the main health-related parts of the government (in fact just about anything that might help people) while increasing funding for what's really important: the military and the wall.

One effect is the shockingly belated and limited testing, well below others, making it impossible to implement the successful test-and-trace strategies that have prevented the epidemic from breaking out of control in functioning societies. Even the best hospitals lack basic equipment. The US is now the global epicenter of the crisis.

This only skims the surface of Trumpian malevolence, but there's no space for more here.

It is tempting to cast the blame on Trump for the disastrous response to the crisis. But if we hope to avert future catastrophes, we must look beyond him. Trump came to office in a sick society, afflicted by forty years of neoliberalism, with still deeper roots.

The neoliberal version of capitalism has been in force since Ronald Reagan and Margaret Thatcher, beginning shortly before. There should be no need to detail its grim consequences. Reagan's generosity to the super-rich is of direct relevance today as another bailout is in progress. Reagan quickly lifted the ban on tax havens and other devices to shift the tax burden to the public, and also authorized stock buybacks—a device to inflate stock values and enrich corporate management and the very wealthy (who own most of the stock) while undermining the productive capacity of the enterprise.

Such policy changes have huge consequences, in the tens of trillions of dollars. Quite generally, policy has been designed to benefit a tiny minority while the rest flounder. That's how we come to have a society in which 0.1 percent of the population hold 20 percent of the wealth and the bottom half have negative net worth and live from paycheck to paycheck. While profits boomed and CEO salaries skyrocketed, real wages have stagnated. As economists Emmanuel Saez and Gabriel Zucman show in their book, *The Triumph of Injustice,* taxes are basically flat across all income groups, except at the top, where they decline.

The US's privatized, for-profit health care system had long been an international scandal, with twice the per capita expenses of other developed societies and some of the worst outcomes. Neoliberal doctrine struck another blow, introducing business measures of efficiency: just-on-time service with no fat in the system. Any disruption and the system collapses. Much the same is true of the fragile global economic order forged on neoliberal principles.

This is the world that Trump inherited, the target of his battering ram. For those concerned with reconstructing a viable society out of the wreckage that will be left from the ongoing crisis, it is well to heed the call of Vijay Prashad: "We won't go back to normal, because normal was the problem."

Yet, even now, with the country in the midst of a public health emergency unlike anything we have seen in a very long time, the American public continues to be told that universal health care is not realistic. Is neoliberalism alone responsible for this peculiarly unique American perspective on health care?

It's a complicated story. To begin with, for a long time, polls have shown favorable attitudes toward universal health care, sometimes very strong support. In the late Reagan years, about 70 percent of the population thought that guaranteed health care should be in the Constitution, and 40 percent thought it already was—the Constitution taken to be the repository of all that is obviously right. There have been referenda showing high support for universal health care—until the business propaganda offensive begins, warning of the heavy if not astronomical tax burden, much as what we have seen recently. Then popular support fades.

As usual, there is an element of truth to the propaganda. Taxes will go up, but total expenses should sharply decline, as the record of comparable countries shows. How much? There are some suggestive estimates. One of the world's leading medical journals, *The Lancet* (UK), recently published a study estimating that universal health care in the US "is likely to lead to a 13% savings in national health-care expenditure, equivalent to more than US$450 billion annually (based on the value of the US$ in 2017)." The study continues:

> The entire system could be funded with less financial outlay than is incurred by employers and households paying for health-care premiums combined with existing government allocations. This shift to single payer health care would provide the greatest relief to lower-income households. Furthermore, we estimate that ensuring health-care access for all Americans would save more than 68,000 lives and 1.73 million life-years every year, compared with the status quo.

But it would raise taxes. And it seems that many Americans would prefer to spend more money as long as it doesn't go to taxes (incidentally killing tens of thousands of people annually). That's a telling indication of the state of American democracy, and of the force of the doctrinal system crafted by business power and its intellectual servants. The neoliberal assault has intensified this pathological element of the national culture, but the roots go much deeper and are illustrated in many ways, a topic very much worth pursuing.

While some European countries are doing better than others in managing the spread of COVID-19, the countries that appear to have had greater success with this task lie primarily outside the Western (neo)liberal universe. They are Singapore, South Korea, Russia, and China itself. Does this fact tell us something about Western capitalist regimes?

There have been various reactions to the spread of the virus. China itself seems to have controlled it, at least for now. The same is true of the countries in China's periphery where the early warnings were heeded, including democracies no less vibrant than those of the West. Europe mostly temporized, but some European countries acted. Germany appears to hold the global record in low death rates, thanks to spare health facilities and diagnostic capacity, and rapid response. The same seems to be true in Norway. Boris Johnson's reaction in the UK was shameful. Trump's US brought up the rear.

Germany's solicitude for the population did not, however, extend beyond its borders. The European Union proved to be anything but. However, ailing European societies could reach across the Atlantic for succor. The Cuban superpower was once again ready to help with doctors and equipment. Meanwhile, the US cut health aid to Yemen, where it had helped create the world's worst humanitarian crisis, and used the opportunity of the devastating health crisis to tighten its cruel sanctions to ensure maximal suffering among its chosen enemies. Cuba is the most longstanding victim, back to the days of Kennedy's terrorist wars and economic strangulation, but miraculously has survived.

It should, incidentally, be profoundly disturbing to Americans to compare the circus in Washington with Angela Merkel's sober, measured, factual report to Germans on how the outbreak should be handled.

The distinguishing feature in responses seems not to be democracies versus autocracies, but functioning vs. dysfunctional societies—what in Trumpian rhetoric are termed "shithole" countries, like what he is working hard to craft under his rule.

What do you think of the $2 trillion coronavirus economic rescue plan? Is it enough to stave off another possible Great Recession and to help the most vulnerable groups in American society?

The rescue plan is better than nothing. It offers limited relief to some of those who desperately need it, and contains an ample fund to help the truly vulnerable—the piteous corporations flocking to the nanny state, hat in hand, hiding their copies of Ayn Rand and pleading once again for rescue by the public after having spent the glory years amassing vast profits and magnifying them with an orgy of stock buybacks. But no need to worry. The slush fund will be monitored by Trump and his treasury secretary, who can be trusted to be fair and just. And if they decide to disregard the demands of the new inspector-general and Congress, who is going to do anything about it? Barr's Justice Department? Impeachment?

There would have been ways to direct aid to those who need it, to households, beyond the pittance included for some. That includes those working people who had authentic jobs and the huge precariat who were getting by somehow with temporary and irregular employment, but also others: those who had given up, the hundreds of thousands of victims of "deaths of despair"—a unique American tragedy—the homeless, prisoners, the great many with such inadequate housing that isolation and storing food is not an option, and plenty of others that are not hard to identify.

Political economists Thomas Ferguson and Rob Johnson put the matter plainly: while the universal medical care that is standard elsewhere may be too much to expect in the US, "there is no reason why it should have one sided single payer insurance for corporations." They go on to review simple ways to overcome this form of corporate robbery.

At the very least, the regular practice of public bailout out of the corporate sector should require stiff enforcement of a ban on stock buybacks, meaningful worker participation in management, an end to the scandalous protectionist measures of the mislabeled "free trade agreements" that guarantee huge profits for Big Pharma while raising drug prices far beyond what they would be under rational arrangements.

Sanders Threatens the Establishment by Inspiring Popular Movements

C. J. POLYCHRONIOU: The impeachment trial of Donald Trump is nearly over, and what a farce it has been—something you had predicted from the start, which is also the reason why you thought that an impeachment inquiry was a rather foolish move on the part of the Democrats. With that in mind, what does this farcical episode tell us about the contemporary state of US politics, and do you anticipate any political fallout in the 2020 election?

NOAM CHOMSKY: It seemed clear from the outset that the impeachment effort could not be serious, and would end up being another gift by the Democrats to Trump, much as the Mueller affair was. Any doubts about its farcical nature were put to rest by its opening spectacle: Supreme Court Chief Justice John Roberts struggling to keep a straight face while swearing in senators who solemnly pledged that they would be unmoved by partisan concerns. They at once proceeded—as everyone knew they would—to behave and vote along strictly party lines. Could there be a clearer exhibition of pure farce?

Are the crimes discussed a basis for impeachment? Seems so to me. Has Trump committed vastly more serious crimes? That is hardly debatable. What might be debatable is whether he is indeed the most dangerous criminal in human history (which happens to be my personal view). Hitler had been perhaps the leading candidate for this honor. His goal was to rid the German-run world of Jews, Roma, homosexuals, and other "deviants," along with tens of millions of Slav *"Untermenschen."* But Hitler was not dedicated with fervor to destroying the prospects of organized human life on Earth in the not-distant future (along with millions of other species).

Trump is. And those who think he doesn't know what he's doing haven't been looking closely.

Is that a wild and ludicrous exaggeration? Or the very simple and apparent truth? It's not difficult to figure out the answer. We've discussed it often before. There is no need to review what is happening on Trump's watch while he devotes every effort to accelerating the race to catastrophe, trailed by such lesser lights as Brazil's Jair Bolsonaro and Australia's Scott Morrison.

Every day brings new forebodings. We have just learned, for example, that the gigantic Thwaites Glacier in West Antarctica has been eroding from warm water below. The *Washington Post* describes this as "a troubling finding that could speed its melt in a region with the potential to eventually unleash more than 10 feet of sea-level rise," adding, "Scientists already knew that Thwaites was losing massive amounts of ice—more than 600 billion tons over the past several decades, and most recently as much as 50 billion tons per year." It has now been confirmed, as suspected, that "this was occurring because a layer of relatively warmer ocean water, which circles Antarctica below the colder surface layer, had moved closer to shore and begun to eat away at the glaciers themselves, affecting West Antarctica in particular." The chief scientist involved in the study warns that this may signal "an unstoppable retreat that has huge implications for global sea-level rise."

That's today. Tomorrow will be something worse.

What's causing the warmer water? No secret. This is only one of the likely irreversible tipping points that may be reached if "the Chosen One," as he modestly describes himself, is granted another four years to carry out his project of global destruction.

We have just witnessed an extraordinary event at the January Davos meeting of the masters of the universe, as they are called; for Adam Smith, they were only "the masters of mankind," but 250 years ago it was just British merchants and manufacturers.

The conference opened with Trump's oration about what a fabulous creature he is. The encomium was interrupted only by a comment that we should not be "alarmist" about the climate. His Magnificence was followed by the quiet and informed comments of a seventeen-year-old girl instructing the heads of state, CEOs, media leaders, and grand intellectuals about what it means to be a responsible adult.

Quite a spectacle.

Trump's war on organized life on Earth is only the barest beginning. More narrowly, in recent days, the Chosen One has issued executive orders ridding the country of the plague of regulations that protect children from mercury poisoning and preserve the country's water supplies and lands, along with other impediments to further enrichment of Trump's primary constituency, extreme wealth and corporate power.

On the side, he has been casually proceeding to dismantle the last vestiges of the arms control regime that has provided some limited degree of security from terminal nuclear war, eliciting cheers from the military industry. And as we have just learned, the great pacifist who is committed to end interventions "dropped more bombs and other munitions in Afghanistan last year than any other year since documentation began in 2006, Air Force data shows."

He is also ramping up his acts of war—which is what they are—against Iran. I won't even go into his giving Israel what the Israeli press calls "a gift to the right," formally giving the back of his imperial hand to international law, the World Court, the UN Security Council, and overwhelming international opinion, while shoring up the evangelical vote for the 2020 election. The prerogative of supreme power.

In brief, the list of Trump's crimes is immense, not least the worst crime in human history. But none merited a nod in the impeachment proceedings. This is hardly a novelty; rather the norm. The current proceedings are often compared with Watergate. Nixon's hideous crimes were eliminated from the charges against him despite the efforts of Rep. Robert Frederick Drinan and a few others. The Nixon impeachment charges focused on his illegal acts to harm Democrats.

Any resemblance to the farce that is now winding up? Does it suggest some insight into what motivates the powerful?

Speaking of the 2020 election, the corporate Democratic establishment and the liberal media are once again mobilizing to undermine Bernie Sanders, even though he may very well be the most electable Democrat. First, can you summarize for us what you perceive to be the core of Sanders's politico-ideological gestalt, and then explain what scares both conservatives and liberals—the possibility of someone like Sanders leading the country?

The core of Sanders's "politico-ideological gestalt" is his long-standing commitment to the interests of the large majority of the population, not the top 0.1 percent (not 1 percent, 0.1 percent) who hold more than 20 percent of the country's wealth, not the very rich who were the prime beneficiaries of the slow recovery from the 2008 disaster caused by financial capital. In this regard, the US far surpasses other developed countries, so we learn from recently released studies, which show that in the US, 65 percent of the growth of the past decade went to the very rich; next in line was Germany, at 51 percent, then declining sharply. The same studies show that if current trends persist, in the next decade all growth in the US will go to the rich.

The welfare of these sectors has never been Sanders's concern.

The Democratic establishment and liberal media are hardly likely to look kindly on someone who forthrightly proclaims, "I have no use for those—regardless of their political party—who hold some foolish dream of spinning the clock back to days when unorganized labor was a huddled, almost helpless mass. . . . Only a handful of unreconstructed reactionaries harbor the ugly thought of breaking unions. Only a fool would try to deprive working men and women of the right to join the union of their choice." By "right to work" laws, for example, or by hiring scabs, or by threatening to ship jobs to Mexico to undermine organizing efforts, to sample the bipartisan political leadership.

That's surely the kind of socialist wild man whom the country is not ready to tolerate.

The wild man in this case is President Dwight Eisenhower, the last conservative president. His remarks are a good illustration of how far the political class has shifted to the right under Clintonite "New Democrats" and the Reagan-Gingrich Republicans. The latter have drifted so far off the political spectrum that they are ranked near neofascist parties in the international spectrum, well to the right of "conservatives."

Even more threatening than Sanders's proposals to carry forward New Deal–style policies, I think, is his inspiring a popular movement that is steadily engaged in political action and direct activism to change the social order. The movement is made up of mostly young people who have not internalized the norms of liberal democracy—that the public are "ignorant and meddlesome outsiders" who are to be "spectators, not participants in action," entitled to push a lever every four years, but are then to return to their TV sets and video games while the "responsible men" manage serious matters.

This is a fundamental principle of democracy, as expounded by prominent and influential liberal 20th-century American intellectuals, who took cognizance of "the stupidity of the average man" and recognized that we should not be deluded by "democratic dogmatisms about men being the best judges of their own interests." They are not; we are—the "responsible men," the "intelligent minority." The "bewildered herd" must therefore be "put in their place" by "necessary illusions" and "emotionally potent simplifications." These are among the pronouncements of the most influential 20th-century public intellectual, Walter Lippmann, in his "progressive essays on democracy"; Harold Lasswell, one of the founders of modern political science; and Reinhold Niebuhr, the admired "theologian of the (liberal) establishment." All highly respected Wilson-FDR-Kennedy liberals.

Inspiring a popular movement that violates these norms is a serious attack on democracy, so conceived, an intolerable assault against good order.

I believe we witnessed something similar in the last UK elections in the case of Jeremy Corbyn. Do you agree? And, if so, what does this tell us about liberal democracy, which is nowadays in serious trouble itself on account of the rise and spread of authoritarianism and the far right in many parts of the world?

There are definite similarities. Corbyn, a decent and honorable man, was subjected to an extraordinary flood of vilification and defamation, which he was unable to confront. At the same time, polls indicated that the policies that he put forth—and that had led to a remarkable victory for Labour in 2017 —remained popular. A special feature in the UK was Brexit. I won't go into it in great detail here, my personal opinion, for what it's worth, is that it is a serious blow to both Britain and the EU, and is likely to cause Britain—or what remains of it—to become even more of a vassal of the US than it has been under Blair's New Labour and the Tories, whose social and economic policies have caused the country great harm. Corbyn's vacillation on the Brexit issue, which became a toxic one, surely contributed to the negative feelings about him that seem to have been a major factor in the electoral disaster for Labour, but it was only one.

As in the case of Sanders, I suspect that the prime reason for the bitter hatred of Corbyn on the part of a very wide spectrum of the British establishment is his effort to turn the Labour Party into a participatory organization that would not leave electoral politics in the hands of the Labour bureaucracy and would proceed beyond the narrow realm of electoral politics to far broader and constant activism and engagement in public affairs.

More generally, much of the world is aflame. As the men of Davos recognized with trepidation at their January meeting, the peasants are coming with their pitchforks. The neoliberal order they have imposed for the past forty years, while ultra-generous to them and their class, has had a bitter impact on the general population. A leading theme at Davos was that the masters must declare that they are changing their stance from service to the rich to attending to the concerns of "stakeholders"—working people and communities. Another theme was that while not "alarmists," they acknowledge the threat of global warming.

The unstated implication is that there is no need for regulations and other actions about climate change: *We Big Boys will take care of it. Greta Thunberg and the other children demonstrating out there can go back to school. And now that we see the flaws in our neoliberal model of capitalism, you can put aside all those disruptive political programs calling for health care, rights of workers, women, the poor. We're taking care of it, so just go back to your private pursuits, keeping to democratic norms.*

As the neoliberal order is visibly collapsing, it is giving rise to "morbid symptoms" (to borrow Gramsci's famous phrase when the Fascist plague was looming). Among these are the spread of authoritarianism and the far right that you mention. More generally, what we are witnessing is quite understandable anger, resentment, and contempt for the political institutions that have implemented the neoliberal assault—but also the rise of global, activist movements that seek to stem and reverse the race to destruction.

The confrontation could hardly have been exhibited more dramatically than by the appearance of Greta Thunberg immediately after the most powerful man in the world—the leader in the race to destruction—had admonished the masters to disdain the "heirs of yesterday's foolish fortune tellers" (virtually 100 percent of climate scientists) and to take up his wrecking ball.

US Is a Rogue State and Suleimani's Assassination Confirms It

C. J. POLYCHRONIOU: Noam, the US assassination of Iran's Quds Force commander Qassim Suleimani has reaffirmed Washington's long-held obsession with Tehran and its clerical regime, which goes all the way back to the late 1970s. What is the conflict between US and Iran all about, and does the assassination of Suleimani constitute an act of war?

NOAM CHOMSKY: Act of war? Perhaps we can settle on reckless international terrorism. It seems that Trump's decision, on a whim, appalled high Pentagon officials who briefed him on options, on pragmatic grounds. If we wish to look beyond, we might ask how we would react in comparable circumstances.

Suppose that Iran were to murder the second-highest US official, its top general, in the Mexico City international airport, along with the commander of a large part of the US-supported army of an allied nation. Would that be an act of war? Others can decide. It is enough for us to recognize that the analogy is fair enough, and that the pretexts put forth by Washington collapse so quickly on examination that it would be embarrassing to run through them.

Suleimani was greatly respected—not only in Iran, where he was a kind of cult figure. This is recognized by US experts on Iran. One of the most prominent experts, Vali Nasr (no dove, and who detests Suleimani), says that Iraqis, including Iraqi Kurds, "don't see him as the nefarious figure that the West does, but they see him through the prism of defeating ISIS." They have not forgotten that when the huge, heavily armed US-trained Iraqi army quickly collapsed, and the Kurdish capital of Erbil, then Baghdad and all of Iraq were about to fall in the hands of ISIS [also known as Daesh], it was Suleimani and the Iraqi Shia militias he organized that saved the country. Not a small matter.

As for what the conflict is all about, the background reasons are not obscure. It has long been a primary principle of US foreign policy to control the vast energy resources of the Middle East: to *control*, not necessarily to use. Iran has been central to this objective during the post–World War II period, and its escape from the US orbit in 1979 has accordingly been intolerable.

The "obsession" can be traced to 1953, when Britain—the overlord of Iran since oil was discovered there—was unable to prevent the government from taking over its own resources, and called on the global superpower to manage the operation. There is no space to review the course of the obsession since in detail, but some highlights are instructive.

Britain called on Washington with some reluctance. To do so meant surrendering more of its former empire to the US and declining even more to the role of "junior partner" in global management, as the foreign office recognized with dismay. The Eisenhower administration took over. It organized a military coup that overthrew the parliamentary regime and re-installed the Shah, restoring the oil concession to its rightful hands, with the US taking over 40 percent of the former British concession. Interestingly, Washington had to force US majors to accept this gift; they preferred to keep to cheaper Saudi oil (which the US had taken over from Britain in a mini-war during World War II). But under government coercion, they were forced to comply: one of those unusual but instructive incidents revealing how the government sometimes pursues long-term imperial interests over the objections of the powerful corporate sector that largely controls and even staffs it—with considerable resonance in US-Iran relations in recent years.

The Shah proceeded to institute a harsh tyranny. He was regularly cited by Amnesty International as a leading practitioner of torture, always with strong US support, as Iran became one of the pillars of US power in the region, along with the Saudi family dictatorship and Israel. Technically,

Iran and Israel were at war. In reality, they had extremely close relations, which surfaced publicly after the overthrow of the Shah in 1979. The tacit relations between Israel and Saudi Arabia are surfacing much more clearly now within the framework of the reactionary alliance that the Trump administration is forging as a base for US power in the region: the Gulf dictatorships, the Egyptian military dictatorship and Israel, linked to Modi's India, Bolsonaro's Brazil, and other similar elements. A rare semblance of a coherent strategy in this chaotic administration.

The Carter administration strongly supported the Shah until the last moment. High US officials—[Henry] Kissinger, [Dick] Cheney, [Donald] Rumsfeld—called on US universities (mainly my own, MIT, over strong student protest but faculty acquiescence) to aid the Shah's nuclear programs, even after he made clear that he was seeking nuclear weapons. When the popular uprising overthrew the Shah, the Carter administration was apparently split on whether to endorse the advice of de facto Israeli Ambassador Uri Lubrani, who counseled that "Tehran can be taken over by a very relatively small force, determined, ruthless, cruel. I mean the men who would lead that force will have to be emotionally geared to the possibility that they'd have to kill ten thousand people."

It didn't work, and soon Ayatollah Khomeini took over on an enormous wave of popular enthusiasm, establishing the brutal clerical autocracy that still reigns, crushing popular protests.

Shortly after, Saddam Hussein invaded Iran with strong US backing, unaffected by his resort to chemical weapons that caused huge numbers of Iranian casualties. His monstrous chemical warfare attacks against Iraqi Kurds were denied by Reagan, who sought to blame Iran and blocked congressional condemnation.

Finally, the US pretty much took over, sending naval forces to ensure Saddam's control of the Gulf. After the US-guided missile cruiser *Vincennes* shot down an Iranian civilian airliner in a clearly marked commercial corridor, killing 290 passengers and returning to port to great acclaim and awards for exceptional service, Khomeini capitulated, recognizing that Iran could not fight the US. President Bush then invited Iraqi nuclear scientists to Washington for advanced training in nuclear weapons production, a very serious threat against Iran.

Conflicts continued without a break, in more recent years focusing on Iran's nuclear programs. These conflicts ended (in theory) with the Joint Comprehensive Plan of Action (JCPOA) in 2015, an agreement between Iran and the five permanent members of the UN, plus Germany, in which Iran agreed to sharply curtail its nuclear programs—none of them weapons programs—in return for Western concessions. The International Atomic Energy Agency, which carries out intensive inspections, reports that Iran fully lived up to the agreement. US intelligence agrees.

The topic elicits much debate, unlike another question: Has the US observed the agreement? Apparently not. The JCPOA states that all participants are committed not to impede in any way Iran's reintegration into the global economy, particularly the global financial system, which the US effectively controls. The US is not permitted to interfere "in areas of trade, technology, finance and energy" and others.

While these topics are not investigated, it appears that Washington has been interfering steadily.

President Trump claims that his effective demolition of the JCPOA is an effort to negotiate an improvement. It's a worthy objective, easily realized. Any concerns about Iranian nuclear threats can be overcome by establishing a nuclear weapons-free zone (NWFZ) in the Middle East, with intensive inspections like those successfully implemented under the JCPOA.

As we have discussed before, this is quite straightforward. Regional support is overwhelming. The Arab states initiated the proposal long ago, and continue to agitate for it, with the strong support of Iran and the former nonaligned countries (G-77, now 132 countries). Europe agrees. In fact, there is only one barrier: the US, which regularly vetoes the proposal when it comes up at the review meetings of the Non-Proliferation Treaty countries, most recently by Obama in 2015. The US will not permit inspection of Israel's enormous nuclear arsenal, or even concede its existence, though it is not in doubt. The reason is simple: under US law (the Symington Amendment), conceding its existence would require terminating all aid to Israel.

So the simple method of ending the alleged concern about an Iranian threat is ruled out and the world must face grim prospects.

Since these topics are scarcely mentionable in the US, it is perhaps worthwhile to reiterate another forbidden matter: The US and UK have a special responsibility to work to establish a NWFZ in the Middle East. They are formally committed to do so under Article 14 of UN Security Council Resolution 687, which they invoked in their effort to concoct some thin legal basis for their invasion of Iraq, claiming that Iraq had violated the resolution with nuclear weapons programs. Iraq hadn't, as they were soon forced to concede. But the US continues to violate the resolution to the present in order to protect its Israeli client and to allow Washington to violate US law.

Interesting facts, which, unfortunately, are apparently too incendiary to see the light of day.

There's no point reviewing the years that followed in the hands of the man "sent by God to save Israel from Iran," in the words of the serious figure of the administration, Secretary of State Mike Pompeo.

Returning to the original question, there's quite a lot to contemplate about what the conflict is about. In a phrase, primarily imperial power, damn the consequences.

The term "rogue state" (used widely by the US State Department) refers to the pursuit of state interests without regard to accepted standards of international behavior and the basic principles of international law. Given that definition, isn't the US a star example of a rogue state?

State Department officials are not the only ones to use the term "rogue state." It has also been used by prominent American political scientists— referring to the State Department. Not Trump's, Clinton's.

During the era between Reagan's murderous terrorist atrocities in Central America and Bush's invasion of Iraq, they recognized that for much of the world, the US was "becoming the rogue superpower," considered "the single greatest external threat to their societies," and that, "In the eyes of much of the world, in fact, the prime rogue state today is the United States" (Harvard professor of the science of government and government adviser Samuel Huntington; President of the American Political Science Association Robert Jervis. Both in the main establishment journal *Foreign Affairs*, 1999, 2001).

After Bush took over, qualifications were dropped. It was asserted as fact that the US "has assumed many of the very features of the 'rogue nations' against which it has . . . done battle." Others outside the US mainstream might think of different words for the worst crime of the millennium, a text-book example of aggression without credible pretext, the "supreme international crime" of Nuremberg.

And others sometimes express their opinions. Gallup runs regular polls of international opinion. In 2013 (the Obama years), it asked for the first time, which country is the greatest threat to world peace. The US won; no one else even came close. Far behind in second place was Pakistan, presumably inflated by the Indian vote. Iran—the greatest threat to world peace in US discourse—was scarcely mentioned.

That was also the last time the question was asked, though there needn't have been much concern. It does not seem to have been reported in the US.

We might ponder these questions a little further. We are supposed to revere the US Constitution, especially conservatives. We must therefore revere Article VI, which declares that valid treaties shall be "the supreme law of the land" and officials must be bound by them. In the postwar years, by far the most important such treaty is the UN Charter, instituted under US initiative. It bans "the threat or use of force" in international affairs; specifically, the common refrain that "all options are open" with regard to Iran. And it bans all uses of force unless explicitly authorized by the Security Council or in defense against armed attack (a narrowly construed notion) and then only until the Security Council, which must be immediately notified, is able to act to terminate the attack.

We might consider what the world would look like if the US Constitution were considered applicable to the US, but let's put that interesting question aside—not, however, without mentioning that there is a respected profession, called "international lawyers and law professors," who can learnedly explain that words don't mean what they mean.

Iraq has struggled since the US invasion in 2003 to maintain a balanced situation with both Washington and Tehran. However, the Iraqi parliament has voted after Suleimani's assassination to expel all US troops. Is this likely to happen? And, if it does, what impact would it have on future US-Iraq-Iran relations, including the fight against ISIS?

We don't know whether it will happen. Even if the Iraqi government orders the US to leave, will it do so? It's not obvious, and as always, public opinion in the US, if organized and committed, can help provide an answer.

As for ISIS, Trump has just given it another lease on life, just as he gave it a "get out of jail free" card when he betrayed Syrian Kurds, leaving them to the mercy of their bitter enemies Turkey and Assad after they had fulfilled their function of fighting the war against ISIS (with 11,000 casualties, as compared with a half-dozen Americans). ISIS organized at first with jail breaks and is now free to do so again.

ISIS has been given a welcome gift in Iraq as well. The eminent Middle East historian Ervand Abrahamian observes:

The killing of Soleimani . . . has actually provided a wonderful opportunity for ISIS to recover. There will be a resurgence of ISIS very much in Mosul, northern Iraq. And that, paradoxically, will help Iran, because the Iraqi government will have no choice but to rely more and more on Iran to be able to contain ISIS [which led the defense of Iraq against the ISIS onslaught, under Suleimani's command]...Trump has pulled out of north Iraq, of the area where ISIS was, pulled the rug out from the Kurds, and now he's declared war on the pro-Iranian militias. And the Iraqi Army has not been in the past capable of dealing with ISIS. So, the obvious thing is now, the Iraqi government, how are they going to deal with the revival of ISIS? . . . they will have no choice but to actually rely more and more on Iran. So, Trump has actually undermined his own policy, if he wants to eliminate Iran's influence in Iraq.

Much as W. Bush did when he invaded Iraq.

We shouldn't forget, however, that enormous power can recover from muddle-headedness and failure—if the domestic population permits it to.

Putin appears to have outmaneuvered the US not only on Syria, but almost everywhere else on the Middle East front. What is Moscow after in the Middle East, and what's your explanation for the often-infantile diplomacy displayed by the United States in the region and in fact around the world?

One goal, substantially achieved, was to gain control of Syria. Russia entered the conflict in 2015 after advanced weapons provided by the CIA to the mostly jihadi armies had stopped Assad's forces. Russian aircraft turned the tide, and without concern for the incredible civilian toll, the Russian-backed coalition has taken control of most of the country. Russia is now the external arbiter.

Elsewhere, even among Washington's Gulf allies, Putin has presented himself, apparently with some success, as the one trustworthy outside actor. Trump's bull-in-a-China-shop diplomacy (if that is the right word) is winning few friends outside of Israel, on which he is lavishing gifts, and the other members of the reactionary alliance taking shape. Any thought of "soft power" has been pretty much abandoned. But US reserves of hard power are enormous. No other country can impose harsh sanctions at will and compel third parties to honor them, at cost of expulsion from the international financial system. And, of course, no one else has hundreds of military bases around the world or anything like Washington's advanced military power and ability to resort to force at will and with impunity. The idea of imposing sanctions on the US, or anything beyond tepid criticism, borders on ludicrous.

And so, it is likely to remain even as "in the eyes of much of the world, in fact, the prime rogue state today is the United States." This is considerably more true than twenty years ago when these words were uttered, and will continue to be the case unless and until the population compels state power to pursue a different course.

Democratic Party Centrism Risks Handing Election to Trump

C. J. POLYCHRONIOU: The 2020 US presidential election is less than a year from now, and, while most polls seem to indicate that Trump will lose the national vote, the electoral vote is up for grabs. What manner of a democracy is this, and why isn't there a public outcry in this country about the antiquated institution of the Electoral College?

NOAM CHOMSKY: Preliminary comment. I find it psychologically impossible to discuss the 2020 election without emphasizing, as strongly as possible, what is at stake—survival, nothing less.

Four more years of Trump may spell the end of much of life on Earth, including organized human society in any recognizable form. Strong words, but not strong enough.

I would like to repeat the words of Raymond Pierrehumbert, a lead author of the startling [Intergovernmental Panel on Climate Change] report of October 2018, since replaced by still more dire warnings: "With regard to the climate crisis, yes, it's time to panic. We are in deep trouble." These should be the defining terms of the 2020 election.

Environmental catastrophe is an imminent threat. Much of the world is taking steps to deal with it—inadequate, but at least something. Trump and the political organization he now virtually owns are taking steps too—to exacerbate the crisis. Some may recall [George] W. Bush's infamous call, "bring it on," directed to Iraqis preparing to "attack us" (in what happened to be their country, but put that aside). Bush later apologized, with regret, but Trump is proud to outdo him, calling on the rising seas and burning Earth to put an end to the human experiment.

In fairness, we should add that Trump is also pursuing ways to avert the environmental threat—he seeks to destroy us first by nuclear war. That is the simple logic of his demolition of the Reagan-Gorbachev Intermediate-Range Nuclear Forces Treaty (INF) followed at once by testing of missiles that violate it; the threat to dismantle the (Eisenhower-initiated) Open Skies Treaty, and finally, New START. These final blows to the arms control regime constitute, very simply, a call to other nations to join in creating new and even more horrendous weapons to destroy us all, to the unrestrained applause of weapons manufacturers.

Those are the highly likely consequences of more of Trump and the party that grovels at his feet, terrified of his adoring base. They provide the essential background for the 2020 elections.

Turning finally to your question, the Electoral College is not the most serious anachronism—even worse is the radically undemocratic Senate. These problems are severe, and remediable only by constitutional amendment that is sure to be blocked by the small states. All of this is part of more fundamental problems. A variety of demographic, structural, and policy factors are converging to a situation where a small minority—white, rural, Christian, traditional, older, fearful of losing "their America"—will be able to dominate the political system.

These considerations raise further questions about worship of a document from centuries ago that was in some ways progressive by the standards of its day, but would very likely lead to rejection of an appeal for membership in the European Union by a country bound by it.

Speaking of political culture, Donald Trump's rise to power has not only unleashed some very dangerous forces, but seems to have altered in significant ways the political culture of this country. Can you talk a bit about this?

The dark forces were gathering long before Trump appeared to mobilize them. It's worth recalling that in previous Republican primaries, candidates that emerged from the base—Michele Bachmann, Herman Cain, Rick Santorum—were intolerable to the conservative establishment and were crushed. In 2016, those efforts failed. None of this is too surprising. In recent years, the Republican Party has dedicated itself [with] such fervor to its constituency of wealth and private power that a voting base had to be mobilized on grounds unrelated to its primary policy objectives—with many dark forces. And it's also worth recalling that there are parallels elsewhere, notably in Europe, with the collapse of centrist parties. Much of what has been happening can be traced to the neoliberal assault on the general population launched a generation ago, leaving in its wake quite understandable anger, frustration, and search for scapegoats—terrain that can readily be plowed by demagogues and con artists of the Trump variety. Matters we've discussed elsewhere.

What can the state elections of the last two weeks ago tell us about 2020?

It seems that relatively affluent suburban sectors that are part of the usual Republican voting base were having second thoughts about Trump, while his grotesque behavior energized voters who normally don't participate. Much, seems to me, uncertain about 2020.

The power brokers in the Democratic Party are out to kill the left wing, and this time includes not only Bernie Sanders but also Elizabeth Warren. If that happens, how will it impact Trump's chances of getting reelected?

The donor class is clearly perturbed by Warren's critique of wealth and corporate power, and even more so by Sanders, who committed a major crime—inspiring a popular movement that doesn't just show up every four years to push a button and then leave matters to their betters, but continues its activism and the engagement in public affairs that is none of their business, according to long-standing democratic theory. The intense hatred of [Labour Party leader Jeremy] Corbyn in England, I think, has a similar basis. These have been concerns of the self-described "men of best quality" since the first modern democratic revolution in 17th-century England, and they haven't abated.

The consequences are hard to predict. If the donor class succeeds in nominating a centrist candidate, progressive activist forces might be disillusioned and reluctant to do the work on the ground that will be needed to prevent the tragedy—repeat, *tragedy*—of four more years of Trumpism. If a progressive candidate does gain the nomination, centrist power and wealth may back away, again opening the path to tragedy. It will be a fateful year. It will be even more important than usual to remain level-headed and to think through with care the consequences of action, and inaction.

Aside from activists, no one is talking about Trump's crimes. What does this tell us about contemporary US political culture?

And the culture of the more privileged sectors of the world generally.

It's not something new. It's common now to invoke Watergate—when President Nixon's terrible crimes, domestic and international, were ignored, while elite opinion agonized over the attack on the foundations of the republic—thankfully overcome in a "stunning vindication of our constitutional system" (according to famed liberal historian Henry Steele Commager). What was the attack? A break-in at the Democratic Party headquarters by some thugs organized by Nixon. That's half of the US system of political power, which doesn't take such offenses lightly. Turning to today, the prime charge so far is the abuse of presidential power to implicate a leading figure of the Democratic Party [Joe Biden] in some concocted scandal ["Ukrainegate"]. Does that suggest some conclusions about what matters to elite opinion?

One final question: Much has been written about the resurgence of democratic socialism in the United States. Do you see such a resurgence, or are people confusing traditional social democratic ideas with democratic socialism?

I'm not sure how helpful the categories are. There are a variety of serious concerns that are engaging substantial sectors of the population, mostly young people. Some have to do with existential crises; the September climate strike brought many millions to the streets, just one phase of ongoing activism. Others cover a wide range of critical issues, including the scandalous health care system; a society in which 0.1 percent hold over 20 percent of wealth while half the population has negative net worth and homeless people try to survive amidst fabulous luxury; and numerous other social ills. There are also promising efforts to develop cooperatives and worker-owned enterprises that challenge fundamental hierarchic structure more directly. That's a bare sample of considerable ferment that could open the way to a much more free and just social order—if imminent looming catastrophe can be overcome.

Coup Attempt Hit Closer to Centers of Power Than Hitler's 1923 Putsch

C. J. POLYCHRONIOU: Noam, you had been warning all along of a potential coup in the event that Trump would lose the 2020 election. In this context, are you surprised at all by what took place on Capitol Hill on the Electoral College vote count?

NOAM CHOMSKY: Surprised, yes. I'd expected a strong reaction from Trump's voting base, raised to a fever pitch by his latest antics. But hadn't expected the attempted coup to reach this level of violence, and I suspect most of the participants didn't either. Many seemed to have been caught up in the excitement of the moment when the leaders of the crowd surged into the hated Capitol to drive out the demons who were not just "stealing the election" but "stealing" their country from them: their white Christian country.

That it was an attempted coup is not in question. It was openly and proudly proclaimed as just that. It was an attempt to overturn an elected government. That's a coup. True, what was attempted was not the kind of coup regularly backed by Washington in its dependencies, a military takeover with ample bloodshed, torture, "disappearance." But, nevertheless, it was an attempted coup. True, the perpetrators regarded themselves as defending the legitimate government, but that's the norm, even for the most vicious and murderous coups, like the US-backed coup in Chile on the first 9/11—which was actually much worse in virtually every dimension than the second one, the one that we remember and commemorate. The first one is best forgotten on the principle of "wrong agents": us, not some radical Islamic fundamentalists.

The emotions of those attempting the [Capitol] coup were apparent. Belief that the election was stolen was plainly held with real fervor. And it is understandable among people who live in passionately pro-Trump areas where he is revered as their savior, and for some, even chosen by God, as he once declared. Many may scarcely have seen a Biden sign, or heard anything from Fox News or Rush Limbaugh to suggest some possible flaw in their beliefs.

In some respects, these beliefs are not as bizarre as they may look at first. A shift of tens of thousands of votes in a few counties might have swung the election the other way in a deeply undemocratic system such as ours, where 7 million votes can be swept aside along with an unknown number of others eliminated by purging, gerrymandering, and the many other devices that have been devised to steal the election from the "wrong people," effectively authorized by the Supreme Court in its shameful 2013 decision nullifying the Voting Rights Act (*Shelby County v. Holder*).

As we've discussed before, the malevolent figure in charge deserves credit for his talent in tapping the poisonous streams that run not far below the surface of American society, with sources that are deep in US history and culture.

I have to say that I was also surprised by the quick reaction of those who own the country and have a large share of responsibility for the malaise that broke forth on January 6. In no small part, it is a consequence of the neoliberal assault since Ronald Reagan, amplified by his successors, that has devastated the rural areas that are the homes of many who stormed the Capitol. Those who hold the levers of the private power that dominates the society and political system never liked Trump's behavior, which harmed the image they project as humanists dedicated to the common good. But they were willing to tolerate the vulgar performance as long as Trump and his accomplices delivered the goods, lining their pockets by robbing the public.

And that they did. The "transfer of wealth" from the lower 90 percent to the ultra-rich since Reagan opened the doors for highway robbery reaches almost $50 trillion, according to a recent Rand corporation study. No one can place numbers on the vastly greater cost of environmental destruction that was a high priority of the Trump-McConnell years of service to the very rich and corporate sector.

But January 6 was apparently too much, and the marching orders were delivered swiftly by the Big Guns.

One has to have some sympathy for the legislators caught between powerful contending forces. On the one hand, they see the angry hordes whipped to a frenzy by Trump's performances, and still in his pocket, poised to wreak vengeance on those who betray their leader. And on the other hand, looking down on them from above, are the captains of finance and industry who fund their elections and dangle before them many other privileges to keep them in line. (How many members of Congress leave office to become truck drivers or secretaries?)

The dilemma is particularly harsh for senators, who are more reliant on the large donors. And their defection from the ranks of obsequious Trump loyalists has been somewhat greater.

Apparently, DC Council members had been briefed by the US Attorney for the District of Columbia that Donald Trump might invoke the Insurrection Act to seize control of the city police, but did not expect an attack on the Capitol itself. In your own view, what explains the enormous security failures that led to the Capitol siege, and do the events of January 6, 2021, qualify as a putsch?

An attempted putsch, though the connotations of the term *putsch* may be too strong. The events reminded many, including historians of Fascism, of Hitler's failed Beer Hall Putsch of 1923, which actually did not so easily penetrate the centers of power as the attempted coup of January 6.

The reasons for the security failures are being debated. I have no special insight. Black members of the Capitol police, who showed great courage, along with many of their white colleagues, have charged for years that the force has been infiltrated with white supremacists. There may have been some collusion, and possibly serious corruption higher up the chain of command.

If Trump incited an insurrection against elected officials of the US government, is it enough that he has been impeached again? Shouldn't he be

facing sedition charges since inciting an insurrection against the government is a criminal act under Title 18 of the US Code?

I presume the Joint Chiefs of Staff chose their words carefully in their message on the "violent riot" on January 6, "a direct assault on the US Congress, the Capitol building, and our Constitutional process," an act of "violence, sedition and insurrection." They surely considered the fact that incitement to sedition and insurrection carries a heavy prison sentence. I presume that they also weighed the evidence that such incitement took place from the Oval Office.

Many questions arise about how to pursue such barely concealed charges, but we should be careful to avoid the Watergate trap. The Nixon impeachment procedures were initiated by [Massachusetts] Rep. Robert Drinan SJ, charging him with the bombing of Cambodia, a truly monstrous crime, of Nuremberg Trial caliber. That charge was struck down by Congress. The prime charge against Nixon was that he organized thugs to invade one of two seats of political power in the country, the Democratic Party headquarters. This attack on the foundations of the Republic was overcome in a "stunning vindication of our constitutional system" (famed liberal historian Henry Steele Commager).

In short, the powerful can rise to their own defense. The victims of truly monstrous crimes can look elsewhere for recourse. Maybe history, with luck.

Incitement of an attempted coup is no laughing matter, but it scarcely weighs in the balance against a dedicated effort to destroy the environment that sustains life on Earth or demolition of the arms control regime that mitigates the threat of nuclear war.

Do you believe that Trump is finished as a political figure? Or, to put the question slightly differently, was the Washington putsch of January 6, 2021, the beginning of the end of the rise of Trumpism?

Far from it. Whether Trump will survive the error of judgment that turned major power centers against him is unclear. He may well do so. The voting base of the party seems to remain loyal, maybe with even greater fervor after this attack on their hero by the "deep state." Local officials too. He was cheered on his visit to the Republican National Committee the day after the Capitol riot. He has other resources.

Whatever the fate of the individual, Trumpism will not be so easily contained. Its roots are deep. The anger and resentment raised to a frenzy by this talented con man is not limited to the US The $50 trillion robbery is only the icing on the cake of the neoliberal disaster, which itself is built on foundations of deep injustice and repression. We are not out of the woods, by far.

Trump Has Revealed the Extreme Fragility of American Democracy

C. J. POLYCHRONIOU: US election officials have declared the 2020 election "the most secure in American history." Yet, the Trump campaign continues to mount legal challenges to the electoral process, pushing outrageous falsehoods, while Rudy Giuliani has gone so far as to make outlandish claims of a vast global conspiracy to steal the election from the Great Leader. In your view, what is really behind Trump's legal challenges?

NOAM CHOMSKY: Speculation of course, but I'll indulge in a bad dream—which could become reality if we are not on guard, and if we fail to recognize that elections should be a brief interlude in a life of engaged activism, not a time to go home and leave matters in the hands of the victors.

I suspect that Trump and associates regard their legal challenges as a success in what seems a plausible strategy: keep the pot boiling and keep the loyal base at fever pitch, furious about the "stolen" election and the efforts of the insidious elites and the "deep state" to remove their savior from office.

That strategy seems to be working well. According to recent polls, "three-quarters (77%) of Trump backers say Biden's win was due to fraud" and "the anger among Trump's base is tied to a belief that the election was stolen." Rejection of the legal challenges with ridicule may please liberal circles, but for the base, it may be simply more proof of the Trump thesis: the hated elites will stop at nothing in their machinations.

Meanwhile, this strategy requires keeping the wrecking ball—Trump's symbol—actively at work. Do nothing to deal with the pandemic, even delay in providing data to Biden's team while a top nurse's union warns of "catastrophic death" in the growing chaos while "our hospitals are knowingly still not prepared" and the government is on vacation.

Viewed through the lens of this vile strategy, if the pandemic gets worse, so much the better. Then local officials will try to impose restrictions and even lockdowns to control patriotic Americans—in line with the plans of the supposed "Communist-run deep state"—leading to economic harm and intrusions on normal life. Meanwhile, Trump and his associates could abandon other normal governmental activities so that when Biden establishes what they describe as a "fake government" on inauguration day, the immediate problems will be severe and failure likely.

On that day, which will live in infamy among the faithful, Trump might set up what he claims is an authentic government in Mar-a-Lago, with Mitch McConnell's Senate in his pocket and a furious popular base. The next step would be to make the country ungovernable, a specialty that McConnell has been perfecting for a decade and that an accomplished demagogue like Trump can manage reflexively. Everything that goes wrong can be blamed on the treacherous "elites."

Trump and associates might, as some have speculated, set up an alternative media empire, incorporating talk radio and other far-right outlets but perhaps not Fox, which has shown occasional signs of disobedience. Then they could come roaring back into power in 2022–2024, feeding on growing discontent.

They would then be free to destroy the environment with abandon and maximize short-term profit for their primary constituency, impose discipline on what remains of government, tame the media, institute harsh authoritarian measures elsewhere, and continue with their abject service to their masters—the real elites, the very rich and the corporate sector, the decision makers, as recent academic research once again establishes very clearly.

It's of no little interest that we have to turn to the world's leading business journal, the very respectable London *Financial Times*, to read some elementary truths about what could once claim to be a leading democracy: "Anyone with a pulse," *Financial Times* Associate Editor Rana Foroohar writes, "knows that in the US today the system is rigged in favour of the wealthy and powerful." Foroohar adds:

One particularly illuminating paper [just cited] found that considering the opinions of anyone outside that top 10 per cent was a far less accurate predictor of what happened to government policy. The numbers showed that: 'not only do ordinary citizens not have uniquely substantial power over policy decisions; they have little or no independent influence on policy at all'. We have had decades of legislative tweaks to everything from tax policy to corporate governance and accounting standards that have favoured capital over labour. Supreme Court decisions such as the Citizens United case have also dramatically increased the amount of money funneled into political campaigning. This has left the nature of America's political economy perilously close to an oligopoly.

If the Trump strategy is anything like the speculation outlined above, the prevailing oligopoly might look like a fond memory.

Anger and contempt for "elites" is not a mistake, even if the real elites are effectively concealed by the propaganda machine.

The masters do not much like Trump. His vulgar antics undermine their preferred image as humane and benign figures who labor tirelessly for the common good, directing "soulful corporations," trustworthy guardians in whose hands our future is safe. But they may find it hard to fault someone whose major legislative achievement is a tax scam designed to enrich the very rich while imposing a heavier tax burden on the undeserving (and unwitting) majority.

Trump's hopes for denying a Biden election win lie with a legislative revolt—that is, by overturning the certification process. Experts indicate that such an outcome has a very slim chance of taking place, yet the fact that it is even considered as a possibility surely reveals something utterly problematic about the way democracy functions in the United States. Can you share your views with us on this matter, and discuss what it would take to make the democratic process in the US actually democratic?

Whatever the validity of my speculation about the goals and success of the Trump strategy, the whole election reveals the extreme fragility of American democracy. It is amazing enough that someone whose malevolent decision to provoke an out-of-control pandemic has just killed tens of thousands of Americans can even run for office, even carry much of the country with him, and that the political party that virtually shines his shoes can win a resounding victory at every level apart from the White House. That's putting aside Trump's major "achievements": driving to near-term environmental catastrophe and sharply increasing the threat of terminal war, crimes that scarcely registered in the electoral process.

Trump's rejection of the election results is just the coda to his quite impressive campaign to accomplish an authoritarian takeover, with the executive purged while his close associate Mitch McConnell converts the Senate into a joke, functioning almost entirely to enrich the rich and stack the judiciary with young, far-right justices whose task will be to impose the ultra-reactionary Trump-McConnell agenda for a generation.

But that is only the icing on the cake. Foroohar of the *Financial Times*, whom I quoted earlier, is quite right that the malaise cuts far deeper. It traces back as far as the constitutional order, which was established on the principle that "those who own the country ought to govern it" (first Chief Justice John Jay) and that a prime duty of government is to "protect the minority of the opulent against the majority" (leading framer James Madison).

Hard struggles ensued to overturn the "Framers' Coup" against democracy—the title of the gold standard of scholarship on the framing of the Constitution, by Michael Klarman. There have been periods of progress and of regression. We have just endured forty years of regression, the neoliberal regime, a bitter assault against democracy and on the kind of society that can sustain it. An estimate of the monetary cost to the general population was recently given by the Rand Corporation: $47 trillion transferred from the working and middle classes (90 percent of the population) to the super-rich; the top 0.1 percent doubled their share of wealth to 20 percent of the total since Ronald Reagan.

The Rand figures are a considerable underestimate. Tens of trillions more were "transferred" after Reagan opened the spigots for tax havens, shell companies, and other devices to rob the public. More were developed under Clinton's deregulatory mania. Reagan and his partner Margaret Thatcher moved at once to undermine the labor movement, setting in motion the campaigns to deprive working people of the primary means to resist the assault. The serious decline of functioning democracy is a virtual corollary of the radical concentration of wealth and dispatch of much of the general population to stagnation and precarity.

There is no need to review the rest of the sordid story once again. But it is important to remember the deep roots of the undemocratic structure of the government. In the 18th century, despite the Framer's Coup, the US Constitution was an important step toward democracy, so much so that the great statesmen of Europe invoked the venerable domino theory. They feared that "the pernicious doctrines of republicanism and popular self-rule" spread by "the apostles of sedition" who had freed themselves from Britain's grip might encourage similar "vicious principles" beyond.

That was then. A lot has happened in 250 years. If the US were to apply for membership in the European Union today, it would probably be rejected. The radically undemocratic character of the Senate would be sufficient reason. There is surely something a little odd about the respected doctrine of "originalism," holding that we should be bound by the ideas of a group of wealthy white slaveowners 250 years ago, even putting aside the cynical ways "originalist" and "textualist" doctrines are often applied in practice.

Even without Trump, the United States would still be facing a severe constitutional crisis. But that is only a fraction of the problem. Democracy is at best a fragile reed when people spend most of their waking lives under the rule of a master with virtually absolute power. That was understood very well by working people in the early days of the Industrial Revolution, who struggled hard against this attack on their fundamental rights and personal dignity. They also expressed their concern that a day might come when wage slaves "will so far forget what is due to manhood as to glory in a system forced on them by their necessity and in opposition to their feelings of independence and self-respect," a day they hoped would be "far distant."

Thoughts worth contemplating.

Millions of Trump's supporters seem to believe that their leader actually won the election. In fact, there have even been signs claiming, "World Knows Trump Won." In light of this, it seems to me that the contemporary United States is not simply a divided and polarized nation on political and ideological issues alone, but that we also have alternative epistemologies in operation: one segment of the population believes in actual facts and relies on science for an explanation of the world, while another segment of the citizenry is under the spell of falsehoods, disinformation

and deception. How do you explain this peculiar phenomenon, especially since we are talking about a very rich and technologically advanced country?

A little caution is needed here.

This is the country of the Scopes trial. When I was a student at an Ivy League college, lectures on the theory of evolution were introduced with the professor's warning that you don't have to believe this but it's important to know what some people think. Today, "both Protestants and Catholics are considerably more likely to say evolution was guided or allowed by God than they are to say that humans evolved due to processes such as natural selection, or to say that humans have always existed in their present form." Over 40 percent of Americans expect the Second Coming by midcentury, while over 80 percent of the population believe in miracles.

In some ways, we're not that far from centuries ago.

It's also important to consider the devastating impact of the neoliberal regime on much of the country, with particular severity in rural areas that were also major centers of manufacturing. After steady growth for many years, employment in manufacturing declined from its 1979 peak of almost 20 million to under 13 million 40 years later. The decline was in large part the result of policy choices: bipartisan investor rights agreements, mislabeled "free trade agreements," which provided unparalleled protection and other rights to corporate power while setting working people in competition with the most poorly paid and repressed workers in the world. That has been a large factor in the devastation of rural America: towns depopulated or abandoned, no jobs or hospitals or other services, general malaise and a justified sense of having been abandoned. That's hardly conducive to participation in the most advanced sectors of global culture.

The sources of the divide you mention are complex. The split, however, is very real. And it has major impacts. Right now, the country is in the grip of a severe pandemic. It was understood by scientists in 2003, after containment of the SARS epidemic, that another coronavirus was likely. The cultural divide soon emerged. When Obama took office in 2009, one of his first acts was to convene the president's scientific advisory council to request them to provide a pandemic response plan. They did. It was implemented, and remained in force until January 2017, when one of Trump's first acts was to dismantle it, opening the most anti-science administration in modern history, with consequences that we have seen on many fronts—and with effects on popular culture.

The conflict of epistemologies is real. It is no simple matter to explain or to deal with it. The future will depend substantially on how the conflict is resolved.

One way or another, Trump will leave office soon. But the question that still lingers in the air is whether Trumpism will also be gone. In your view, is there Trumpism without Trump?

Returning to my original speculation, I think both Trump and Trumpism will remain with us for a long time, both the individual himself and the poisonous currents he has unleashed. These poisons may be virulent enough to bring civilization to a horrifying end. There are workable solutions to the crises that humans face in this uniquely dangerous moment of human history. What happens within the most powerful country in human history cannot fail to have an overwhelming impact on what eventuates—an impact even on survival of human society in any recognizable form.

Voting Is Not the End of Our Work. It's Only the Beginning.

C. J. POLYCHRONIOU: Although Biden has won the election, the Democrats failed to materialize a blue-wave landslide, and it is clear we will continue to deal with large-scale Trumpism. Given that you were extremely skeptical of the polls from day one, what do you think contributed to the massive turnout for Trump, even as Biden saw an even more massive turnout? Or, to phrase the question differently, why is nearly half the country continuing to support a dangerous charlatan leader with such a feverish passion?

NOAM CHOMSKY: The very fact that someone could be considered a serious candidate after just having killed tens if not hundreds of thousands of Americans through a disastrous response to COVID-19 is an extraordinary victory for Trump—and a defeat for the country, for the world, and for hopes for a decent future.

Some of Trump's victories are very revealing. A report on NPR discussed his victory in a solid Democratic county on the Texas-Mexico border with many poor Latinos that hadn't voted Republican for a century, since Harding. The NPR analyst attributes Biden's loss to his famous "gaffe" in the last debate, in which he said that we have to act to save human society from destruction in the not very distant future. Not his words, of course, but that's the meaning of his statement: that we have to make moves to transition away from fossil fuels, which are central to the regional economy. Whether that's the reason for the radical shift, or whether it's attributable to another of the colossal Democratic organizing failures, the fact that the outcome is attributed to the gaffe is itself indicative of the rot in the dominant culture. In the US, it is [considered] a serious "gaffe" to dare to hint that we have to act to avoid a cataclysm.

Poor working people in the border area are not voting for the predictable consequences of Trump's race toward cataclysm. They may simply be skeptical about what science predicts. Sixty percent of conservative Republicans (35 percent of moderate Republicans) believe that humans are contributing "not too much/not at all" to global warming. A poll reported in *Science* found that only 20 percent of Republicans trust scientists "a lot . . . to do what is right for the country." Why then believe the dire predictions? These, after all, are the messages pounded into their heads daily by the White House and its media echo chamber.

South Texan working people may not be ready to sacrifice their lives and communities today on the basis of claims in elite circles that they are instructed not to trust. These tendencies cannot be blamed solely on Trump's malevolence. They trace back to the failure of the Democratic Party to bring to the public a serious program to fend off environmental catastrophe while also improving lives and work—not because such programs don't exist; they do. But because they don't appeal to the donor-oriented Clintonite neoliberals who run the Democratic Party.

There's more. Trump has shown political genius in tapping the poisonous currents that run right below the surface of American society. He has skillfully nourished and amplified the currents of white supremacy, racism, and xenophobia that have deep roots in American history and culture, now exacerbated by fear that "they" will take over "our" country with its shrinking white majority. And the concerns are deep. A careful study by political scientist Larry Bartels reveals that Republicans feel that "the traditional American way of life is disappearing so fast that we may have to use force to save it," and more than 40 percent agree that "a time will come when patriotic Americans have to take the law into their own hands."

Trump has also skillfully tapped reservoirs of anger and economic resentment among the working and middle classes who have been subjected to the bipartisan neoliberal assault of the last forty years. If they feel that they have been robbed, they have good reason. The Rand Corporation recently estimated transfer of wealth from the lower 90 percent to the very rich during the four neoliberal decades: $47 trillion, not small change. Looking more closely, the transfer was primarily to a small fraction of the very rich. Since Reagan, the top 0.1 percent has doubled their share of the country's wealth to an astonishing 20 percent.

These outcomes are not the result of principles of economics or laws of history but of deliberate policy decisions. If decisions are shifted from government ("Government is the problem," as Reagan claimed), they do not disappear. They are placed in the hands of the corporate sector, which must be guided solely by greed (per neoliberal economic guru Milton Friedman). With such guidelines in place, results are not hard to anticipate.

On top of the near $50 trillion train robbery, the international economy ("Globalization") has been structured to set American working people in competition with those in low-wage countries with no workers' rights while the very rich are granted protection from market forces, by exorbitant patent rights, to take one example. Again, the effects of this bipartisan enterprise are not a surprise.

Less educated workers may not know the details or understand the mechanisms that have been designed to undermine their lives, but they see the outcomes. The Democrats offer them nothing. They long ago abandoned the working class and have been full collaborators in the racket. Trump in fact harms workers even more than the opposition, but he excoriates "elites"—while slavishly serving the super-rich and corporate sector, as his legislative program and executive orders amply demonstrate.

Apart from almost daily steps to chip away at the environment that sustains life and to pack the judiciary top-to-bottom with far-right young lawyers, the main achievement of the Trump-McConnell administration has been the tax scam of 2017: "a delayed tax increase dressed up as a tax cut," economist Joseph Stiglitz explains. "The Trump administration has a dirty little secret: It's not just planning to increase taxes on most Americans. The increase has already been signed, sealed and delivered, buried in the pages of the 2017 Tax Cuts and Jobs Act."

The law was carefully designed to lower taxes initially so as to "hood-wink" Americans to think their taxes were being reduced, but with mechanisms to ensure that tax increases "would affect nearly everyone but people at the top of the economic hierarchy. All taxpayer income groups with incomes of $75,000 and under—that's about 65 percent of taxpayers—will face a higher tax rate in 2021 than in 2019." It's the same device that the George W. Bush Republicans used to sell their 2001 "tax cut"—for the rich.

What happens if Trump refuses to accept a Biden victory and seeks to settle the matter in the Supreme Court? And when corporate lawyers and the militias end up doing their thing, is it even remotely possible that the country could end up under martial law?

My uneducated guess is that it won't come to that, but it's a speculation with little basis or credibility. Trump has strong reasons—maybe even his personal future—to hold on to office by any possible means. We are not in the days of Richard Nixon, who had good reasons to question the legitimacy of the vote he lost in 1960, but had the decency to put the welfare of the country about his personal ambitions. Not Donald Trump. And the organization that grovels at his feet is not the political party of sixty years ago.

Trump still has two months to wield the wrecking ball that has already diminished the United States, harmed the world and severely threatened the future. His penchant for wrecking everything he did not create, whatever the cost, is hard to miss. He might decide to go for broke.

What are the next steps for the left?

For the left, elections are a brief interlude in a life of real politics, a moment to ask whether it's worth taking time off to vote—typically against. In 2020, the choice was transparent, for reasons not worth reviewing. Then back to work. Once Trump is fully removed, the work will be to move forward to construct the better world that is within reach.

INDEX

About Haymarket Books

Haymarket Books is a radical, independent, nonprofit book publisher based in Chicago.

Our mission is to publish books that contribute to struggles for social and economic justice. We strive to make our books a vibrant and organic part of social movements and the education and development of a critical, engaged, international left.

We take inspiration and courage from our namesakes, the Haymarket martyrs, who gave their lives fighting for a better world. Their 1886 struggle for the eight-hour day—which gave us May Day, the international workers' holiday—reminds workers around the world that ordinary people can organize and struggle for their own liberation. These struggles continue today across the globe—struggles against oppression, exploitation, poverty, and war.

Since our founding in 2001, Haymarket Books has published more than five hundred titles. Radically independent, we seek to drive a wedge into the risk-averse world of corporate book publishing. Our authors include Noam Chomsky, Arundhati Roy, Rebecca Solnit, Angela Y. Davis, Howard Zinn, Amy Goodman, Wallace Shawn, Mike Davis, Winona LaDuke, Ilan Pappé, Richard Wolff, Dave Zirin, Keeanga-Yamahtta Taylor, Nick Turse, Dahr Jamail, David Barsamian, Elizabeth Laird, Amira Hass, Mark Steel, Avi Lewis, Naomi Klein, and Neil Davidson. We are also the trade publishers of the acclaimed Historical Materialism Book Series and of Dispatch Books.

Also Available from Haymarket Books

Chronicles of Dissent: Interviews with David Barsamian
David Barsamian and Noam Chomsky

Consequences of Capitalism: Manufacturing Discontent and Resistance
Noam Chomsky and Marv Waterstone

Fateful Triangle: The United States, Israel, and the Palestinians
Noam Chomsky, foreword by Edward W. Said

Gaza in Crisis: Reflections on the US-Israeli War Against the Palestinians
Noam Chomsky and Ilan Pappé

Masters of Mankind: Essays and Lectures, 1969-2013
Noam Chomsky, foreword by Marcus Raskin

On Power and Ideology: The Managua Lectures
Noam Chomsky

Optimism over Despair: On Capitalism, Empire, and Social Change
Noam Chomsky and C.J. Polychroniou

Propaganda and the Public Mind
David Barsamian and Noam Chomsky

Rogue States: The Rule of Force in World Affairs
Noam Chomsky

Turning the Tide: U.S. Intervention in Central America and the Struggle for Peace
Noam Chomsky

Year 501: The Conquest Continues
Noam Chomsky